WEAPONS OF OUR WARFARE

PASTOR GREG LOCKE

Global Vision Press™

CHARISMA
HOUSE

WEAPONS OF OUR WARFARE by Greg Locke
Published by Charisma House, an imprint of Charisma Media
600 Rinehart Road, Lake Mary, Florida 32746

Unless otherwise noted, all Scripture quotations are from the King James Version of the Bible.

Scripture quotations marked ESV are from the Holy Bible, English Standard Version. Copyright © 2001 by Crossway Bibles, a division of Good News Publishers. Used by permission.

Scripture quotations marked NIV are taken from the Holy Bible, New International Version®, NIV®. Copyright © 1973, 1978, 1984, 2011 by Biblica, Inc.® Used by permission of Zondervan. All rights reserved worldwide. www. zondervan.com. The "NIV" and "New International Version" are trademarks registered in the United States Patent and Trademark Office by Biblica, Inc.®

Scripture quotations marked NKJV are taken from the New King James Version®. Copyright © 1982 by Thomas Nelson. Used by permission. All rights reserved.

Cover design by Locke Media.

Photography and original graphics by Locke Media and Wayne Caparas.

While the author has made every effort to provide accurate internet addresses at the time of publication, neither the publisher nor the author assumes any responsibility for errors or for changes that occur after publication. Further, the publisher does not have any control over and does not assume any responsibility for author or third-party websites or their content.

For more Spirit-led resources, visit charismamedia.com and the author's website at LockeMedia.org.

Cataloging-in-Publication Data is on file with the Library of Congress.

International Standard Book Number: 978-1-63641-343-3
E-book ISBN: 978-1-63641-344-0

23 24 25 26 27 — 987654321
Printed in the United States of America

Most Charisma Media products are available at special quantity discounts for bulk purchase for sales promotions, premiums, fund-raising, and educational needs. For details, call us at (407) 333-0600 or visit our website at www. charismamedia.com.

Charisma House gratefully acknowledges the partnership of Global Vision Press in the publication of this book.

DEDICATION

My first book, This Means War, *was affectionately dedicated to the love of my life, my beautiful wife, Taisha. But for this work, I felt it necessary to give recognition and absolute dedication to the amazing people of Global Vision Bible Church.*

I have never known a faith fellowship that was so eager to learn the truth of God's Word. I feel more than privileged every day that I wake up to serve and shepherd the most amazing church on the planet. I am humbled and overwhelmed to be a part of this unbelievable and unexplainable move of God in our midst.

The sacrifice of our church family makes my traveling, preaching, and writing possible, and together we're changing the lives of countless people around the world, all for the sake of the kingdom of God and the proclamation of the gospel of Jesus Christ. Whether you are in-house or online, we are family. We stand together, and we fight together. We weep together, and we laugh together. There is no place on earth I would rather be.

May the face and favor of God rest upon each of you like never before. I love you, Global Vision family. I truly love you.

CONTENTS

FOREWORD

I'M THANKFUL TO be married to a pastor who stands boldly through all the deception and controversy in these evil days. His courage and wisdom in writing this timely book have encouraged me greatly. I believe it will take all who read it through a spiritual boot camp—the urgently needed equipping and training for the army of God. We are undoubtedly living in the last days—days where lawlessness is out of control, both in the high places and in the streets. It's time for the church to stand, step into the spiritual realm, and fight.

We are taught in God's Word that the weapons of our warfare are not carnal but mighty through God to the pulling down of strongholds. During this season, when the church has gone into retreat and fallen silent, we need to pray that God will raise up an army of believers—an exceeding great army—that will go to war for the souls of this world. The harvest is plentiful, but the laborers are few. We need to suit up and boot up and take the war to the enemy in the spiritual realm. It's time, friends. As we journey through this together, let us all be reminded to pray without ceasing, see all things through a spiritual lens, and glorify the Father in all we do. For that, please join me in prayer:

Father, Lord, we thank You so much for Your Word. We thank You for proving that Your Word is true, Lord, and for revealing that we can look to Your Word at any time and find You there. As we navigate these times of great uncertainty and chaos—when so many call good, evil, and evil, good—oh Lord, we ask You to resurrect Your church. Breathe Your Spirit into these dry bones and raise up an exceeding great army of soldiers for Christ. Lord, guide us and teach us all Your ways and only Your ways. Your Word says that Your people are destroyed for a lack of knowledge. Give us Your knowledge and wisdom, oh God, and teach us to stand and fight according to Your Word—fully knowing that no weapon formed against us will ever prosper. May we be reminded every day to put on the whole armor of God and do all to stand against the wiles of the devil in this evil day, ensuring You receive all glory and honor. In Jesus' name, amen.

—TAISHA LOCKE

INTRODUCTION

Wherefore seeing we also are compassed about with so great a cloud
of witnesses, let us lay aside every weight, and the sin which doth
so easily beset us, and let us run with patience the race that is set
before us, looking unto Jesus the author and finisher of our faith; who
for the joy that was set before him endured the cross, despising the
shame, and is set down at the right hand of the throne of God.
—HEBREWS 12:1–2

THE SPIRITUAL WARFARE raging today—on the earth and in the heavenly realms—has been going on from the beginning. It is by no means a new phenomenon, but we're clearly approaching its climax. Through it all, the modern American church has led many Christians to believe that every day should be a Friday as you strive to live your best life now—absent any supernatural opposition or demonic persecution. I hope you know that's a lie from hell, but fear not.

The Bible tells us that Jesus is the "author and finisher of our faith," and that's not merely a poetic metaphor. If it exists, He wrote it into existence. He is the Creator of all. Through the Bible, He uses Judeo-Christian history, teachings, and prophecy to reveal His deity and prepare all humanity for what is soon to come. In the greatest true story ever told, where the Author Himself endures great suffering to bring world history to its stunningly beautiful crescendo of an ending, there must be a supernaturally powerful antagonist to oppose and tempt us. You can call him the devil, Satan, the enemy, Lucifer, or any other demonic names recorded in the Bible, but don't you ever fear him. While he has the power to move invisibly through our lives in his search for souls to steal, he is still just a created being. He's no more than ink on a scroll compared to the Author, but the Lord assured he is a formidable foe to us, nonetheless.

FEAR NOT, BUT TAKE HEED

The great preacher Charles Spurgeon compared the devil and his demons to vicious dogs on a leash. Spurgeon's point is that the devil, his demons, and his human minions can do nothing outside the permissive will of God. Instead of fearing them, we should fear God, who holds all their leashes. However, the fact that the top dog has been so brazen and desperate that he has begun revealing himself through every willing participant and every institution he can infiltrate—the church included—should alarm and awaken the sleeping body of Christ.

This is the primary message Jesus delivered in His end-times apocalyptic teaching, commonly called the Olivet Discourse (Matt. 24–25). Though Jesus already defeated Satan on the cross, the devil and his minions haven't been cast into hell yet, so the story continues as it is written. A lot must happen before the devil's final day of reckoning, but it's drawing near at an accelerating rate, and he knows it.

With all that in mind, it's well past the time for the American church and conservative Christians around the globe to stop cooperating with his schemes and start fighting back as God instructs. We are all part of a God-sized story written by God Himself. And by His amazing grace, He wrote Himself into each of our personal stories. But don't ever be mistaken. While God uses literary terminology to disclose how He supernaturally wrote all creation into existence, the heavenly dimensions and angelic beings He speaks of are positively real.

Don't ever be fooled into believing that the enemy is a mythological or fictional character of man's making or man's control. Across the millennia, many saints were used by God to verbally spread His word and eventually pen the Bibles we read, but man authored none of this. The devil is as real in this world as you and me and the institutions he controls. We ignore this fact at our own peril.

Centuries of born-again believers have recognized that the enemy is present, active, and powerful. Proof of his existence is undeniable for anyone with eyes that see and ears that hear. The Bible tells us he has a massive army of demons desperately working with him to take as many of us to hell with them as possible.

I believe the devil hopes God will rewrite the prophetic narrative if they can steal enough of His children, so none of us is exempt from his schemes. Though he can only be in one place at a time, his demons (and their human minions) are doing his bidding everywhere they find open doors to the vulnerable. If you make the mistake of dismissing the reality of these dark forces in your life, they will charm and consume you into their plans, and they'll turn to destroy you in the end.

I believe most of you realize that 2020 was a mere glimpse of what the devil has planned for this generation. Right before our eyes, the church in America has unwittingly fallen under his spell, but God has provided us with all we need as born-again believers to bear our crosses while crushing the enemy under our feet. If there is a zillion-dollar question in this battle for our souls, it is this: Will you fight the good fight as the Lord has instructed, or will you succumb to the devil? Every single one of us is doing one or the other, and contrary to pop-culture heresy, there is no middle ground in the battle for your soul.

SIGNS OF THE TIMES

In the Bible, Jesus says that the enemy is hell-bent on killing, stealing, and destroying the children of God and our high calling in this world (John 10:10). If you read just that single verse, you'll either be consumed by fear, or you'll dismiss the devil's very existence and fall right into his hands. Regardless, intense fear will eventually overtake you, and before you know it, you'll be cowering in isolation far from all other people—even your loved ones— wearing latex gloves, a full-face shield, and an industrial-strength mask while shopping online for an affordable hazmat suit.

I've already seen many wayward believers in this condition, and the enemy is just warming up. It's tragic that so few professed Christians practice any form of defensive spiritual warfare, and even fewer answer the call of Christ to go on the offensive. This book aims to correct all of that while there's still time. When you take the full counsel of the Word of God to heart, you learn that He has equipped us with every weapon needed to fight from His place of victory—the victory He secured for us on the cross.

EQUIPPING THE SAINTS

Few believers ever access the supernatural power of God's spiritual weapons—weapons designed to cast out every dark imagination and every evil spirit that aims to distract us from gaining the knowledge of God (2 Cor. 10:4–5).

I originally wrote this as the second book in a trilogy on spiritual warfare. But the Lord has opened so much new revelation to me about spiritual warfare and deliverance that I have revised the entire trilogy. I encourage you to read all three books: *Weapons of Our Warfare, Accessing Your Anointing,* and *Cast It Out.*

You see, when I first put pen to paper, I lacked the fullness of understanding that the Holy Spirit has since given me. But through prayer, diligent study, and a willingness to step out in faith and let go of old ways of thinking, my eyes have been opened wider than ever before. I've dug deep into the Word, witnessed the power of deliverance firsthand, and sought counsel from brothers and sisters in Christ who have fought the good fight.

I now offer you this revised edition with a fire in my soul, written to reflect the breadth and depth of the knowledge the Lord has graciously poured into me. My prayer is that within its pages you find a treasure trove of divine insights, a guide for your spiritual battles, and a beacon of hope in this world of darkness. You are among the remnant of men and women who see and hear the deepest truths God gave us through the Bible.

It's evident that generations of Christians have been fed a lot of lukewarm milk along with their chocolate chip cookies—and, yes, lots of cotton candy and Skittles. Meanwhile, only a small remnant has been fed the meat of God's instructions in due season, as Jesus commanded in Matthew chapter 24. So we need to get ready for the dark days ahead and fast.

My job as a watchman, teacher, and pastor is to properly warn, instruct, and equip the church for the spiritual warfare we're facing in nearly every area of life today. Jesus warned us that the destructive onslaught of the devil would only increase as the unknown day of His return swiftly approaches, but fear not; He did not leave us as orphans (John 14:15–18). The Holy Spirit will never leave us. Praise God!

WHY AREN'T WE ARMORED UP?

The Apostle Paul is the primary teacher the Lord used to pen the finer points of the Spirit-filled born-again life. Most scholars believe Paul penned half the books of the New Testament, and he was the right man for the job. His letter (or epistle) to the church at Ephesus, better known as the Book of Ephesians, contains the most revelatory, encouraging, supernaturally charged teaching on God's weaponry found anywhere in the Bible.

This book will take you piece by piece through Paul's discourse on the armor of God in Ephesians 6:10–18. I've discovered that most Christians today have no clue how to *put on* the armor in a way that unleashes its supernatural power in their daily lives. Sure, putting on the armor of God has become a battle cry in the church, but what good are words made empty by the lack of understanding or made lifeless by the lack of action? You might even have the armor memorized, but are you wearing it?

Most have never had an expository teacher reveal the mysteries and full depth of the life-transforming power gained when someone puts on the whole armor of God as God instructs. Most churches leave this crucial subject to children's ministry leaders and Sunday school teachers. These churches lump the armor in with other supernaturally charged teachings in the Bible—as if only children can appreciate the supernatural—seldom, if ever, exploring these teachings with their sophisticated adult "audiences." All the while, this lost and dying world is most starving for the supernatural, but the enemy has somehow succeeded at quenching it from most churches.

The harnessing of God's supernatural power can't effectively be taught in a thirty-minute puppet show, a flannel-graph storytelling scene, or a coloring book exercise. Nor can it effectively be taught through a handful of seeker-sensitive sermons. These approaches are, of course, better than nothing—but not much. Mysteries so deep and meaningful can only be found through the full counsel of the Bible—from Genesis to Revelation.

GAINING SUPERNATURAL POWER

Have you ever wondered why you lack the power to overcome the enemy's schemes or why you struggle to advance your dreams and visions in these dark days? Are you praying for the power to take back the ground you and your family may have lost to the enemy in recent years? Do you hope to end the butchering of babies, the sex trafficking of children, and the promotion of perversion to the vulnerable? Are you ready to stand firm against lawlessness and those stripping away our rights and liberties as Christians and citizens? Do you believe revival and the greatest awakening in history are needed to rescue the church and reclaim this nation for the sake of a lost world? Do you hope this book will take your faith and Christlikeness to a higher level? Or might you simply want to ensure you and your loved ones are prepared for Jesus' sudden return?

If you answered yes to any of these questions, I believe the Lord led you to this book to arm you with the full supernatural power of the whole armor of God in ways you never imagined. Once you complete this book, I believe you will be equipped, inspired, hopeful, activated, and overflowing with the glorious power of "Christ in you" like never before (Col. 2:8–9). Be assured the whole armor of God is not just a divinely designed memory tool. Though it is among the most unique visual teachings in all the Bible, it is—above all—the living Word of God. So please know this and never forget it. Putting on the whole armor is not a mere suggestion but a divine command from God.

TAKING INVENTORY

Many who grew up in the church remember their parents teaching them to take a daily inventory of the armor. Some were taught to visualize putting it on piece by piece every morning. Many were taught about the six physical pieces, and some were also taught that prayer is the activator of each piece, making prayer the seventh piece of God's supernatural armor. For this, many of us already know about the belt of truth, the breastplate of righteousness, the shoes of the gospel of peace, the shield of faith, the helmet of salvation, and the sword of the Spirit, which is the Word of God.

It all seems so simple when considered at the surface level. Many have a mindset that says, "Okay, I need truth, righteousness, peace, faith, salvation, and the Word of God. Check. And I need to pray. Roger that. Over and out!" But most go through life never truly taking any of it to heart and never even trying to *put it on* until a crisis strikes. Then—once things calm down—most return to the world unarmored, and the cycle continues.

While this sort of cursory attention given to the armor of God is good memory milk for kids and new believers alike, it takes a far deeper study to receive the life-transforming meat and sustainable, nourishing power found in each piece of armor. Most adult Christians I know—even among those who claim to be born again—admit that their daily habit of putting on the armor has waned as they've grown older. Many say that wearing the armor of God has become more of a battle cry to inspire than a command to obey. If that's you, you've been leaving the supernatural power of these weapons in your closet as you've headed out into the enemy's territory unarmored—and unarmed. Through this book, I aim to help you change all that.

ARE YOU READY?

For all the above and more, I encourage you to get excited in advance. If you take to heart all the Scripture explored in this book, I believe you will be enriched with God-given understanding and the supernatural power you need to defeat the enemy wherever you face him—for the sake of this present generation and those to come.

Everyone with breath has a role to play in this spiritual war. Dark forces in high places are trying to destroy the church and cancel the Bible—on our watch. In these last of the last days, we all must answer God's call to arms and persevere in battle against evil. Don't let the enemy tempt you and lull you into comfortably silent surrender. In Matthew 24:13, Jesus said, "He that shall endure unto the end, the same shall be saved." When we truly put on the armor of God as He instructs, we are supernaturally invincible, we endure, and—on the day of His return—we'll rise to join Him for all eternity. Don't miss it.

> Blessed is the man that endureth temptation: for when he is tried, he shall receive the crown of life, which the Lord hath promised to them that love him.
>
> —JAMES 1:12

CHAPTER ONE

The Power of His Might

Finally, my brethren, be strong in the Lord, and in the power of his might.
—EPHESIANS 6:10

IDON'T TEACH ABOUT spiritual warfare to impress you. I teach the whole Bible to impact you with the full power of the Gospel. I want to ensure you understand that we are not fighting *for* victory; we are fighting *from* a victory that Jesus has already secured for us. He has already provided all the power and authority we need.

Before we discuss each piece of spiritual armor identified in the armor of God discourse, we first need to explore the introductory verses and discuss the source of our power in Ephesians 6:10. Paul opens the discourse with, "Finally, my brethren...." Have you ever noticed that a man's final words on a subject are his most important? Leading up to the mayhem that broke out in 2020, I finished a two-year verse-by-verse expository teaching series on the Book of Ephesians. Because of this, our church was especially well prepared for all we faced in those dark days. It's another sign of His presence in our ministry, which prepared me to write this book.

In his letter to the church at Ephesus, Paul begged the elders and the new converts alike to ensure they understood redemption and salvation and were theologically correct about holiness and separation from the world (Eph. 2:1–2). Then Paul went on to teach the fullness of the Holy Spirit and what that looks like in our lives. He compelled all to be "full of the Spirit" and then discussed marriage and other relationships. As he began to discuss the local church issues, he deviated for a moment to talk about family and work life. Why? Because nothing will bring out the fullness of the Holy Spirit or the lack thereof like your home and workplace.

If you want to convince a pastor like me that you're filled with the Holy Spirit, don't tell me about it; let me visit your home and talk to your spouse for five minutes. Let me talk to your kids. Let me talk to your dog. Let me talk to your boss. Let me talk to your coworkers. They will tell me if you have what you say you have. So don't go to church and pretend to be a Christian if you don't go to work and live like one. If it's not fresh in your mind, I strongly encourage you to read Ephesians in its entirety at your first opportunity, as it offers context to speed up your learning curve concerning the armor.

THE ULTIMATE POWER SOURCE

With all this incredibly rich theology laid out before us in Ephesians, Paul suddenly pens, "Finally...." He was, in effect, saying that everything he wrote preceding this verse was building up to this big reveal. "Finally, my brethren...." Even with all these critically important teachings—and maybe *because* of them—the Book of Ephesians would have been sorely lacking without this epic climax. Paul brings the jet in for its landing and says, "Finally, my brethren, be strong in the Lord, and in the power of his might."

No one can wield spiritual weapons or put on the armor of God without the Holy Spirit. His indwelling is the power source for every piece of God's armor. This is why the Bible tells us that when we prepare for spiritual warfare, we must be filled with the power of His might—the Holy Spirit. As we will discuss in detail in the coming chapters, far too many people don't recognize the real enemy, so they fight the wrong things and the wrong people in the wrong way. No wonder people are exhausted in their spirit. No wonder people go to church, get their hands dirty for three months, and go up like a rocket only to crash back to earth like a meteorite, suddenly so deep in hiding that not even an FBI agent with a pack of bloodhounds can find them.

People who get burned out in the ministry typically fight the wrong battles in the wrong way because they lack the discernment and sustaining power of the Holy Spirit. If you cannot identify the real enemy, you'll shoot at the wrong people, and more often than not, you'll shoot the people you love the most. You will find yourself fighting the wrong war against the wrong antagonists, and you'll inevitably lose the fight hands down every single time. For this, before he ever said to "put on the whole armor of God," Paul first compels us to ensure we are filled with the power of the Holy Spirit—saved by the grace of the gospel—and thereby born again of the Spirit as Jesus commands.

> Nicodemus saith unto him, How can a man be born when he is old? Can he enter the second time into his mother's womb, and be born? Jesus answered, Verily, verily, I say unto thee, except a man be born of water and of the Spirit, he cannot enter into the kingdom of God.
>
> —JOHN 3:4–5

THE HOLY GHOST

For some folks, hearing that we must recognize the indwelling of the Holy Spirit (also called the Holy Ghost) makes them queasy. Sometimes this reality frightens folks and makes them a little skittish. Having grown up in a Baptist congregation, I remember whenever someone started talking about the Holy Spirit, the people in my circles got spooked. Sometimes they even got angry or creeped out. But you should *never* be afraid of the supernatural work of the Holy Spirit within you!

As you will quickly learn through this book, you will never be able to harness the supernatural power in God's holy arsenal if you are not filled with the Holy Ghost. Jesus plainly stated that we cannot even enter the kingdom of God without the Holy Spirit—the third person of God's holy Trinity—actively dwelling within us (John 3:3–8).

Never forget that when we speak of the Holy Spirit, we speak of God Himself. Surely you want Him dwelling within you, yes? This is the supernatural marker of born-again believers, and in John 3, Jesus reveals that your answer can only be yes if you hope to see the kingdom of God. As Paul penned in Galatians 2:20, once born again, it is no longer we who live, but Christ who lives in us. If you're not there yet, I believe and pray you will be by the time you finish this book. Likewise, if the meaning of born again is still a bit of a mystery to you, I believe this book will help you immensely.

WALK IN THE SPIRIT, EXPECT SPIRITUAL WARFARE

I know spiritual warfare can freak people out. I get it. We've all seen silly movies about exorcisms and demons and angels. Hollywood has dumbed down the supernatural in every way possible, but don't you doubt the supernatural dimensions for a second. If you could somehow cut a window into the heavenly realms and see what's going on in the fight for the souls of humanity (yours included), it would shake you to your very core. It would rock your foundations. It would change you forever. So put aside childish views about the heavenly dimensions where angels and demons travel to and fro.

If you don't believe in the ongoing spiritual warfare and demonic activity that has been raging since the beginning of time, you don't believe a thimbleful of the Bible. Evil is very real and active, but so is God's power to defeat it and deliver us. Believers can face any demonic threat without fear when we are fully armored and armed with prayer and the power of God. If this discussion scares you or makes you nervous, rise above it. Get over it. "Greater is he that is in you, than he that is in the world" (1 John 4:4). "If God be for us, who can be against us?" (Rom. 8:31). "Yea, though I walk through the valley of the shadow of death, I will fear no evil: for thou art with me; thy rod and thy staff they comfort me" (Ps. 23:4).

We truly have nothing to fear. When the devil is at his strongest, he's still nowhere near as strong as the power of the gospel of Jesus Christ in us, and he's entirely powerless before God, who created him and keeps him—as Spurgeon pointed out—on a leash. The name of Jesus still silences demons, so you should say it often throughout the day and never shy away from an opportunity to do so. Why? Because even Christians can be influenced or oppressed by demons. They try to creep into our lives, mess with our minds, and turn us away from the path of righteousness. But fear not, my friend, Jesus' name is our mighty weapon in this spiritual battle. It's not about our own strength or smarts, no! It's about the authority and power that resides in that blessed name, the name of Jesus! When we call upon it, when we speak it with faith and conviction, the demons have to flee! They have to run and hide because they know they've got no chance against the power of the Son of God.

Even more, though I know that many folks in the modern church are afraid to say this, I also need to remind you (or inform you) that the blood of Jesus Christ is still powerful enough to save people and destroy the enemy's schemes. For this, you should recognize the supernatural power of the *blood of Jesus* over the devil whenever you are under attack.

> And they overcame him by the blood of the Lamb, and by the word of their testimony; and they loved not their lives unto the death.
> —REVELATION 12:11

Spiritual warfare is now and always has been a reality, and the Bible says it's all coming to a head very soon. Why did Paul emphasize our need to be strong in the Lord and the power of His might?" Because when you are filled with the Spirit of God, He allows the devil to come against you and do all he can to deceive you and uproot you. God allowed the same attacks against Jesus while He walked the earth as a man, so don't get mad at God for allowing the same refining fire in your life.

A DESPERATE TYRANT

The devil doesn't care what you believe as long as it's not the truth. Consider that. In his second letter to the church at Corinth, Paul wrote:

> In whom the god of this world hath blinded the minds of them which believe not, lest the light of the glorious gospel of Christ, who is the image of God, should shine unto them.
>
> —2 CORINTHIANS 4:4

"The god of this world" refers to the devil, not God, thus the little *g*. The devil wants to keep you blinded to the reality of *who* Jesus is, just as he attempted with Jesus. That's the easiest way he can remain your god. If he can no longer rule you here, he plans to rule you in hell. If you have been saved by Jesus and filled with the power of the Holy Spirit, the devil will not take it lying down. He knows born-again believers are the greatest threat to his plan, so he's not letting you go without a fight. He'll do all he can to destroy you. The devil gets ticked off when you are delivered from the enemy's kingdom into God's kingdom (Col. 1:13). This is why the Lord gives you His Spirit and the weapons needed to fight back.

> Therefore rejoice, ye heavens, and ye that dwell in them. Woe to the inhabiters of the earth and of the sea! for the devil is come down unto you, having great wrath, because he knoweth that he hath but a short time.
>
> —REVELATION 12:12

As the end of the age approaches, the devil is desperately trying to drag you, your loved ones, and every last one of us into the fire with him. Have you ever noticed that professional crooks never get arrested alone? They almost always take other people down with them. In the same way, like a crazy, rabid dog, the devil still thinks he can break free from his master, so we must expect spiritual warfare every day.

WALKING WITH GOD

Consider this about the life of Jesus. He came as a substitute, but He lived as an example. The Bible tells us that Jesus unexpectedly showed up at one of John the Baptist's baptismal celebration services in the muddy River Jordan. John was dunking them, dunking them, and dunking them when he looked up and saw Jesus approaching, to which he said, "Behold, the Lamb of God, which taketh away the sin of the world" (John 1:29).

So John baptized Jesus, and when He came up, *the voice* of God the Father parted the clouds and said, "This is my beloved Son, in whom I am well pleased" (Matt. 3:17). At the same time, the Spirit of God flew down and lit on His shoulder in the form of a dove. This moment is one of the most revealing in all the Bible, but do you remember what happens next? "Then was Jesus led up of the Spirit into the wilderness to be tempted of the devil" (Matt. 4:1). For forty long days and nights—temptation, temptation, temptation—but Jesus didn't try to theologically argue His way around the devil. He didn't try to sound philosophically superior, and He didn't post stupid stuff on Facebook. He said, "It is written," "It is written," "It is written." "Man shall not live by bread alone, but by every word that proceedeth out of the mouth of God....Thou shalt not tempt the Lord thy God....Thou shalt worship the Lord thy God, and him only shalt thou serve" (Matt. 4:2–10).

While He walked as a man, Jesus knew exactly where the power came from. It came from the Spirit within, and it came from the Word of God, which is infused with the power of the Spirit. When Jesus came out of that baptismal water, He, in effect, made a public declaration, "My ministry begins now," and the devil immediately came after Him. The Apostle Matthew didn't even record half a verse before the devil attacked because spiritual warfare is an inescapable reality when you are *truly* walking with God.

You might be reading this book and thinking, "Woo! I'm telling you, Pastor Locke; I'm glad the devil has not messed with me in a long time." If that's you, then shame on you for what that reveals. If you walk with God, the enemy's attacks will be relentless. Look at the world today. Have we ever seen more proof of this reality than we do right now?

A GOOD FIGHT

If you're right with God and find yourself asking why you're going through a battle, you should recognize that the struggle is evidence that God is working in your life. The more you embrace it, the more powerful you become in the Spirit. Don't discount spiritual warfare just because you're discouraged. Discouragement is a choice. You can choose to live there if you want to, but you can also choose to get up and move on for the glory of God. As we'll see in the context of Ephesians 6, a big part of the problem is that we tend to grow weary and discouraged and simply don't want to fight anymore. That's why Paul later wrote, "I have fought a good fight, I have finished my course, I have kept the faith" (2 Tim. 4:7).

This letter to Timothy was Paul's final known writing before he was taken by the executioner's sword. Reading that helps me, so I hope it helps you. God makes it clear that life is a supernatural fight, and Paul fought a good fight to the end. Some of us fight stupid fights and ultimately give up. I know I've fought my share of stupid fights and learned I couldn't die on every hill of contention. I've determined that if I'm going to fight, I'm going to fight a good fight, and I'm going to fight to the very end.

If I ever go to jail over an issue, you can trust it will not be over something stupid. It's going to concern something biblical, like our ability to gather for the fellowship of believers, or my right to preach the gospel and speak out against evil wherever and whenever I'm led by the Holy Spirit, or the rights of babies to live and not get murdered by a doctor who took an oath to protect its life. Walking with God will always lead you into battles over justice and mercy in these last days. Are you fighting a good fight? Are you contending for the faith?

> He hath shewed thee, O man, what is good; and what doth the LORD require of thee, but to do justly, and to love mercy, and to walk humbly with thy God?
>
> —MICAH 6:8

CONTENDING FOR THE FAITH

> Beloved, when I gave all diligence to write unto you of the common salvation, it was needful for me to write unto you, and exhort you that ye should earnestly contend for the faith which was once delivered unto the saints. For there are certain men crept in unawares, who were

7

before of old ordained to this condemnation, ungodly men, turning the grace of our God into lasciviousness, and denying the only Lord God, and our Lord Jesus Christ.

—JUDE 3–4

While some of us fight the wrong fight, others don't fight at all. They're biblical pacifists, which isn't biblical at all. You may ask, "But Jesus is love, right?" Yes, and Jesus is also holy. God teaches us exactly how to fight for holiness from a place of love—for the sake of the gospel. We already know that the Apostle Paul was led to *fight* by the Holy Spirit, but even a casual study of the New Testament reveals the call to an ongoing, active fight against the forces of darkness, both outside and inside the church. On the outside, we battle with those who try to silence us and outlaw the commands of God and His commission to preach the gospel to all nations and all people (Matt. 28:18–20). On the inside, we battle those who pervert the Word of God with heretical or lukewarm teachings and lifestyles. In both cases, we aren't fighting or "contending" for carnal gains but only for "the faith"—the gospel of Jesus Christ.

While the prophetic Book of Revelation closes out the Bible with battle instructions for these last days and beyond, we find the very short Book of Jude immediately preceding it. This book is the Bible's final instructional writing for the ongoing church age, so it's no coincidence (no such thing) that it speaks directly to the unprecedented warfare we face today. Like James (who penned the Book of James), Jude was a younger half-brother of Jesus (Mary and Joseph were their birth parents). The brothers had infamously refused to follow Jesus during His ministry, but—like the Apostle Paul—both became passionate and vocal converts to the faith shortly after Jesus' resurrection. It can be said that the Book of Jude serves as a foreword to the Book of Revelation, as the entire letter is loaded with fiery fighting words, all coming from a place of love.

THE SAME WAR YESTERDAY AND TODAY

In the opening passage of Jude, which I cited at the top of this chapter, the Lord exhorts us to earnestly contend (or fight) for the faith. Never let any cowardly pacifists and "ungodly" heretics in the church tell you otherwise. When you read Jude, you'll see the Lord reminds us that He has been empowering His children for victory in battle from the very beginning.

God reminds us of the Israelites' fight for freedom from the Egyptians and how He destroyed the enemy's minions through His prophet Moses (v. 5). He reminds us that He destroyed Sodom and Gomorrah because of their immorality and gross perversions (v. 7). He reminds us that the angels still battle the devil on our behalf (v. 9), and He also reminds us of Enoch's end-time prophecy:

> The Lord cometh with ten thousands of his saints, to execute judgment upon all, and to convince all that are ungodly among them of all their ungodly deeds which they have ungodly committed, and of all their hard speeches which ungodly sinners have spoken against him.
>
> —JUDE 14–15

Keep in mind that *we* are the saints of which He speaks. Do you see any pacifism in the Book of Jude? Peace as God defines it, yes, but never pacifism or peace as the world defines it. I get hammered on social media for being judgmental and for calling out the "ungodly," yet that single prophetic passage (vv. 14–15) uses the word *ungodly* four times in a single sentence, and it speaks to *all* ungodly sinners, inside and outside the church. We need to realize that by silencing the church against these dark forces, the enemy and his minions are trying to silence the Bible, and he's starting with those of us who obey the Lord's commands by demanding our First Amendment right to speak the entire Word of God whenever and wherever He leads us!

The Book of Jude instructs us to fight when godlessness begins to gain influence and control over the church and its ability to spread the gospel worldwide. After giving us an overview of our ongoing battle against evil throughout the history of our faith, Jude ensures we realize the Lord is speaking directly to the final generation by writing, "There should be mockers in the last time, who should walk after their own ungodly lusts" (vv. 17–18). The term *last time* is a reference to the last of the last days that Jesus warns of in the Olivet Discourse (Matt. 24–25). These are those days.

LOVE PEOPLE, FEAR GOD, HATE EVIL

Just before Jude's closing benediction, we're reminded that the weapons (and the methods) of our warfare are indeed founded in the love of God for the sake of the lost, as we share the "mercy of our Lord Jesus Christ unto eternal life...[to] save with fear, pulling them out of the fire; hating even the garment spotted by the flesh" (vv. 21–23). Don't miss the message in that loaded passage. When we fight the good fight outlined in Jude, we are on a rescue mission to save godless folks from the fire of hell. That's love. Also, note that this verse instructs us to hate "the garment spotted by the flesh." This is an example of loving the sinner while hating their sin—and everything their sin permeates. Proverbs 8:13 says, "The fear of the LORD is to hate evil." Don't ever think you can claim to fear God when you make excuses for godless behavior. That's certainly not love. You're dead wrong if you think you can tolerate someone's sin and still help rescue them from hell.

The next time you hear someone criticize pastors who preach about hell, remember that the Bible commands us to do so, as this is the brand of love— the *fear* of the Lord—that can save souls from damnation, including our own (Matt. 10:28). Our corporate motivation is to engage in this spiritual war inside and outside the church. It's also my personal motivation for writing this long-overdue book. If we ignore God's commands to fight and contend for the faith in these last days, we risk losing the lost souls in our families, our nation, and the world. If you're not serious about saving souls, you're not serious about Jesus. It's His Great Commission for our lives (Matt. 28:16–20), so I trust you agree. There are untold numbers of souls whose rescue from eternity in hell depends on our love, our fear of the Lord, and our willingness to fight evil on their behalf.

TIME-OUT: IF NOT NOW, WHEN?

Recall the last time you got upset over evil and corruption in the church or the government but decided it wasn't your job or season to fight back. To that, we must ask, "If not us, then who? If not now, then when?" This saying was coined by Rabbi Hillel, a leading scholar in the Holy Land during Jesus' youth—a season when all of Israel cried out for the Messiah to come and deliver them from Roman persecution and godlessness. History does indeed repeat itself.

If the disciples of the first-century church had not risked their lives to contend for the faith, the church would never have made it to the second century, let alone the twenty-first. Now it's our turn to follow their lead, all the way to our own crosses if necessary (John 21:18–19). I know that makes some people nervous, but I like making folks nervous—for the right reasons.

God is building an army of passionate warriors for Jesus, and I pray that you hear His call. Many who are supposed to be soldiers in this spiritual war are complaining about hangnails or lying down in a valley full of dead men's bones (Ezek. 37:1–2). I'm hoping this book might wake enough of them to make a difference.

THE LAST OF THE LAST DAYS?

Even if you're a cultural Christian who has never been involved in a church, you can feel that something is coming. Even atheists and folks in false religions are beginning to sense its inevitability at some point in this generation. I believe that's why so many non-religious folks are reading my books. You want to see what the Word of God says about how best to defeat the evil working against you and your family. You believe in God. It's the religion of the church that has lost your trust. If that's you, I believe you'll get what you came for.

As we enter this season, the world will be more distracted by deceptions than ever before. Demons thrive in an environment of spiritual darkness and deception. They exploit the openings created by folks who have strayed from the truth, allowing them to slip in and take hold of their lives. This can manifest as oppression, obsession, or possession, depending on a person's engagement with deceptive practices and their susceptibility to the enemy's influence. We need to cultivate a strong foundation in the truth of God's Word, maintain a vibrant relationship with Christ through prayer and worship, and seek discernment through the Holy Spirit if we are to discern truth from deception. When we stray from the truth and dabble in darkness, we open ourselves to a range of spiritual afflictions. Never underestimate the consequences of giving place to the enemy in your life.

The enemy is gearing up in the spiritual realm because this is his moment. We can't minimize that reality for a second. Where Jesus repeatedly foretold the theological and geopolitical signs of the *last* of the last days with undeniable accuracy, He used Paul to detail the cultural and behavioral signs with the same precision. In one of many such passages throughout the New Testament (in this case concerning the condition of the church), Paul wrote:

> This know also, that in the last days perilous times shall come. For men shall be lovers of their own selves, covetous, boasters, proud, blasphemers, disobedient to parents, unthankful, unholy, without natural affection, trucebreakers, false accusers, incontinent, fierce, despisers of those that are good, traitors, heady, highminded, lovers of pleasures more than lovers of God; Having a form of godliness, but denying the power thereof: from such turn away.
>
> —2 TIMOTHY 3:1–5

We're living in days when the Bible literally reads like a newspaper. Please don't take that lightly.

11

CHAPTER TWO

They Know Not What They Do

Then said Jesus, Father, forgive them; for they know not what they do. And they parted his raiment, and cast lots. And the people stood beholding. And the rulers also with them derided him, saying, He saved others; let him save himself, if he be Christ, the chosen of God.
—LUKE 23:34–35

ODERN *CHURCHIANITY* (the man-made religion of church) has trained people to sit in chairs or to sit in pews and to wear the right kind of clothes and to read the right kind of authors and to have the right kind of this and the right kind of that, all based on man-made traditions that can never save or lead to the born-again life in Christ. Most of these folks wouldn't recognize Jesus if He came swooping down from the clouds right before their eyes. How much less would they have recognized Him while His blood-soaked body hung dying on the cross?

God looks on the heart, not the outward appearance (1 Sam. 16:7). And so must we, but the American church has led people to conform to an image-based "perception is reality" counterfeit form of Christianity. Jesus likened these churches to whitewashed tombs, "which indeed appear beautiful outward, but are within full of dead men's bones, and of all uncleanness" (Matt. 23:27). If you don't have Him on the inside, God doesn't care what you have on the outside. Without the Holy Spirit in control from the inside out, it's all vanity.

We've raised a generation of people who want external spiritual power without internal spirituality. They want the benefits of God without God. They have a counterfeit "form of godliness" but unwittingly deny the very power of God (2 Tim. 3:5). They may want to be godly, but they don't have the source, so they don't know how to practice "the way, the truth, and the life" of Jesus (John 14:6) that defines true godliness. They're like a pretty lamp that doesn't have a power source. They lack the oil necessary to keep the lamp burning (Matt. 25:3–4).

Most cultural Christians operate as if everyone who goes to church has access to the same power. If you get nothing else from this chapter, please know that's a lie. I know people who attend every church service possible yet are as spiritually dry and cold as a mother-in-law's kiss. Their spiritual life is barren and dusty like dead men's bones, and there is not one thing within them that has brought about change, transformation, or radical redemption. They can never claim something they don't have—no matter what they say they believe.

SPIRITUAL DISCERNMENT AND THE LACK THEREOF

> But the natural man receiveth not the things of the Spirit of God: for they are foolishness unto him: neither can he know them, because they are spiritually discerned.
>
> —1 CORINTHIANS 2:14

If you find yourself arguing religion and politics with lost people, you're wasting your time. You are blessed to see and hear things that lost folks and cultural Christians simply cannot see or hear, and most will never know what sort of spirit controls their souls until it's too late. If you're still wondering why the world is going so nutso-crazy (most megachurches included), it's because they don't have the Spirit of God within to counsel them in the truth. They simply do not know or obey the Word of God, so the armor of God is powerless to them, leaving them defenseless against the enemy in this spiritual war. Since most people don't even believe there is an actual devil to fight, they become unwitting accomplices in his schemes. When people dismiss or deny the reality of spiritual warfare, they become vulnerable to the subtle tactics and deceptions employed by the devil. The enemy thrives on the ignorance and complacency of those who turn a blind eye to his existence. They become like unsuspecting sheep, and he knows how to disguise himself and infiltrate their lives in subtle ways. Ignorance is not bliss when it comes to spiritual warfare.

By disregarding the existence of the devil, folks unknowingly fall into his traps. They will be more susceptible to false teachings, deceptive ideologies, and worldly temptations. The devil now has the upper hand and sows seeds of doubt, confusion, and moral relativism, removing their standards of right and wrong and pulling them further away from God's truth.

More importantly, without acknowledging the reality of the devil, people will neglect to put on the spiritual armor described in Ephesians 6:10–18. They will fail to engage in prayer and other spiritual disciplines, which leaves them defenseless against the attacks of the enemy and easily swayed by his deceptive whispers. Most of these people don't even believe in the spiritual realm, even though scientific research continues to prove the existence of spiritual dimensions.

We even have so-called pastors and preachers defending and supporting virtually every form of perversion the Bible condemns. It's no surprise that their churches are bowing to lawless lockdown orders and other manifestations of fear and worldly submission.

REAL ZOMBIES?

I never thought there was any possible way we would ever experience any sort of zombie apocalypse. When I saw the leftist-rioters beating innocent senior citizens in the streets while spewing satanic hatred and violence in every imaginable way (and some that were unimaginable), I realized why so many fiction writers and filmmakers are drawn to the zombie concept. In these days, they have a lot of source material to work with. I've long battled this sort of violent hatred as it has been fomented by the media and the godless culture, and I knew it would soon manifest beyond all measure, but not like this.

No coincidence that these are the same people fighting to keep late-term abortion legal all the way up to the delivery date and beyond. They're also the people who fight to keep the harvesting of butchered baby parts and baby blood legal. *Why* they practice such abominable evils is a discussion we'll have to save for a later text, but if there's anything that should convince you that demons are real, this is it. How can a "living" human defend such evil against human babies—even on their birthday—even while they criminalize the accidental destruction of bird eggs and turtle eggs? When did a baby turtle become more important than a human baby? All of this is proof that the enemy and his demons are hard at work. Like the mythical zombies, these people can't possibly realize what they're doing.

15

As we identify the works of the enemy to this end, we need to constantly remind ourselves that the pawns of the enemy are not the actual enemy. Even cultural Christians who support these evils are under the devil's control. Without a genuine faith in Jesus and the indwelling of the Holy Spirit, cultural Christians lack the spiritual discernment, conviction, and power to resist the devil's influence. It's mighty easy to get swept up in the current, and as a result, they conform to the values and patterns of the world, compromising their beliefs and convictions.

However, even when they fall short and find themselves entangled in the web of conformity, they can turn to our heavenly Father in repentance. They can seek His forgiveness, knowing that His mercy knows no bounds. He is eager to cleanse, restore, and guide them back on the right path. For this, we should never view any of them as being beyond all hope, as hard as that may be at times. We just need to ensure we never again submit to them or cower to their demonic lawlessness. This discussion of the devil's minions should help explain why this war often feels more human than spiritual. Historically speaking, unregenerate Christians are the devil's most dangerous pawns. Never forget, they're still human beings in need of deliverance and salvation, so don't ever fear them or hate them.

VICTORY IN JESUS

Never forget that as born-again believers—the true family of God—we are fighting from a place of victory in Jesus. We are already victorious in this war and will receive all His promises because we're among the brethren and the "sistren," if you will, but we still have to fight the battles. I'm in the family of God. I'm in the body of Christ. I'm part of the framework of who Jesus is and all He said I would be in the biblical narrative. If you are truly born again and filled with the Holy Spirit, this is also true of you. Acknowledge and take hold of the Holy Spirit's power within you, or you'll find yourself powerless.

Born-again believers are "members of his body, of his flesh, and of his bones" (Eph. 5:30). We've been washed in the blood of Jesus upon being saved. We've been reborn through the indwelling of the Holy Spirit and His transforming power, and we can expect our lives to produce all the supernatural power and fruit of the Spirit that the Bible promises. Everybody loves to say, "I believe the Bible! I believe what the Word says!" That's great. Now I wish you'd *behave* the Bible. I wish you'd behave what the Word says and produce some fruit with your life. Most of these folks need to receive the Holy Spirit and let Him instill His life-transforming, armor-empowering presence within. Don't be mistaken; being born again is not a ceremony or a confession. It is the recognition of His power within and the subsequent submission to all He instructs.

In James 1:22 (NKJV), we read, "Be doers of the word, and not hearers only, deceiving yourselves." As we continue the discussion of our holy power source, don't just agree with what you read. I urge you to start acting on the Word of God that you read along the way. In our initial key verse, Ephesians 6:10, Paul begins his teaching on the whole armor of God by telling us to be "strong in the Lord."

Too often, we hear "sloganized" scriptures like that and let them come in one ear and go out the other. Commit to doing what the Holy Spirit teaches you through this study of His Word, and He will counsel you on how to live it out in your daily life. Do this, and His power will beautifully manifest in and through you sooner than you think. I love that Paul isn't just *suggesting* that I get stronger through the indwelling of the Holy Spirit—the power of His might. He's putting forth an imperative command from God's lips, backed by God's promises.

> Marvel not that I said unto thee, Ye must be born again. The wind bloweth where it listeth, and thou hearest the sound thereof, but canst not tell whence it cometh, and whither it goeth: so is every one that is born of the Spirit.
>
> —JESUS (JOHN 3:7–8)

POWER TO ENDURE UNTIL THE END

We don't know what's coming in these last days, but God does. And because He knows what's coming, He's telling us we'd better be strong in the spirit, and we'd better be ready. The spiritually weak will not survive what is coming in this nation and around the world. They just won't. That's why Jesus said those who "endure unto the end" will be saved (Matt. 24:13). Someone might ask, "Do you mean to tell me that I'm not saved until I endure to the end?" No. I'm saying that only those who are saved and born again will be able to endure to the end *because* we alone are filled with the supernatural power of God!

Born-again believers don't back down or retreat in the face of godlessness, lawlessness, and perversion. We contend for the faith and supernaturally endure to the end, often moving with mystery like the wind (John 3:8). I know that many pastors (and several large denominations) teach erroneous man-made doctrines on this subject, so if any of this confuses you, stick with me. As we continue to open the Scripture, I believe it will all become beautifully clear.

The spread of apostasy (rejection of biblical truth) among the churches in America revealed the devil's infiltration long before they began bowing to anti-Christian forces. In the past several years, we've seen prominent, outspoken gospel preachers betraying the faith and the commands of God to shocking degrees. As the media and the liberal government continue to pressure churches in every way imaginable, more and more churches will begin to bow to the threats of persecution and choose the path of least resistance—the ways of the world in their new world order.

Increasing numbers of churches and ministries will join the chorus of apostates who defend abortion and other abominations while ignoring the truth of God's Word. They either embrace the whims of mere men, cower in fear, or both. If we don't take back the church now, we'll never again regain our role as the moral compass for the nations.

FOOD THAT NEVER PERISHES

I see it on social media all the time. "Well, I'll tell you one thing, Brother Locke. If you preached like Jesus, people would like you more." The truth is, if I preached like Jesus, nobody would like me. It's important to remember that they didn't kill Jesus because of what He *did*; they killed Jesus because of what He *said*.

People accept stuff they should have never accepted, all in the name of "social justice" and the "common good." Some pastors suggest we quit preaching the gospel to focus on social justice work. I'm all for *biblical* social justice. I believe we ought to feed, clothe, love, and accept people and help people right where they are. Our ministry at Global Vision is known far and wide for our selfless love, charity, and generosity toward needy people. But if we only help them with their temporal needs while leaving them on a highway to hell, we've done more harm than good.

No matter what we do to help people, we haven't done our job if we don't give them the love of the gospel of Jesus Christ. We're called to feed the sheep, not to slop the hogs. Did you know that when Jesus fed the multitudes, He fed them to gather them together to preach to them? It wasn't about the food that perishes but about feeding them the true Word of God, the "meat" that never perishes (John 6:27). Churches these days are surrendering through silence. By doing so, they're falling into the enemy's hands and dragging their congregations with them.

WHEN RIGHT IS WRONG

There's been a line drawn in the sand. The powers of this world have decided we are not allowed to offend anyone except God and His people. You can say anything you want about a Christian. Anything. You can call us lowdown, hypocritical, yellow-bellied, homophobic, Islamophobic, xenophobic sexists, racists, or bigots with zero evidence, and no one will blink an eye. But if you dare whisper and utter a disagreement with the LGBTQ or BLM/Antifa crowd, you are marked with a scarlet letter for life. They call it *virtue signaling*—as if they're the champions of virtue—and vilify Christians as the only threat to their new normal. For them, good is evil, and evil is good (Isa. 5:20).

We're suddenly the antithesis to all they deem virtuous, like lawless rebellion, abortion, and every form of perversion. The tactics used to confuse good and evil in the public-school systems and our nation's universities have become pervasive and insidious. I would never be welcome to go into a public school to read Bible stories to children, but men dressed like women are celebrated as they conduct "Drag Queen Story Hour" for elementary school children. How can this be?

Let's be honest: many believe that standing against these evils is too ambitious or too *spiritual,* especially in the volatile uber-divided environment of post-2020 America. But *real* Bible believers have no choice. We need to do far more than talk if we hope to take back the spiritual ground we've lost. That's where the whole armor of God comes into play. We live in an age when powerful people openly lie with zero accountability, never caring that we can prove they are lying because very few of us even care about the truth.

WHO'S TO BLAME?

Despite all the deceptive evil in their plans and behaviors, they truly believe they're the *good* people and that we—the proponents of the Bible's Judeo-Christian moral code—are the *bad* people. For this, the coming war will be far more than a war of words. Let's face it. It's our fault that America is in this mess. We were once the moral compass of this nation, but somewhere along the way, we abdicated our role.

We ignored our high calling even as we watched their schemes unfold.

19

Jesus said, in effect, "If they hate you, you'd better know they hated Me first." (See John 15:18.) It's time for the church to stir up the atmosphere in America in every way possible.

I posted a YouTube video during the Obama administration after they legalized same-sex marriage in America. In that video, I told our followers that this landmark attack on Judeo-Christian morality would open the door for the government to start protecting pedophiles. And in the middle of the pandemic, California made pedophilia legal for certain groups. At this rate, it won't be long before men and women of any age can buy and sell children, just like Planned Parenthood already buys and sells butchered babies.

If we don't act now, perversions that sound insane today will soon become protected rights. I could go on listing all the formerly illegal (and biblically immoral) perversions we have accepted without a fight. For me, it's heartbreaking and convicting. When I made that video, I honestly believed (or maybe it was just a hope) that the depth of perversion and lawlessness we're currently witnessing was still a decade or two away. But as I've noted before, we leaped fifty years ahead in the prophetic timeline during 2020, so we'd better get busy if we hope to stop the bleeding before it's too late.

JUST OBEY

Tai and I were recently walking the beach hand in hand when I turned to her and said, "Look, honey, I need to be honest about something. Sometimes I think I make you nervous." Most people that follow me on social media hate me. It's a weird reality, but I can handle it. I told her I feel like maybe sometimes I'm just too much. I should dial it back a bit, get my personality out of it, calm down, and let the waters settle.

I figured she'd say, "Yeah, it's probably about that time." Nope. She said, "Not in these last days, honey. God has already prepared you for it, so just obey. Follow the Holy Spirit according to the Bible, and just obey." By saying that, she reminded me of the many members of our church who have overcome demonic attacks over the past few years. These folks are my true family, so I know they'll fight hell by the acre right along with me. There's no doubt about that. We've been trained up, and we continue to get trained up. We're ready to pay the price and make amends for the past failures of the American church.

We can't be afraid to fight back just because it will stir something up. We *need* to stir things up! Come what may, we must boldly contend for the faith and speak out for the gospel's sake, empowered by the Holy Spirit. Life is too short to live like a coward. We're currently facing a tidal wave of demonic activity that will be followed by a massive rip current of God's judgment. It's coming, and there's no way around it.

THAT OTHER ONE

A while back, I read a story about the late preacher Sam Jones, a circuit-riding Methodist evangelist. You might have heard of the Ryman Auditorium in downtown Nashville. Today it's the home of the *Grand Ole Opry*, but it was originally built for Sam Jones revival meetings. That's why the seats are church pews, and the windows have a stained-glass motif. Jones would preach there three times a day—morning, noon, and night—all packed to capacity. Nashville loved Sam Jones so much that they bought him a house and acres of land without telling him, hoping he would permanently move to Middle Tennessee. Though he refused to take it and eventually gave it all away, Nashville thrived through years of a revival led by the powerful preacher.

If you think I'm a little bit crazy and a little too bold sometimes, you should read Sam's wife's memoir about his life. When things would get crazy, and men started acting rowdy during a service, she said Sam would walk down on the main floor and give them a little UFC smackdown before returning to the stage to keep preaching. That's my kind of man right there—not that I'd ever try it! I've got a team of guys who keep the peace and watch my back, praise God. The Bible says a preacher can't be a brawler (Titus 1:7). So I'm not one. I just carry my brawlers with me! But seriously, I trust Sam was much more a peacemaker who broke up more fights than a brawler—although I'm sure he had to take a few blows and dole out a few to get there. Those were raucous times.

On one particular day, Sam was about two hours late taking the platform for a revival meeting. He was already in the Ryman Auditorium, but no one knew what was keeping him. All the denominational men, dressed in fine suits and ties, started getting nervous. For over two hours they sang every song in the hymnbook they knew how to sing until they finally said, "Where in the world is he?" They eventually decided they had no choice but to try knocking on his door, but none of these men dared to disturb the fiery preacher. Instead, they sent a young boy backstage to find Sam and directed the boy to Sam's little dressing room (which was just his prayer closet).

The little boy walked down the hallway and saw the door cracked open about an inch. Just before the little boy could open the door to ask Mr. Jones to come to the platform—albeit two hours late—he could hear the preacher in the room talking to someone.

Sam was saying, "I'm telling You right now, I am not going out there without You tonight! I've done it before, but I will not do it again. Do You hear me? I will not go out there without You. I need Your strength, and I will not go without You." He was laboring in some fiery prayer. "I will *not* go on that stage, no matter how many people are here tonight, not unless You go with me!"

The little boy was so startled that his eyes got as big as saucers. He turned around and walked back up the hallway, climbed back up on the platform, and walked over to those dignified, well-dressed distinguished preachers. Now exasperated, they anxiously asked, "Is he coming?"

And the little boy said, "Yep. And that other one is coming with him too."

Whether your pastor shows up to preach at your church or not, whether you show up at church or not, that other one—the Holy Spirit—*must* show up, or nothing will change.

Finally, my brothers and sisters, let's "be strong in the Lord, and in the power of his might" (Eph. 6:10)!

But ye are not in the flesh, but in the Spirit, if so be that the Spirit of God dwell in you. Now if any man have not the Spirit of Christ, he is none of his.

—ROMANS 8:9

CHAPTER THREE

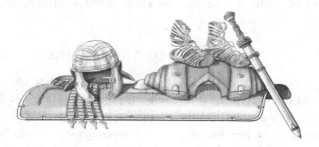

The Whole Armor of God

Put on the whole armour of God, that ye may be
able to stand against the wiles of the devil.
—EPHESIANS 6:11

O NE OF THE major themes of the Bible is spiritual warfare, but you'd never know that if you've been attending the typical church in America most of your life. Evangelical churches tell most new believers to walk an aisle, pray a prayer, sign a card, join a small group, and get baptized. Few are being trained in spiritual warfare, and most are simply set adrift to live however they jolly well please. It's no wonder most would be terrified and run for safety if the devil ever came against them. As previously stated, if the devil *never* comes against you, it's because you're not doing much, if anything, for the kingdom of God.

If you pose no threat to the devil, you're already doing some of his dirty work, even if you don't realize it. He'll just let you rock on because you're unwittingly on his side. But when you make a bold public declaration to follow Jesus and keep your word by putting on the whole armor of God, you'd better know that the devil and his minions aren't going to take it lightly.

It still amazes me that I get attacked by so many so-called Christians and pastors for using biblically sound fighting words while contending for the faith in these dark days. You'd think I was out there calling for violent riots, yet I do nothing of the sort. I can say with total confidence that I fight as the

Bible instructs. The compliant, submissive, tolerant, silent pastor is in error and in need of public rebuke, not the vocal objector pushing back through godly, vocal, nonviolent protest.

THE PLAGUE OF COWARDICE

Sadly, we've raised a generation of people with big yellow stripes down their backs, fearful to the core. They're afraid of spiritual warfare. Most preachers do all they can to avoid offending people, so when they take the pulpit, all they talk about is the love of God, over and over again. It would be beautiful if they gave equal time to the tough stuff God commands of us. I don't let a service go by without talking about His immeasurable love, but my people would boo me off the stage if I left it at that. The love of God doesn't make sense unless you also talk about the justice of God, the wholeness of God, and—yes—the condemnation of God.

Talking about His love while ignoring His firm commands is like teaching about heaven without mentioning hell. You can't have one without the other. The kingdom of heaven is not a playground; it's a battlefield (Matt. 11:12). When we go to church, we should learn how to fight our battles, not compromise the Bible and comply with the devil.

If you believe the Bible, you surely recognize that these are *the last* of the last days. If you're not strong in the Lord, you won't have the power to survive what's coming. Gaining strength in the Lord isn't just about going to church, raising your hands, saying Amen, and giving God your tithes and offerings.

Over the next few years, we will find out who really loves Jesus Christ, the gospel, their neighbor, and the presence of God. You'd better get busy figuring out whose side you're on. Jesus said that if you're not with Him, you're against Him (Luke 11:23).

When Jesus returns, He won't give you a chance to explain why you weren't ready and expectant as He instructed. You might believe you're not bold for Jesus because you're shy when the real reason is that you find it embarrassing to share the gospel. If so, don't forget that Jesus also warned that if you're ashamed of Him before men, He'll be ashamed of you before His Father in heaven (Luke 9:26). That's not written in Greg's letters; it's written in *red letters*, which are the recorded words of Jesus Himself. If you call Jesus Lord, you must do what He says, or He's not your Lord at all—not yet anyway (Luke 6:46).

ONLY YOU CAN PUT IT ON YOU

Have you ever noticed that when we're disobedient to the Bible, we often blame God for the outcome? Maybe we don't express it in words, but we prove it through our lack of worship, our lack of praise, our lack of prayer, and our lack of public expressions of obedience to Him. We need to understand that—although God readily forgives our sins—He does not relieve us from the consequences of choosing sin over obedience. If you make dumb choices, you must live with the dumb results—and the painful consequences.

Look again at our current key verse, Ephesians 6:11, where God wrote, "Put on." Read those two words out loud: "Put on." God doesn't put it on for you. You've got to do it yourself. Everyone wants ready-made instant Christianity and ready-made instant discipleship. You might say, "Well, I'm just gonna pray my prayers, wake up in the morning, pop a pill with my coffee, and do my best to be spiritual." If you're spiritual, it's because you *want* to be spiritual; if you're non-spiritual, it's because you *want* to be non-spiritual. The choice is yours. You are fully responsible for your spirituality and your obedience.

There's something unique about our church at Global Vision and other churches standing ready to fight the good fight. You'll never be able to walk out of one of these living churches and say you didn't get fed meat from the Word of God. If you don't feel like you're getting fed at our church, you aren't paying attention.

You can't just sleep with the Bible under your pillow and wake up knowing what the Psalms teach you. You can't skim through the Book of Proverbs and hope you automatically walk in its wisdom. You must put it on and keep it on. To access the power of the whole armor of God, you must make a conscious, deliberate effort to stand up and put it on. God has a dress code. It's called the whole armor of God.

PUTTING OFF THE OLD

While I'm on the subject of misplaced blame, I may as well ask you now to stop blaming your spouse when you're being a jerk. If you're being a jerk, it's because you *want* to be a jerk. Likewise, you must quit blaming your pastor and the Bible for your problems. If you're not getting the results the Bible promises, it's because you don't obey what the Bible says. If you disobey God, don't you dare blame the president or your boss for your problems. And if you believe all your problems spring from your dysfunctional family, welcome to the club! Adam and Eve jacked it up for all of us. We're all from a dysfunctional family, so don't blame your disobedience on anyone but yourself.

When you want to know who to blame for your lack of spirituality, all you need to do is look in the mirror. Few people want to take personal responsibility or have accountability in their spiritual walk. That's why Christians are falling away left and right, dropping like flies as churches throw in the towel all over America. Everyone wants to talk about accountability until someone calls them out on it.

For some of you to put on the armor of God, you will first have to *put off* some stuff that you've allowed to get into your life. If we could see people's spiritual lives with our eyes, we would see many struggling to drag their junk into the house of God. If you could see it yourself, would you recognize how it's blocking your power? Would you finally get rid of the stuff that's holding you back? Would you release some burdens that are weighing you down? Would you forgive some folks who keep you in bitterness? Paul wrote that if you're going to *put on* the new man, you must first *put off* the old man (Eph. 4:22–24). There's no escaping this reality.

THE WHOLE ARMOR OF GOD

When Paul wrote that we had to put on the *whole* armor of God, he was trying to ensure we didn't think any of it was optional. I like that. We must put on *every piece* of armor intrinsically, through and through. Apparently, the armor only works if you obey the command to put on *all* of it, not just the parts and pieces you pick and choose for any given day or crisis. Just as we need to know the full gospel message and obey the full counsel of the Bible, we must also understand the whole armor of God for any of it to work properly.

The enemy wants Christians to believe we can pick and choose from Scripture. It's one of his most successful and most devastating schemes. People love to pick and choose from the Bible and make it mean whatever they want to believe. This is especially true on social media. Have you noticed how people love to quote Bible verses out of context? They'll quote half a Bible verse and then beat you to death with it even though they clearly don't understand it.

Context is key, and you can't break a verse out of the context of the full message just because the selected words can easily be spun or augmented to support a lie. This is the work of the devil in the lives of those who practice this sort of heresy. The devil attempted this very tactic on Jesus during His forty days of fasting and temptation in the wilderness (Matt. 4:3). But even in this weakened state, Jesus was fully armored up. He drew the sword of the Spirit to shred the devil's scheme.

As the Apostle Peter reminds us, no scripture is of any private interpretation (2 Pet. 1:20–21). It may hit you a little differently. It may move you a little differently. It may do something in your life a little differently by way of application, but there's only one true interpretation. Each verse has a clear meaning, and it doesn't mean what your grandfather said. It means what Jesus said in the context of His full Word.

NO CHERRY PICKING

Consider how the devil deceived Eve in the garden. He took a phrase from the mouth of God, flipped its meaning, and—because Eve was not fully armored up—the rest is history (Gen. 3:4). The Bible is not a "this is what it means to me" book, yet I always hear that. Folks constantly say, "That's how it speaks to me." I don't care how it speaks to you if it does not agree with the Bible's full counsel. It's your job to learn what the Holy Ghost is saying, and it's a serious sin to chop it up to serve your agenda. That's what the devil did to Eve.

For those of you who think, "I like what the Bible says here, but I just don't know if I like what the Bible says there because if I believe what it says there, I may lose some friends and opportunities." You can bank on it. The Bible is not a pick-and-choose manual. In the same way, if you're thinking, "Well, I like this piece of armor, but that piece makes me a little uncomfortable," then you need that piece even more.

I'll add this as a rebuke to my breed of teachers—my ilk of theologians and pastors who preach like the devil in their churches—folks who say, "Well, you know, ladies and gentlemen, that's not really what Jesus meant." Are you kidding me? Likewise, to those who say, "You don't have to believe those parts of the Bible because those parts are no longer relevant." You need to fire that liar. Tar and feather him and run him out of town! The whole Word of God is relevant, ladies and gentlemen. Even the Book of Leviticus offers valuable truth for every generation. All Scripture is given by inspiration of God, not just some of it (2 Tim. 3:16). If it's in the Bible, it's Bible truth—period.

You don't get to say, "Well, I'd like a little of this, I want a little more of that, and give me a great big scoop of that love, love, love, love, love!" Some people in our culture are so fat on being loved and loving others that they're good for nothing. Many believe love is accepting and tolerating everything

27

everyone does. But I can love you and not like what you do. I can accept and love *you*, but that doesn't mean I accept your behaviors or beliefs. Yet we've raised a generation of people who think, "Well, if the Bible says God is love, then that means you have to love me on my terms." Wrong. That's not biblical love. In fact, it's sinful (and hateful) to leave someone in their sin without trying to help them out of it.

Reflect on our discussion of the *rescue mission* in chapter 1. I won't let my or anyone else's kids play on the street with cars zooming by. I will warn them and even assist them to get out of danger's way if necessary. That's an example of love. Leaving them alone to play in traffic wouldn't just be negligent but evil. Day and night for three years, Paul wrote to the elders of the Ephesian church to warn them. He never ceased to weep and cry and warn them with tears about what was to come (Acts 20:31).

BIBLE PROPHECY

The desire to dismiss the tough teachings of the Bible is an especially relevant concern in these last days, as the same tragic error has led many to reject Bible prophecy altogether. Apparently, talking about Jesus coming again scares them. I'm glad. It ought to scare them. My Bible says that once the church really believes that Jesus Christ is coming again, this revelation will purify the church. It will be the truth that purifies our homes. It will spark the regeneration that makes us holy and righteous and reveals the evil in the secular-humanist philosophies of this world.

If you really believed that Jesus Christ was coming at any moment, you would change your tune about a lot of issues. Right? If somehow you knew that Jesus was coming tonight, wouldn't you sound the alarm for the rest of us and immediately get right with the Word of God? For your sake, I sure hope so.

I'll admit that some passages and historic events in the Bible make me nervous and squeamish. There are even some chapters in the Bible that I'm hesitant to preach—but I've got to deal with all of it. As you read this book, if you think that I'm unfairly picking on you and your crowd, you can't put that on me. If the Scripture in the Bible stings, the Holy Spirit is picking on you, not Greg Locke. As the revivalist Sam Jones said, "If you throw a rock into a pack of dogs, the one that chases after you, barking, is the one you hit." If you get angry with me over something I teach from the Bible, don't bark at me.

When discussing the unchanging truth of the Bible, you've got to take it for what it says, not for what you want it to say. "Jesus Christ is the same yesterday, today, and forever" (Heb. 13:8, NKJV). "For I am the LORD, I do not change" (Mal. 3:6, NKJV). Both of those verses, in context, refer to the character of God. His character never changes. Therefore, the Word of God will never change.

I couldn't even imagine compromising the truth of God's Word to draw a bigger crowd or build a bigger audience. The mere thought of it sickens me. We've all seen enough of that counterfeit nonsense over the past few decades, and I've had a gut full of it. I'm not here to dance around it but to expose it. I hope you're starting to realize that the same should be true of you.

> For there is nothing covered, that shall not be revealed; neither hid, that shall not be known. Therefore whatsoever ye have spoken in darkness shall be heard in the light; and that which ye have spoken in the ear in closets shall be proclaimed upon the housetops.
> —JESUS (LUKE 12:2–3)

CHAPTER FOUR

Strength Made Perfect

And he said unto me, My grace is sufficient for thee: for my strength
is made perfect in weakness. Most gladly therefore will I rather glory
in my infirmities, that the power of Christ may rest upon me.
—2 CORINTHIANS 12:9

Y OU MAY BE wondering why we are instructed through Paul to put on the whole armor of God, even while we are also told through Paul that God's grace is *sufficient*. As stated in Ephesians 6:11, the answer is straightforward: "That ye may be able to stand against the wiles of the devil." Paul says right there—plain as the nose on your face if you've got one—that we have been given the armor of God for this specific reason: "that ye may be able to stand" even in your weakness, even in your wounding, even if you are unable to physically stand. His grace is sufficient to strengthen us for battle, no matter our physical state.

Even if you have a serious health condition, you can still put on the whole armor of God and stand against the enemy—both in your personal battles and in your intercessory prayers for others. Never forget that these weapons are *not* carnal (physical) but supernatural.

The controversies about *grace,* which is God's unmerited favor, reveal a prime example of how folks misappropriate a snippet of Scripture to cover their disobedience. Yet all we need to do is read the context of what Paul penned in that famous coffee-mug verse about grace to get it right. God said, "My grace is sufficient for thee: for my strength is made perfect in weakness."

The words *my strength* point directly to the reason we can't just take the easy road while bowing to a godless culture—certainly not while calling it grace. God's strength is an *explicit* component of His grace, and so is the armor. When we reject His armor, we reject His strength and grace. "For unto whomsoever much is given, of him shall be much required" (Luke 12:48), so we cannot take His grace for granted. Jesus was crystal clear about this.

When God gives us something, He expects us to use it. We don't get to put God's gifts in a closet to break out around the holidays. He gave us His armor to contend for the faith and to do "greater things" in His name, by the power of the Holy Spirit in us (John 14:12). If God's supernatural strength in us is perfected in our weakness, it must actively override our weakness, yes? It wouldn't be perfect if it didn't!

Recall our discussion of Ephesians 6:10 (the initial verse in Paul's armor discourse), where God told us to "be strong in the Lord, and in the power of his might." Doing so is not optional. A born-again believer will never prefer to be spiritually weak when they can be strong, so please take that to heart no matter your circumstances or physical condition.

A GARMENT OF PRAISE

Knowing that the armor of God is a component of God's grace, be assured that He has provided us with the means to gain courage and *strength* to take action and to speak out—even when we can't physically speak, even when we're weak, even when we're persecuted, even when we feel like we have no voice. But we must first put on His armor and stand on the Bible, or we'll inevitably falter. No matter what you're struggling with in your flesh, and no matter what you battle in your spirit, He's ready to do a perfect work *in your weakness*—both because of your weakness and despite your weakness.

His grace is sufficient to make beauty from ashes. His grace is sufficient to bring joy to our mourning. His grace is sufficient to make us stand firm like mighty oaks of righteousness. His grace is sufficient to help broken people find new meaning in life, so let's *put it on* like a garment of praise (Isa. 61:3).

It takes courage to take a stand on the Word of God. Cowardice always results in wickedness. When we boil it all down and get truly transparent about it, do you know why America is in the mess we're in as a nation and a culture? Because the church pulpits in America are full of fear-struck posers who are afraid to speak the truth of the Word of God. Even as churches have slowly begun reopening, pastors have only grown more silent—and eerily so.

I'm still heartbroken by the mass silence of pastors during the lockdowns of 2020, even by men I have long admired. But I'm also convicted. Because of their silence, we must speak out all the louder. When contending for the faith, truth *is* love, no matter how sharply you serve it. See the Bible for proof. Likewise, as noted earlier in this chapter, we can never speak *love* at the *expense* of truth. A lie is a lie, no matter how many *talking heads* repeat it. Love cannot exist in lies, and it's a lie to say otherwise.

STAND UP, STAND OUT, SPEAK UP, SPEAK OUT

We absolutely can and must tell the truth and be loving at the same time. You don't have to be a jerk for Jesus, but love can often sting when it exposes the truth, and sometimes that's necessary. I can be demonstrative and bold, but when all is said and done, I will stand before God and answer for what I said. Can you guess the results when the church goes silent and remains silent, even in the face of clear corruption, lawlessness, and injustice? That is exactly what we're seeing.

Sadly, like a handful of my colleagues, I saw this coming. I believe the fact that I sounded the prophetic alarm (with our Global Vision family in Tennessee and worldwide in full agreement) explains why the Lord is so strong in our church today. We armored up. We lifted the Word. We raised our faith and immediately began fighting the good fight. Maybe your pastor is already fully armored, standing strong, and risking all to speak out against the devil's wiles. If not, I believe the Lord calls you to speak life into his dry bones (Ezek. 37).

Maybe some of these silent pastors think that someone else will do all the dangerous (dirty?) work for them, or maybe they're cowering in fear of what people would think if they got fired up like "that Locke guy." Brethren, we'd better worry about what God thinks and stop worrying about what people think. Amen? We'd better stop fearing men and start fearing God alone (Matt. 10:28). The assumed truth is if you're right with God, you will stand for something in these evil days. Yet even sincere believers hesitate to stand or don't want to.

YOUR PLATFORM

I've heard pastors say, "Oh, that's easy for you. You've got a big social media platform. It's your job to stand up and speak out." That's one lame excuse for playing it safe. First, my social media platform resulted from my bold stance and vocal public opposition to evil. Second, what does the size of my platform have to do with yours? That sort of covetous self-sabotage is of the devil.

These people know better, but the truth doesn't seem to matter to them. They're embracing or surrendering to a world where right is wrong and wrong is right. Carnal feelings matter to these pastors. The approval of man matters to them, and safety matters to them. No matter the size of your platform—even if it's just one person—it's your job as a follower of Christ to stand boldly and speak out for justice, mercy, and faithfulness (Matt. 23:23). It's your job to stand in your home, workplace, church, and community. Just stand for what's right and watch the Lord move on your behalf!

These are like the days of Shadrach, Meshach, and Abednego in Daniel chapter 3. Most everyone is bowing down to the golden idols of the kings of the world, and hardly anyone is standing up for the righteousness found only in Jesus Christ. That's why churches like mine are overflowing with people who are *called*. Believers who hear the call are sick of lukewarm churches. They want to be fed the truth of God's Word by someone unafraid to say what needs to be said in these wicked last days.

Some of our folks have lost friends for their physical proximity or social media "friendship" with me. I get it. But I don't need you to be loyal to me. I need you to be loyal to the truth of God's Word. If I ever divert from the truth of the Bible, you stick with God's Word and confront me head-on. That's the sort of love and accountability in the body of Christ that can move mountains. But if you can remain silent and sit back at ease while three thousand babies per day get ripped from their mothers' wombs by Planned Parenthood—only to be butchered and sold for profit—I'm sorry, but I don't have time for your compliance or your godlessness.

As the old saying goes: if you don't stand for something, you'll fall for anything. Your silence makes you complicit to these abominations, and the devil is pleased with the bed you're lying in. He's the one who made it for you.

GOD HAS OUR BACKS

Sometimes I feel bad for my kids. *Sometimes.* When they start making new friends, the "that guy" conversation eventually comes up, and they have to answer the question, "Is your dad that guy on Twitter that everybody hates?" I know that's not fun for them, but I'm proud of their courage and fortitude. They know I'm not going to compromise the truth of what the Word of God says for anyone, least of all the folks for whom I'm directly responsible. If all this talk about being bold makes you nervous, stick with me, and I'm confident you'll turn a corner before you reach the end of this book.

Once you realize that all the strength and power you need for every battle in your life can be found in God's armor, you'll start putting it on daily. You'll certainly realize that the armor of God is not designed to sit in your closet. In the coming chapters, you'll see that every piece of the armor (except for prayer, which is the activator of the armor) covers just the front side of a believer. There aren't any rear-end covers or back braces. Why? Because the army of God should never retreat from the devil. We're supposed to take the fight to the enemy, fully trusting that God will have our backs! Jesus said the gates of hell will come against us but will not prevail (Matt. 16:18). You can trust Him to keep His promises.

THE WILES OF THE DEVIL

Reflect again on our current key verse in the armor discourse: "Put on the whole armour of God, that ye may be able to stand against the wiles of the devil" (Eph. 6:11). The purpose of the armor is to protect us and empower us as we stand against the *wiles*—the trickery, the deception, and the schemes—of the devil. His subtle tactics can take various forms, including the following:

1. Deception and lies: The devil is the father of lies (John 8:44) and takes the truth and twists it, mixing lies with what's good and godly. He's a master at making wrong seem right, but we can't fall for his tricks!

2. Temptation: The devil knows our weaknesses, and he'll use them against us. He'll dangle all sorts of temptations in front of us, promising pleasure and success.

3. Spiritual attacks and oppression: The devil will tear us down, rob us of our peace, and destroy our faith, so he

creates obstacles and roadblocks that keep us from fulfilling our purpose. He weighs us down with burdens, feelings of despair and hopelessness, and tells us lies straight from the pit of hell.

4. Distraction and worldly allure: The devil knows if he can get our eyes off the things of God, he can lead us astray. So he fills our lives with noise and busyness, causing us to lose our focus and tempting us to prioritize the things of this world over our walk with the Lord.

5. Division and discord: The devil wants nothing more than to see us divided, so he focuses us on our differences rather than our shared values and beliefs. By fueling conflicts, fostering bitterness, and promoting a spirit of division, he attempts to weaken the unity and effectiveness of the church.

6. Counterfeit spirituality: The devil presents false spiritual experiences, counterfeit miracles, and deceptive signs and wonders to mislead and deceive "even the elect" (Mark 13:22). He will try to throw us off course, lead us astray with his smoke and mirrors, and get us chasing after signs and wonders instead of standing firm on the solid rock of God's Word.

Recognizing the wiles of the devil requires spiritual discernment, rooted in a deep understanding of God's Word and a close relationship with Him. If you put on the whole armor of God to stand righteously, you will not fall prey to the devil's wiles, and you'll be equipped to stand through every attack, no matter how threatening or dangerous. You'll be spiritually alert, and you'll be able to recognize his wiles early on.

Spiritually alert people do not fall prey to the enemy's schemes. It's that simple. If you realize you're frequently the victim of deception, you need to get in the Bible, hear some good preaching, and get to a place where you spiritually feed yourself and grow your faith.

The devil doesn't care what you believe as long as it's not the truth, so he uses deception and lies to build pathways into your soul. He strategically constructs these paths by distorting truth, enticing you with false promises, and exploiting your vulnerabilities. His chief aim is to obscure the truth of God's Word and distort your perception of reality. He may present appealing alternatives that align with worldly desires but contradict God's principles. By blurring the line between right and wrong, he causes confusion and weakens your spiritual discernment.

When you buy into his lies, you enable him to manipulate and control you. He fabricates falsehoods that you believe about yourself, others, and even God. He whispers lies about your worth, purpose, and identity, aiming to make you insecure and dissatisfied. These lies can penetrate deeply into your soul, causing emotional and spiritual harm.

He also capitalizes on vulnerabilities such as unhealed wounds, unresolved conflicts, and unguarded areas of your life. Without any spiritual armor to protect you, he exploits these weaknesses to render you powerless for the kingdom of God.

To that end, he doesn't care what you believe, he doesn't care what you do, he doesn't care who you hang out with, and he certainly doesn't care where you go to church as long as you do not hear the truth. He does all he can to ensure you're never confronted with the truth because it is the truth that will make you free (John 8:32).

Even if we're suited and booted with our spiritual armor and fully protected from the enemy's attempts to influence us personally, he's still very much at work in the world around us. It's vital to realize that the devil's deceptions are increasing in scope and power every day. If you think 2020 epitomized the height of the devil's deceptions, you'd better brace yourself for what's coming.

The devil's schemes and lies will continue hitting peaks where we can all see them as clear as day. Though his work is easy to discern, he's always at work where he cannot easily be seen, busy weaving subtle lies and far more destructive deceptions where they can grow like cancer. No matter how calm things may seem on any given day, you can be sure that he'll continue doing what he does at an ever-increasing rate with ever-increasing intensity.

The Bible says that the church is going to get sucked right into the vortex of the enemy's master plan, so anyone who is trying to tell you otherwise is a liar. Even if every one of the devil's pawns and minions gets arrested for their crimes over the past fifty years, this is still the beginning of the enemy's end game. He's the master of deception, and he's not going down without a fight of biblical proportions (Rev. 12:12).

"And No Marvel…"

When the devil finally shows himself in person, he isn't going to look like that dude in the cartoons. He won't be wearing a red leather suit, he won't

37

have a long tail with a spearhead at the end of it, he won't have a slithering snake tongue, and he won't have goat horns on his head. The Bible says he'll transform into an angel of light, and in all likelihood, he'll appear standing at a church pulpit. In his second letter to the church at Corinth, Paul told us not to be surprised or "marvel" at this fact when he wrote:

> For such are false apostles, deceitful workers, transforming themselves into the apostles of Christ. And no marvel; for Satan himself is trans-formed into an angel of light. Therefore it is no great thing if his min-isters also be transformed as the ministers of righteousness; whose end shall be according to their works.
>
> —2 CORINTHIANS 11:13–15

I imagine the enemy's preaching will go like this: "Dearly beloved, this archaic and antiquated book belongs in the basement of the Vatican. It's best for the common good if we allow the culture to predicate how we live. We can all rejoice that there are multiple ways to heaven. After all, Oprah said so on multiple occasions. Que será, será, what will be, will be. Let us be accepting of everyone and tolerant of everyone. Let us love others in ways that make them love us! Let people choose their gender identity because—after all—Facebook now freely recognizes 127 different genders!"

That sort of perverse nonsense was already starting up before the lock-downs, and it's only going to get worse as high-dollar churches struggle to reopen with crowds large enough to cover their expenses. After all, they're little more than social-club business ventures, so nickels and noses set their bottom line—not the Word of God.

THE SCHEME OF BINARY GENDER ELIMINATION

Since I mentioned gender, let me go ahead and address this now. There are just two different genders. Just *two*. When a baby is born, you have a little boy or girl. I know there are rare cases of birth defects, but these anomalies don't constitute a new gender.

There are males and females, and there is nothing else in between. The Bible says so, science says so, and even the eye test says so. No gray area exists, and anyone with an ounce of common sense knows so. I could write endlessly about the long-range goals of this insidious scheme, and I'll touch on it a bit before we wrap up this chapter, but I'll have to save most of it for another text. Just know this: Whenever people start trying to destroy a foundational truth of life, you know the devil is afoot.

As hard as it is to believe, the uneducated, deluded masses are swallowing it all—hook, line, and sinker. They're conditioned to believe whatever the media, the government, and their unregenerate Bible-ignoring pastors tell them to believe, so here we go. I'm confident that you can see this isn't a conspiracy theory or a myth. This prophetic Word of God is coming to life in real time.

TIME-OUT: IT'S TIME TO MAN UP

I want to say something directly to men. Guys, I love you enough to tell you I do not care about your feelings. I love you even more by telling you that God doesn't care about your feelings, either. Feelings generally reflect your flesh, and He commands us to crucify that (Gal. 5:24). He cares about your faith, calling, and spiritual growth. That about covers it.

Have you noticed that manhood has been so beaten down in the American culture that suddenly, we're all supposed to be sensitive to how a man *feels* about something? Not what he thinks or theorizes, and not about his convictions, but how he feels emotionally. If you're a man who wants people tiptoeing around the truth with you to avoid hurting your feelings, you'd better get over yourself quickly. Quit whining, crying, and pouting. Get over it, man! You're under a spiritual attack, but you call it being sensitive? That's your flesh talking. Gentlemen, I'm an emotional guy, so I get it. But 1 Peter 3:7 says we're supposed to be the stronger vessel, ready for spiritual warfare with the calm of a well-trained soldier, so shake it off and man up!

We'd better rein in our delicate feelings and replace them with more faith. We can't let that scheme of the enemy destroy our calling. Our families are counting on us, as are our churches, communities, nations, and the world. Put off your fleshly feelings long enough to put on the whole armor, and you'll never go back to worldly self-absorption again. When you meet a man walking in the whole armor of God, you'll never hear him put his feelings ahead of the Word. Never.

It's no coincidence that the devil is trying to strip gender from the law books and the public discourse. He knows that if he can trick men into abandoning their uniquely masculine roles and responsibilities commanded in the Bible, he will be able to render us powerless. I believe every single man reading this book can take this challenge to heart and still healthily process their feelings in accordance with the Scripture, but it's up to each one of us to renew our minds and adjust our behaviors accordingly. The enemy is trying to emasculate you and your sons, just as he is trying to pervert the minds and harden the hearts of our wives and our daughters. Don't let it happen.

> And be not conformed to this world: but be ye transformed by the renewing of your mind, that ye may prove what is that good, and acceptable, and perfect, will of God.
>
> —ROMANS 12:2

CALLING THE REMNANT

We must get trained for what's coming next—both on the global stage and right here in our neighborhoods. It's coming strong, coming soon, and coming fast, so we need to put on the whole armor of God and get spiritually alert. The devil wants you to remain in a state of confusion and chaos. When you rise every morning, you'd better stand on the Bible and nothing more.

The Lord has always had a remnant of believers who are set apart for every battle, and I believe you have every opportunity to join the ranks of His chosen. Throughout history, it has never been the majority that stood for God's mercy, justice, and faithfulness. Instead, it has always been a small minority of people that rose up against tyranny and ungodliness like Shadrach, Meshach, and Abednego, saying in effect, "We will not bend, we will not bow, and we will not burn!"

We need to pray that God will help us be people of the Book who develop our own convictions and not just live on a preacher's or our parents' convictions. As we close this chapter and prepare to seek greater revelation concerning the power and purpose of every weapon God has provided for our battles, I want to challenge each of you.

Husbands and fathers, I challenge you to make the decision—right this moment—to forever put on the whole armor of God for your wives, families, churches, and communities. Armor up, prepare to fight the good fight, and contend for the faith as discussed in the preceding chapters.

Wives and mothers and all you amazing teens reading this book, I challenge you to do the same while also praying that the men in your life answer their unique calling as men. Let's commit before God never to be cowards, comply with lawlessness, or surrender in silence. Let's commit to being bold men, bold women, and bold teens, too; saints who will suit up and boot up, standing firm and looking the culture straight in its eyes while speaking the truth of God's Word, declaring, "We will not bow!"

> Then Nebuchadnezzar spake, and said, Blessed be the God of Shadrach, Meshach, and Abednego, who hath sent his angel, and delivered his servants that trusted in him, and have changed the king's word, and yielded their bodies, that they might not serve nor worship any god, except their own God.
>
> —DANIEL 3:28

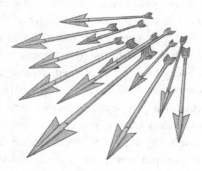

CHAPTER FIVE

Fighting the Right Enemy

And the great dragon was cast out, that old serpent, called the
Devil, and Satan, which deceiveth the whole world: he was cast
out into the earth, and his angels were cast out with him.
—REVELATION 12:9

I THINK IT'S A sin to make the Bible boring. There will always be news reported in the morning that is fresh and timely, but it will never be more fresh or more relevant than the book we call the Bible. I don't know about you, but that excites me. As we continue plumbing the deeper mysteries of spiritual warfare, we'll soon start zooming in on each piece of the whole armor of God, but first, Paul ensured we understood the urgent dual nature of the armor and exactly what it is that we battle against. If you are saved by the glorious grace of the gospel of Jesus Christ and have been filled with the Holy Spirit, you will walk every day in spiritual warfare.

> For we wrestle not against flesh and blood, but against principalities, against powers, against the rulers of the darkness of this world, against spiritual wickedness in high places.
> —EPHESIANS 6:12

In this, our next key verse from Paul's armor of God discourse, we see that we—God's people—don't wrestle against flesh and blood but against far more dangerous forces. We are in a UFC smackdown battle (spiritually speaking) against principalities, powers, rulers of the darkness of this world, and spiritual wickedness in high places. That's a lot of opposition. Meanwhile, people of the liberal/socialist persuasion insist things are just going to get better and better and better because the government is going to keep us safe at home and give us everything we ever need, free of cost, all to usher in a utopian society. You are stone-cold ignorant if you believe that.

Not only has world history repeatedly proven that socialism (and all its tyrannical derivatives) erases liberty and ends in devastation, but the Bible also proves it. It doesn't say things will get better; it says evil men and seducers shall wax worse and worse and worse, and there will be an apostasy—a great falling away (2 Tim. 3:13). We are in that season of the falling away, and churches today are full of apostates who accept sin that would have never been accepted thirty years ago in the United States of America.

Before you get too much angrier at the liberty-stealing liberals, you need to realize you can't win the right battle by fighting the wrong enemy. We are in a fight for our lives, a fight for our souls, a fight for Judeo-Christian morality, and a fight for New Testament principles. The only way to fight a good fight and to fight the *right* fight is to know who the real enemy is.

Most of us (myself included) fight the wrong people all the time. You're not wrestling with your spouse. You're not fighting with your jerk boss. You're not fighting with ridiculous church members. You're not fighting with Democrats or Republicans. Okay? The Bible says we wrestle *not* against flesh and blood. The person you're mad at is not the person you ought to be fighting. In fact, you shouldn't even be mad at them, as that serves no one but the enemy. You ought to be mad at the devil and fight only against him and the dark powers that serve him, but always pray for the people he uses.

TIME-OUT: IT'S NOT TOO LATE

I addressed this in *This Means War*, but I need to ensure we're on the same page before I proceed. People are often uber-critical of preachers like me who stand on Bible prophecy. They say things like, "You people have been talking about the rapture of the church and the return of the Lord for almost two thousand years! Where are the signs of His coming in this generation?"

Let me remind you, it took Jesus three thousand years to show up the first time, but He still kept His promise! Sure, in this dimension, it's been two thousand years since He told us to keep watch for His return, but to the Lord, a day is like a thousand years, and a thousand years are like a day (2 Pet. 3:8). Remember, He is not constrained by space or time as we know it.

On our calendars, He has delayed His return for two thousand years, but that's like two days to Him, and on that scale, now that we're in the third millennium, we've begun the *third day*. Recall that after His death on the cross, Jesus remained in the grave—outside space and time—for two days and rose again on the morning of the third day. When I consider that, I hear, "Get ready for the morning has come." Praise God. It's an interesting alignment from any perspective.

Considering all that, I have a red-hot principle you should never forget. You'd better be glad the Lord is delaying His return because, by doing so, He's giving everyone proper time to repent and believe the gospel. He is long-suffering for us, "not willing that any should perish," but tarrying (delaying) so "that all should come to repentance" (2 Pet. 3:9).

You might be religious but still lost, so you'd better be glad Jesus hasn't returned yet. He's giving you a chance to get saved by the grace of God, and if you don't believe that, then you don't believe an ounce of the Bible. He *is* coming again, and you need to erase any doubts you have about that, or you'll never understand the urgent purpose of the armor. You might say, "Well, you can't take the Bible and prove He's coming tonight." True, but you can't take the Bible and prove that He *isn't* coming tonight, either. Are you willing to gamble with your eternity, knowing that Jesus told us He would come at a time we least expect Him, like a thief in the night (Matt. 24:43)? Jesus is coming—soon.

THE PRINCE OF THE POWER OF THE AIR

The Bible tells us in no uncertain terms that the devil is "the prince of the power of the air" (Eph. 2:2), and it's obvious that the airwaves are his playground and his pipeline into our senses. We must get prepared, fight while he's striking, and fight *where* he's striking. In 1 Peter, we read:

> Be sober, be vigilant; because your adversary the devil, as a roaring
> lion, walketh about, seeking whom he may devour.
>
> —1 PETER 5:8

Most Christians, even those who know that verse well, don't take it seriously. These believers live in the flesh—in the natural—not the supernatural.

45

They never want to talk about what is happening around them in the spiritual world. They have no interest in studying all the Lord tells us about angels and demons and the heavenly dimensions. They say they believe in heaven and hell but never want to discuss their implications in the natural world. They don't believe what they cannot see, never realizing that their unbelief is the absence of faith.

If we could see everything going on in the spiritual dimensions, it would freak us out to the core. It would unveil the spiritual forces at work behind human actions, decisions, and circumstances, shedding light on the unseen influences that shape our world. It would undoubtedly challenge our preconceived notions of reality and confront us with the gravity of the spiritual dynamics impacting our lives. Seeing the magnitude of demonic activity would be unbearable were it not for the fact that we would also see the actions, missions, and interventions of angels, the victorious power of God to defeat every work of the enemy, the authority of the name of Jesus that causes every knee to bow in heaven and on earth, and the impenetrable divine protection we walk in when wearing the whole armor of God.

If you still have doubts that we live in a multi-dimensional universe where angels and demons are warring all around us, you need to suspend that disbelief long enough to take the Bible seriously, maybe for the first time in your life. If you are a doubter and scoff at or dismiss that simple mental exercise while reading this book, you'll continue your life unchanged and unarmed.

Give the Word of God a chance to speak to you as the God-given guide it is, or you'll never stop fighting the wrong enemies. And at the end of the day, you'll have run the loser's race, wasting your life by "beating the air" (1 Cor. 9:26). If you are on that path, over time, the real enemy will steal, kill, and destroy everything you hold dear.

SHOOTING AT DUMMIES

Just before all hell started breaking loose in March of 2020, I read about an especially interesting strategy deployed during World War II. Have you ever heard of the dummy paratroopers? These weren't paratroopers that were stupid or uneducated. They were fake humans. The military put these rubber dummy soldiers in airplanes, and when they got to a densely populated area where they knew the enemy was lying in wait, the American army would parachute these dummies out of the airplanes. It was a diversionary tactic, a ruse to waste the enemy's bullets.

The enemy would start shooting like crazy, and while they were shooting at the dummies, our boys came in with a ground attack and took care of business against a depleted enemy. In the same way, the devil triggers us into fights with other people, and while we're distracted, he comes in on the fronts we're not watching and starts wreaking havoc. Today in the church and our culture, we're wasting our weapons on straw men, puppets, and dummies while the real enemy advances.

I'll confess that I've been as guilty of that as anyone because it's easy to get angry with people who attack you or your loved ones. It's easy to get vindictive. It's easy to feel the need to get revenge, even when you know that nothing good will come from getting back at them. "Vengeance is mine; I will repay, saith the Lord" (Rom. 12:19). Don't ever try to do through your flesh what only God can do righteously in the Spirit. Trying to fix something without Him—operating in the flesh—always ends up worse than it started.

RULERS IN HIGH PLACES

Our key verse also teaches what we are fighting and wrestling against, starting with principalities. Most of us best know the word *principality* as an entity relating to a governmental seat of power of some sort. We talk about the principalities of a community—the leaders, the agency heads, the mayors, the governors, the elected officials, and the other people in high positions that have some semblance of authority over us as citizens.

Ephesians 6:12 further identifies the enemy we fight against as "powers... rulers of the darkness of this world...spiritual wickedness in high places." This gives us non-negotiable New Testament principles that put steel in the armor. There are dark powers and spirits in this world because of the depravity of man's heart, and there are rulers over that darkness who are stirring it up while perpetrating spiritual wickedness in high places. Their goal is to lord over us in every way possible.

The term *high places* is not referring to other planets or the moon, and it's not referring to God's abode in His heavenly dimension. Remember, the Bible calls the devil the "prince of the power of the air" (Eph. 2:2), so he has dispatched his forces in the high places of authority and communications. Before 2019, most folks didn't want to believe the devil had so effectively infiltrated the high places in this world. But 2020 changed all that. Very few born-again believers today doubt that the devil is deeply involved in the governments and communications giants (big tech) that rule this planet. Even cultural Christians are starting to see that there are indeed dark "shadowy" powers manipulating these entities. When the Bible warns us that the devil controls "high places" and rules over "the air," you can take it literally.

Consider who controls the transfer of information in your life. The devices we use for entertainment, social media, and digital communications transfer this information primarily through the air (on the airwaves). When I started raising the alarm about these concerns in 2019, even some of my folks at Global Vision thought I was overreaching, but not now. Anyone can see that evil powers are behind all the corruption, deception, and lawlessness that took hold during 2020 and continues to wreak havoc on our country. When the devil puts the next wave of deceptive schemes into play, we'd be wise to be better prepared. Don't ever grow numb to all that 2020 revealed.

The devil has always put his minions in high places of authority and information control, and the Bible told us that it would all become blindingly clear in the last of the last days, and so it is. The devil is a big evil bully who enters through the airwaves and high places he commands, so you'd better be careful what you and your family dabble in. Be careful what you allow into your home, what you allow into your marriage, and what you allow through your media devices.

THE GROUND ATTACK

Though many of you have come to realize that there are very real high places full of wickedness in this nation and around the world, all controlled by territorial spirits of darkness, don't think for a moment that the same dark powers haven't found a way to creep into your life. If you've ever experienced a spiritual heaviness, doubt, and fear that makes it difficult to believe God's truth or walk in your calling, these are signs of being under a spiritual attack. If your guard is down, the enemy can cause an atmosphere of moral decay in your home or neighborhood that manifests as immorality, dishonesty, addictions, violence, and other destructive behaviors and attitudes. By opposing the work of God, these influences can negatively impact the well-being of a community and hinder the spiritual effectiveness of the church in that area, making it difficult to spread the gospel or see the Spirit of God move in people's lives.

While we've been distracted by the revealing of all the evil forces working at the higher levels, the enemy has been coming after every soul he can, right here on the ground where we live. This sort of deception through distraction has always been a primary tactic in his ground assault against the body of Christ, but it's never been this easy to see.

You can visit towns that are squeaky clean as a hound's tooth, where everyone seems to get along well, and the community is on a relatively healthy trajectory. Meanwhile, just across the tracks, the adjacent town can be immersed in lawlessness, with methamphetamines or opioids burning families to the ground and law enforcement agencies seemingly powerless against it all. These devastated communities also lack leaders, churches, and any form of addiction program that can effectively help. This geographic paradox reveals a demonic force controlling the air—the high places—over that area. Absent a real move of the Spirit among the army of God in that town or county, it will only worsen.

If the church doesn't get busy ensuring the light of the gospel begins to shine in these oppressed communities, the darkness will eventually consume every town and every home within its reach. Like yeast spreading through the dough, this spiritual wickedness spreads like cancer, and the local leaders will eventually fall victim to it and fall in line, as will every citizen who foolishly places their trust in them (Mark 8:15). That's what my Bible is saying, so I know that's what yours is saying.

But God

In the post-2020 world, even secular folks are crying out about wickedness, but the enemy has deceived many into believing it's all coming from Christians and conservatives in America—along with Israel and the Jews on the global scene. I am convinced there are wicked actors in high places in our government who are making decisions to destroy this nation and ultimately destroy this world—even as the masses remain in denial or are simply blind to the truth. On and on we go, and there's no end in sight.

It might surprise you to hear that revealing this sort of delusion among these powerful entities gets me fired up, even while it's profoundly discouraging to most. I've learned that when the devil is fulfilling his role in this prophetic timeline, it's really God Almighty—the Author—fulfilling His Word in His amazingly bittersweet story that we're all living (2 Thess. 2:11).

As the great preacher Martin Luther once said, "Even the devil is God's devil."[1] As I noted in my introduction, Satan is the antagonist (the adversary) God wrote into the Bible and our personal stories, and he's little more than a dog on God's leash. He can only bite when God says he can bite. The Lord allows these attacks to advance the prophetic timeline, but don't ever think He has left us unprotected. "Greater is he that is in you, than he that is in the world" (1 John 4:4). But as we fully explored earlier, we must fully embrace the Holy Spirit's presence within us for His power to work through our lives.

The devil has limited power, but God is omnipotent, and His unlimited power to fight the enemy is ours when we put on the whole armor of God.

THE PROPHET DANIEL AND THE ANGELS

We talk a lot about fasting these days, and not always for the right reasons, but here's a very interesting thing about fasting and prayer. You've probably heard of the twenty-one-day Daniel fast. That twenty-one-day idea comes from the Book of Daniel, chapter 10. Daniel was praying for an answer from God concerning Israel's captivity in Persia. As he prayed, the Bible says it took twenty-one days for Daniel to receive the answer from God.

We learn that God had answered Daniel on the very first day of his fast. God didn't wait until day eighteen, seven, two, or twenty-one. The Bible says God dispatched an angel to answer Daniel's prayer on day one. Why did it take twenty-one days of prayer and fasting before he finally realized he had the answer all along? The Bible tells us that the king of Persia—the political and governmental authority over that area—was under the control of a demonic force so strong it could thwart Daniel's ability to receive the answer from the angel.

The Bible says that the devil was so powerful against this unnamed angel that the Lord dispatched the Archangel Michael—the very angel who cast the devil out of heaven in Revelation 12:7–9—to step in and flex his spiritual muscles and finally get the answer to Daniel.

You might read this and think, "That sounds like a scene from *The Avengers.*" But this isn't coming from a comic book. It's from the Word of God. The Author who wrote each of us into this supernatural story constantly reminds us that reality is far stranger and more powerful than fiction. Part of the reason we're drawn to supernatural fiction and superhero movies is that their themes ring true in our spirits. Deep inside, we all know we are not the most highly evolved beings in the universe, let alone other dimensions, not even close.

THE ANGELS AROUND YOU

Both angels and demons have been dispatched on your behalf. Angels for good and demons for evil. The demons are coming to serve up evil regardless, so don't miss out on the good. As long as we're not bowing to the enemy in ignorance or fear, God has our backs. And when needed, He'll send angels to help us. Why would anyone want to dismiss that reality when the evidence of their existence is so pervasive throughout history? I don't get it. Lost folks will readily believe in advanced aliens visiting our planet, but they scoff at the possibility of angels. It's crazy.

The Bible says you may "have entertained angels unawares" (Heb. 13:2), so you'd be wise to walk through your day assuming you'll unknowingly encounter angels from time to time. Angels and demons are at work everywhere in this world. Don't ever doubt it. Have you ever been in a situation where you walked away and thought, "Where did that person go? They were here for a moment, but now they're gone." I'll bet most of us have.

Jesus said that some of us would be honored, rewarded, and blessed because we fed Him, clothed Him, housed Him, visited Him, or gave Him something to drink. We're going to say, "When did we feed You? When did we clothe You? When did we house You? When did we visit You in prison or the hospital?" And He'll say, "When you did it unto one of the least of these." (See Matthew 25:34–40.)

Through this beautiful passage, the Lord commands us to care for and comfort the neediest among humans. I suggest starting with the unborn, newborns, the infirm, the homeless, prisoners, orphans, and widows. But you'd better know there are spiritual forces (both good and bad) all around God's people, and they can masquerade as normal folks at will. You'll struggle to know the difference without the Holy Spirit's discernment. Through the power of the Spirit, putting on the whole armor of God ensures you're in tune with the activity of the spiritual realm around you. As born-again believers, we shouldn't need the realization of angels and demons to remind us to love the least as commanded, but if it helps you start taking the supernatural more seriously, praise God.

JUST GEARING UP

As mentioned earlier, Jesus said that "the gates of hell shall not prevail against" His church (Matt. 16:18). The "gates of hell" is a metaphor for the full force of the devil and his demons in their final offensive on their turf. Jesus' church consists of born-again believers who do as He instructs in the Bible, not those who merely identify with the words *church* and *Christian*. Notice that Jesus didn't say that the gates of hell wouldn't take ground from the church. Instead, He said it wouldn't *prevail* when the devil makes his final desperate assault. So—like it, love it, park it, pay rent, it doesn't matter to me—I believe if the gates of hell will rise against us regardless of what we do, we might as well give the devil something to be mad about, right?

Will I lie around on a Sunday morning while the sun warms my feet and just wait for the devil to show up at *my* house? Not a chance. I will take the fight *to him* at the point of his attack, and I will be suited up and booted up when I get there, fully expectant that the angels will work on my behalf if ever needed, just as they have done many times before. What about you?

> For by him were all things created, that are in heaven, and that are in earth, visible and invisible, whether they be thrones, or dominions, or principalities, or powers: all things were created by him, and for him: And he is before all things, and by him all things consist.
> —COLOSSIANS 1:16–17

CHAPTER SIX

The Dual Purpose of the Armor

Wherefore take unto you the whole armour of God, that ye may be able to withstand in the evil day, and having done all, to stand.
—EPHESIANS 6:13

THE NEXT KEY verse in Paul's armor discourse opens with the word *wherefore*. When we see *wherefore*, we should always ask what it's there for. *Wherefore* means because of this fact, this absolute fact. So the text is saying, because of the darkness of this world and the spiritual wickedness in high places, take unto you the whole armor of God. If you hope to survive the attacks of these dark forces, putting on the *whole* armor is not an option. Paul already touched on these themes earlier in the armor discourse (in Ephesians 6:11), and he mentions them again two verses later for a good reason.

Repetition is a powerful teaching device that the Lord uses throughout the Bible, so whenever I double back to reinforce the intent of His instructions, I hope you'll recognize it's for good reason. You have to take the whole armor as a single unified suit, or you take none of it at all. Each piece depends on the others. They're both interconnected and interdependent, so we're left vulnerable and virtually powerless if we don't have all seven elements of the armor working together in unison.

The Lord also used our key verse to ensure we know "the evil day" is indeed coming and that only the whole armor of God can help us survive it. Don't miss that. The armor of God has always provided the framework for living the Spirit-filled life as a warrior for God, but in the last of the last days—the evil day—the armor is essential for believers. We'll take a deeper look at that day later in this chapter.

I love that the Holy Spirit doesn't mince words. I get sick and tired of hearing people say, "I have this habit, I have this addiction, I have this devilish thing in my life, but God understands me... He's got me." Let me tell you what God understands and what He's got. God understands that He is holy and righteous and that His Son died not to aid you in your sin but to deliver you from your sin. He's got you when you get that, and you'll struggle to get that until you get born again in the Spirit. Until then, you'll remain in rebellion even if you don't realize it, and the armor remains powerless even if you try to put it on ten times a day.

Every day you delay is another day you're left vulnerable to enemy attacks. Titus 1:2 tells us that God cannot lie. So you either believe all the Bible, or you believe none of the Bible. As I unapologetically wrote earlier in the book, you only *believe* the parts you *behave*. If you say you believe the Bible, but your life stands in stark contradiction to the Bible, then you don't believe the Bible. It is that simple.

DEFENSE AND OFFENSE

In our key verse, Paul repeats that the armor empowers us to stand. Again, repetition in the Bible always conveys the urgency of the message. Paul already told us to stand just two verses earlier, and then he ends this verse by repeating that command. But notice this. In the middle of verse 13, Paul writes that we need the armor to "withstand." *Stand* and *withstand* are two different words, but they're used in the same context for good reasons. The armor was not created solely to empower us to stand and fight the devil in active battle. It was also created to ensure we can withstand (survive) what the devil throws against us even when we aren't in battle mode.

That points directly to the fact that He will cover us defensively even when we are weak and have no offensive fight in us—if we would ensure to put on the whole armor. We can only *stand* to fight if we can *withstand* the enemy's never-ending attacks. In other words, you won't be able to stand up and speak if you can't withstand the evil and persecution that comes against you—before, during, and after making your stand.

Knowing there is no such thing as a Bible-believing pacifist, be reminded that none of us gets a pass on spiritual warfare—defense and offense. You are either standing under His covering or cowering apart from it. The choice is yours.

THE BEST DEFENSE

As you'll soon see, the armor of God represents the active expression of the born-again life in Christ, so you can't say you believe the Bible if you don't believe that God requires us to put on the armor daily. Even now, you are in a battle, and the Word of God says you must stand in the battle to withstand the enemy's mounting attacks.

An adage commonly attributed to George Washington says, "The best defense is a good offense." It's hard to disagree with that. I think the adage helps explain why the armor discourse uses the offensive term *stand* three times and the defensive term *withstand* just once. When we're boldly standing in an offensive posture, it's much easier to withstand the enemy's attacks. Don't forget that he is powerless against God, so when we go on the offensive by God's command, the enemy has no choice but to retreat. When was the last time you went on the offensive against evil?

Far too many Christians wither away when problems and persecution come. I'm not trying to be a doomsday prophet, just preaching gloom and doom. On the contrary, I'm looking for Jesus Christ, not the Antichrist. But we are already living in days of intense spiritual persecution. If things continue the way that they are going in the United States, many souls hang in the balance.

REAL PERSECUTION

Some of us began talking about spiritual persecution long before it started breaking out everywhere. Many agreed with us, but most Christians are so ignorant of the workings of real persecution that they never take it seriously enough to get armored up. That's why they're crumbling in fearful compliance to tyranny today. They have no power to stand or withstand even the weakest attacks.

Visit a communist or socialist nation, and you'll discover how bad persecution can get. Go to most Islamic-led nations, and you'll learn what Christian persecution is. I'm sorry if you got unfriended on Facebook because you posted a picture of the cross. That is not spiritual persecution. Spiritual persecution is when they round you up for what you wrote on Facebook, throw you in prison, and want to hang you on a cross for opening your mouth about Jesus. When that day comes, we'll find out who loves Him. We'll find out how many "I go to church on Sunday but do whatever I jolly well please on Monday" Christians we have in America.

Jesus told us that the road that leads to eternal destruction is broad, while the road that leads to eternal life is narrow. He also told us that most choose the broad road while few choose the narrow one (Matt. 7:13–14). I'm not trying to be negative and judgmental, but I'm telling you the truth, and I care about your salvation. As a gospel preacher, I'm always contending for the faith on your behalf, even if it angers you.

Most churches in the United States of America are filled with people entertained by religion while never being born again a natural day in their lives. When it all comes crashing down, they will roll with whatever makes them feel safe and comfortable—the path of least resistance—the broad road. Most Christians will not *stand* because they won't be able to *withstand* what's coming.

THE PROPHESIED EVIL DAY

From our key verse, we know the whole armor of God enables us to withstand the evil day. If you don't believe we're already in the evil day, I trust you believe it's on the horizon. Scripture instructs every generation to live as if it were the last, ours included, but no generation has ever witnessed the unfolding of the full prophetic timeline until ours. The *evil day* points directly to the last of the last days, the "due season" Jesus spoke of in His Olivet Discourse (Matt. 24:45). As you know by now, I am thoroughly convinced that we are now in that due season, and most theologians and preachers who stand on the Word of God—and only the Word of God—fully agree.

There has always been pornography in this world. There has always been perversity and violence on top of violence in this world. The devil has always destroyed lives. He has been on a rampage, and he doesn't play fair. He causes pain, brokenness, and devastation as he seeks to steal, kill, and destroy everything good in this world. But, my friend, we serve a mighty God. In the midst of pain and brokenness, He brings healing. In the midst of devastation, He brings deliverance and restoration.

We don't have to fight this battle on our own. We can lean on God's strength and thank Him that He's already won the victory for us through His Son. The sacrifice of Jesus on the cross and His resurrection provide victory over sin, death, and the power of the enemy. Through faith in Jesus and the indwelling of the Holy Spirit, deliverance from the destructive influence of the devil is possible.

The topic of deliverance has filled many books, and indeed, I am in the process of writing one myself. But it's worth taking a moment here to list the basic forms deliverance can take:

1. Salvation: By accepting Jesus as Lord and Savior, we are rescued from the dominion of darkness and brought into the kingdom of God, experiencing forgiveness, restoration, and eternal life.

2. Healing and restoration: God offers healing for those who have been wounded or broken by the devil's schemes. Through prayer, repentance, and seeking God's guidance, individuals can find healing from emotional, spiritual, and physical wounds inflicted by the enemy.

3. Spiritual warfare and authority: Believers have been equipped with spiritual weapons and authority to resist and overcome the devil's attacks. By putting on the armor of God, engaging in fervent prayer, and relying on the power of the Holy Spirit, believers can stand against the enemy, experiencing victory and deliverance in spiritual battles.

4. Deliverance ministry: God has also provided the gift of deliverance ministry within the church. Trained individuals can help guide and assist those struggling with demonic oppression or influence, using biblical principles and the power of prayer to bring freedom and restoration.

While the devil seeks to destroy lives, the name of Jesus sets the captives free! No matter how many fiery darts the enemy throws at you, you can experience freedom, restoration, and victory over his destructive schemes. So be encouraged! This world is overrun with wickedness, but there will never come a time or a season on this side of heaven when we lose our ability to live godly and stand up for what is right, so do not fear the evil day. There will never be a season that we will be unable to stand against evil in this world, so stop using lazy, Laodicean church excuses, like, "The days are so wicked we can't publicly live for the Lord" or, "If the enemy is the ruler of this world, we might as well just make a safe place for ourselves and wait him out." If you're a true Jesus follower, you can only obey the Lord amid this wickedness.

Very soon, there will be no place for the cowards to hide from the persecution. They'll simply be forced to reject the Bible as hate speech as the pedophiles, Satanists, Luciferians, LGBTQs, communists, anarchists, and all the other biblically perverse subcultures of humanity continue to gain power in high places. Right under our noses, these groups and the spirits that control them have crawled out of the shadows—over just the past twenty years or so—to lord over us in this evil day, just as the Bible foretold.

Few could have imagined America tolerating such darkness in the '90s, much less giving authority to principalities and high places. The devil has deceived his puppets into worshiping him while mocking God, and our children and the masses of unbelievers are being influenced by their demonism no matter what they claim their motives to be. Jesus said we must boldly obey Him and stand for what is right no matter the cost (Matt. 10:32–38). So don't crumble when you're called to go on the offensive.

TIME-OUT: THE GREAT FALLING AWAY

If you've been around the things of God for more than a handful of years, you've watched a demonic shift in the American church—a literal apostasy beyond anything that we could have ever imagined before this generation. You can read about it in the Bible, but watching it play out on the world's stage can be terribly demoralizing. Leading up to 2020, it seemed every month, another major leader in evangelical Christianity—people who wrote *New York Times* best-selling books about God—was denying His existence or the existence of hell, or both. What some call "the great falling away" had become a rapid growth movement within modern Christianity.

Even before the illegal pandemic lockdowns, most churches had become little more than glorified stage shows and social clubs. I can enjoy a degree of entertainment in all areas of life. I don't mind telling a joke in a message to help make a point of relatable truth, so I get it. But most major market churches have evolved into microwave rock concerts, comedy shows, and self-help seminars where the gospel makes an occasional half-hearted cameo appearance. So we shouldn't be surprised that many of these same churches now bow to principalities and rulers of darkness in this evil day.

Regarding the Word of God, I'm not compromising for you, your mama, or my mama. I'm not compromising the truth for anyone, "for what fellowship hath righteousness with unrighteousness? and what communion hath light with darkness?" (2 Cor. 6:14). Revival is breaking out at our church, and that wouldn't have been the case if I had bowed to the commands of ungodly principalities or other powers of darkness during the lockdown of 2020. Whether future lawmakers say churches should be opened or closed, all I can hear in the Spirit is, "As for me and my house, we will serve the LORD" (Josh. 24:14–15).

It doesn't matter if Facebook and Twitter throw me under their jail and permanently shut down our accounts. God established our platform out of thin air, so He'll reestablish it just as quickly if the need arises. Like so many of you, I have reached a place where I refuse to cater to the appetites of the masses or compromise with people who bow to the lawless evil running wild in America. These are dangerous days, and I'm under constant attack for standing firm on the Bible. God won't fail those of us who put on His armor daily. In the power of His might, I can withstand it all.

THUS SAITH THE LORD!

Even before the enemy started his attack against the church, I was already sick of cotton candy preachers leading their congregations into tolerating and celebrating sinful perversions in the name of love. In these dark days, we need pastors to contend for the faith by thundering out the whole Word of God without compromise. We need pastors to shout, "Thus saith the Lord! Thus saith the Lord! Thus saith the Lord!"

It's not "thus saith the Baptists" or "thus saith the Pentecostals." It's not "thus saith Greg Locke" or "thus saith Global Vision." It's "thus saith the Lord!" And for those who believe preachers ought to stay out of politics, I challenge you to show me one preacher in the Bible that refused to call out wicked, evil, perverse ungodliness in the governments of their day. You will not find one. Every preacher and prophet in the Bible that was worth his salt went on the offensive against the culture and spoke out against spiritual wickedness among the priests, the princes, and the kings—the rulers in high places—no matter the cost. We must do all we can to stand, and we must do all we can to withstand. We must fearlessly speak up and speak out in this demonic culture for the sake of the gospel.

Being the Remnant

If you're bold enough to confront that nonsense in public, you'd better be sure the Holy Spirit led you there, and you'd better be armored up! I'm not saying you need a PhD in Old Testament studies or you have to be some New Testament theologian. All you need is to be infused with the power of the Holy Spirit. He will give you a hunger for the meat of the Word of God, and He will tell you what to say (Matt. 10:19). You don't have to fret about it. You don't have to get it all scripted out and rehearsed. Just be willing to stand firm no matter who walks away from your life, no matter who threatens you to be silent, and no matter what they take from you.

There is a hungry remnant of people who pray and fast for the people of God to stand up like John the Baptist, to be a voice that cries out to this wicked cultural wilderness, already "having done all, to stand" (Eph. 6:13). This is why you must be trained in the proper purposes and acts each piece of the armor of God was designed for. You can't sustainably withstand or stand in this evil day until you've already done all that is necessary to stand.

Here We Are

Though we would all love to see a Christ-centered culture leading this demon-oppressed world into the love, kindness, and unity we have long prayed for, that's not in the biblical narrative the Lord has written. We must accept that reality and stop acting like we can somehow outrun His prophecies. The days of great tribulation are on their way, as foretold in Matthew 24:21. I briefly discussed the millennial reign in *This Means War,* and that joyous season is still to come, but it is not going to start in the day and age in which we live. (See Revelation 20:4.)

No matter how difficult these days become, I often remind folks that we live in the days that the apostles of the first century prayed for. Their greatest hope was that this evil day would come before they died. They wanted to be here to stand and withstand while contending for the faith until the day Jesus returns. Don't let it escape you how blessed we truly are to be alive in this due season.

I'm not asking you to be like me. I'm not even asking you to be like the first-century apostles. I'm simply asking that you be biblical in all ways and pray to be more like Jesus every day. Paul taught us to follow him only to the extent that he followed Jesus (1 Cor. 11:1). But how many believers are doing *that*?

LET'S DO THIS!

As we now turn to unlock the supernatural power found in each element of the whole armor of God, piece by piece, let's reflect on what Paul wrote to help prepare us for the process. We're in a spiritual battle, and we need to recognize and identify the *real* enemy. We need to realize that there is a daunting amount of demonic activity around us in every individual, institution, and principality that is not operating by the full counsel of the Word of God. And we've got to recognize that there is no cost too high to stand for Jesus Christ as we fight this good fight for the gospel's sake.

In these last of the last days, I'm convinced that serving Jesus will not cost you *something*; it will cost you *everything*. If you're unwilling to pay the price as a true follower of Christ, don't just go to church and pretend you are. Why bother? Jesus called His disciples to leave everything and follow Him. We must be honest with ourselves and ask if we really want to be born-again followers of Jesus Christ because He'll accept nothing but our all.

> If any man will come after me, let him deny himself, and take up his cross daily, and follow me.
>
> —JESUS (LUKE 9:23)

CHAPTER SEVEN

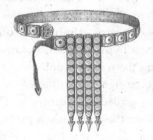

Belt of Truth

I have given them thy word; and the world hath hated them,
because they are not of the world, even as I am not of the
world. I pray not that thou shouldest take them out of the
world, but that thou shouldest keep them from the evil.
—JESUS (JOHN 17:14–15)

A SIDE FROM REJECTING Christ, the worst thing a believer can ever do is ignore the supernatural and prophetic realities we're exploring in this book. Spiritual warfare is something that affects us all. None of us can escape it. Jesus said, "In the world ye shall have tribulation: but be of good cheer; I have overcome the world" (John 16:33). He has made a way for us to overcome every attack, even when there seems to be no way (Isa. 43:19).

Jesus often prayed for us to be *delivered* and protected from evil. In the context of spiritual warfare, He was praying specifically for the saints who obediently stand in His armor. The hunker-down-in-your-bunker mentality that most believers have will never work in a spiritual battle. We are not called to follow Jesus in this work by running away from the battle or hiding in fear. We are called, as God's people, to go on the offensive as well as the defensive—out in the world. We are to fight back against the workers of iniquity wherever they exist, in accordance with the truth of God's Word. We are to *stand*.

> Stand therefore, having your loins girt about with truth.
> —EPHESIANS 6:14

In our next key verse from the armor discourse, Paul wrote, "Stand therefore." Now let me stop and tell you what the word *therefore* is there for. Because we wrestle not against flesh and blood but against principalities and spiritual wickedness in high places; because we must recognize the real enemy to avoid putting the wrong people in our spiritual crosshairs; and because we are in an ongoing fight, stand *therefore* having your loins—your midsection and your guts—girded up with truth. This reveals that we can't stand if we're not covered in the truth. It's a prerequisite, if you will. That said, there is another aspect of truth that the belt is designed to protect.

In the context of the armor discourse, Paul is not referring to the *truth* of the full counsel of the Bible or the truth about what is going on in the world. While those truths are inescapable and required in spiritual battle, your head knowledge of these truths cannot protect you from evil. We'll indeed deal with these aspects throughout the book, but there is a far more vulnerable aspect of truth that the belt is designed specifically to gird. The virtue of personal truth that the Lord has placed within each of us—our honesty and personal integrity—provides protection.

> Howbeit when he, the Spirit of truth, is come, he will guide you into all truth: for he shall not speak of himself; but whatsoever he shall hear, that shall he speak: and he will shew you things to come.
> —JESUS (JOHN 16:13)

Jesus taught us that the truth of the Bible doesn't just set us free, but rather it *makes* us free (John 8:32), yet you could have the entire Bible memorized and still be imprisoned in sin. It is your possession of this truth that makes you free. This is the transformative shackle-breaking truth placed within us through the power of the Holy Spirit. As born-again believers, though we lived a life of deception in our former lives, once we gained the light of the glory of the gospel of Christ revealed unto us, we no longer live in deception but in truth (2 Cor. 4:4).

THE FATHER OF LIES AND HIS CHILDREN

> Ye are of your father the devil, and the lusts of your father ye will do.
> He was a murderer from the beginning, and abode not in the truth,

because there is no truth in him. When he speaketh a lie, he speaketh
of his own: for he is a liar, and the father of it.
—JESUS (JOHN 8:44)

Jesus tells us that the devil was a murderer from the beginning, and he "abode
not in the truth, because there is no truth in him." When the devil is speaking
a lie, he speaks of his own—those in the world that he controls—for he is a
liar and the father of all liars and all those who lust after the things of this
world. When born again, we are translated from the kingdom of darkness into
the kingdom of God's dear Son (Col. 1:13). If you are born again, why would
you ever risk putting your life back into the deception that the gospel brought
you out of? In his letter to the church at Ephesus, Paul is not just talking
about the truth of God's Word; he's talking about the truth that needs to be
lived and told—the honesty, integrity, fidelity, and the character of our heart,
mind, soul, and strength.

THE PURPOSE OF THE WARRIOR'S BELT

The truth God has placed in you is not predicated on your beliefs. Truth is
still the truth, no matter what you believe. The Bible says we know faith
comes by hearing and hearing by the Word of God (Rom. 10:17). Once we've
been saved through the truth, we need to walk in that truth continuously and
with conviction. For that, Paul teaches us that the first piece of armor you
must wear is the belt that girds around your loins and midsection.

To understand why this belt represents honesty, integrity, fidelity, and the
other facets of truth the Lord has put inside us, let's look at the purposes of
the combat belts warriors have worn throughout history. Since we live in
the modern era, a quick zoom through Paul's discourse on the armor of God
doesn't instantly speak to many of us because modern-day warriors don't
dress the way they did during biblical times. However, today's soldiers and
police officers wear an equally important utility belt for parallel purposes.

If you know anything about the comic book hero Batman, you know he
wouldn't even head out to fight crime without his utility belt. Even in these
modern and fictional contexts, something about a warrior's belt is undeniably
powerful and valuable. The modern warrior's belt holds all the defensive and
offensive utilities and instruments, including knives, pistols, handcuffs, flashlights, ammo, tasers, you name it—all in the most secure and readily accessible place on their body. Like their comic book counterpart, modern warriors

would feel naked without belts, but there is an even deeper meaning to the belt that we'll miss if we don't return to the context of ancient warriors.

WHY OUR LOINS?

Paul wrote that we are to gird up the loins, which consist of your entire mid-section (your gut). In ancient times, virtually every male of fighting age was expected to fight for the king whenever needed. Hand-to-hand armored combat was a way of life for men in those times. So, though we like to picture a well-armored Roman soldier (like the one sketched in this book) or a temple guardsman, many soldiers throughout history were regular working folk drafted into the army as secondary fighters.

The best of these citizen soldiers were the rugged woodsmen, farmers, and shepherds of their day who seldom owned any armor. When they would enter battle, it was usually with a club or a farming tool in their hands. They adapted whatever they could find to serve the purpose of each piece of armor. These draftees were indeed girded up, but not with an armored belt like the one at the top of this chapter. Instead, they would tightly tie up their robes with some rope to ensure none was dangling as a trip hazard or an easy handle for the enemy to seize.

If a soldier tripped and fell during battle or was ever pulled down to the ground by a combatant, they would typically become defenseless. When Paul used this analogy of the belt in his day, the Roman soldiers and the citizen draftees completely understood what he meant. The belt was critically important and couldn't just be strapped on willy-nilly. It had to be tied up and buckled down tightly.

TIGHTEN YOUR BELT

You've probably noticed that many young people these days wear their belts loose enough that their pants sag way down around their thighs. You can't do that if you're a warrior in battle. The enemy could grab that poorly fitted belt and yank you to the ground. Once there, he could easily chop off your head and drive a dart through your heart.

For this, the Bible says to gird it up and make sure the belt remains tightly girded. What He's saying is that we must make sure we're telling the whole truth and that our conscience is truly clear. Once you do that, your armor will begin to fit properly, and you'll also begin to sleep well at night (much more on that in the coming chapters). If, however, you continue playing loose with the truth in these dark days, the devil is going to take hold of that dark secret and that dishonesty and yank you down until you're destroyed.

FRONT AND CENTER

God tells us to get that belt of truth and gird up our loins, which makes it both the first piece and the centerpiece of the armor. When not actively engaged in battle, the sword of the Spirit hangs on that belt. If the belt isn't on, isn't tight, or isn't worn correctly, then the sword itself is difficult to draw in battle. It's not because the sword loses its power but because you're not caring for it or keeping it at the ready as God instructs (2 Tim. 2:15).

Just like a police officer or a soldier (or just like Batman in our comic book metaphor), you must have a good belt that properly serves its purpose to stand ready for battle. The problem is, however, that this first piece of armor is the one we'd like to be able to ignore because it's the most uncomfortable to put on properly. We can enjoy talking about the Bible. We can enjoy talking about faith. We can enjoy saying we're saved and made righteous by Him. We can enjoy talking about prayer. We can even enjoy handing out gospel tracts, telling people about Jesus, and inviting them to church. You can enjoy all that, but absent the whole truth, you'll live a powerless life of fruitless religion.

PUT THIS ON FIRST

Why do you think Paul begins the process of putting on the whole armor of God by saying that we first should be girded with the belt of truth? The answer is simple. Without the belt, none of the other armor or offensive accessories properly fits the soldier. For this, in the broader sense of the analogy, none of the other armor can prove effective.

Without the belt of truth—without your conscience being clear and girded with the truth permeating every single area of your life—the rest of the armor is virtually useless in battle. The breastplate of righteousness won't work well. The shoes of the gospel, the shield of faith, and the helmet of salvation won't work well. Even the sword of the Spirit and prayer will fail to work properly if you lack integrity in your life. The Lord will not hear my prayers if I hold iniquity and falsehood in my heart (Ps. 66:18). So there is no escaping the fact that you must put on the belt of truth. All is lost if we don't walk in it.

Dishonesty will never lead to victory, and you are circumventing your spiritual power if you are harboring lies or lying to yourself about them. Sometimes we have this strange idea that nobody knows our dark secrets if we keep them to ourselves. As long as you and God know, that's the majority where your salvation is concerned, and that's all that matters in your life.

Benjamin Franklin famously said, "A clear conscience is a continual Christmas." It's an amazing blessing to walk through life having confessed and repented of your sin nature. When you know you're girded up in truth, you can walk boldly, never looking over your shoulder and never worrying if they will find you out. You don't live in fear that they'll someday see your web browser history, find out who you've been texting or calling, or learn of the crazy, destructive (or illegal) things you've done. A clear conscience in Christ is preeminent in spiritual warfare. Don't miss that.

THE CORE ISSUE

Deception and dishonesty are sins that the devil has mastered. If he can get you to live in darkness, he's got you. When the light of the gospel of Christ first shines in your life, you have immediate access to victory, but you cannot receive that victory if you're continually lying to yourself and the people around you. One of the greatest problems in the American church today is dishonesty, and I'm not saying that the people holding the microphones have a monopoly on the lying that goes on in our churches.

You can talk a good talk about the fight. You can talk all about the place of victory we fight from. You can talk knowledgeably about the whole armor of God. You can raise your hands and shout in praise. You can bend your knees, cry at the altar, and give magnanimously, but you will never access His power if you do not get humble and honest before God. He simply doesn't bless liars.

In every congregation in the world—even in a congregation like ours at Global Vision, where the Bible is thunderously preached, and people clap and shout and get excited about the presence of the Holy Spirit—some people are extraordinarily dishonest with themselves. If that's you, even in part, don't despair. Please don't throw the book down and walk away. You can get right with God this very moment, after you finish this chapter, or even after you finish this book and beyond. Don't ever give up, but don't delay either. If you're feeling conviction, don't let this moment pass. Get right with God and all the people who have been hurt by your deceptions, and the full armor of God will again be yours to wear in power. If you stick with me and finish this book, I'm confident you'll find greater courage through each chapter to do the right thing. Repentance begins with recognition, so prepare your heart for a breakthrough.

JACOB AND ESAU

God the Father, the Son, and the Holy Spirit have always been, and they have always communicated as one. In the very first chapter of the Bible, when God said, "Let us make man in our image," He was revealing His triune nature straight out of the gate (Gen. 1:26). Though we know Jesus came to earth in the form of a man just two thousand years ago, just as we know He taught us of the outpouring of the Holy Spirit to unprecedented degrees following His resurrection, God in all three persons has been working in concert to lead our ancestors into the truth from the very beginning of creation (John 1:1).

In Genesis 25, we meet a young man named Jacob. He was a grandson of Abraham, and he was stone-cold crazy for most of his early adult life. This dude was full of tricks and secrets and seemed to stay one step ahead of them through every crisis—until he couldn't. I expect seasoned Bible readers to remember Jacob and his twin brother, Esau, very well. The Bible says that during their births, Jacob reached out and grabbed Esau's heel, and trouble, consternation, and divisiveness were triggered from that moment forward.

These guys were twins who didn't look anything alike, inside or out. Three times the Bible says that Esau was a hairy man. If the Holy Ghost goes out of His way to tell me three times that you're hairy, you are one *Duck-Dynasty*-looking dude. There is no doubt about that. The Bible tells us that Jacob wasn't a man of the field like his brother. Esau was a skilled hunter and a rugged outdoorsman, but Jacob was more of a mama's boy who enjoyed domestic activities. Esau liked to hunt and kill stuff to feed the tribe. Jacob liked to stay home and watch Paula Deen and cook stuff, so to speak. The point is they were opposites. They didn't act, dress, or look alike, and all their differences engendered a lot of envy, bitterness, and division between them.

JACOB THE LIAR

You might remember in the context of the story that Jacob stole two things from his brother Esau, starting with his birthright. Then, two and a half chapters later, he stole Esau's blessing. We may look at that in modern times and think, "What's the big deal?" But in the context of biblical history, this was the biggest deal to men of authority. Esau went ballistic once he figured out what Jacob had unjustly taken from him. He said, in effect, "You know what, I'll be avenged of my birthright, and I'll be avenged of my blessing. I will shed the blood of my brother, and I won't be happy until I cut off his head." (See Genesis 27:41.)

For this, Jacob got out of Dodge with no intention of ever returning. We have no idea how long his self-appointed exile lasted, and we have no idea how old he was when he left. When we finally catch up with him in Genesis 32, he has two wives, two women servants, and eleven sons. From this, we know he remained extraordinarily busy for a very long time, and we know he was able to gain a lot of wealth while building a big family of his own. We also learn that, all these years later, he's still running from his brother Esau. But when the time came that he could no longer run, he finally arranged to meet with his estranged brother. Thank God it didn't turn out how Jacob feared all those years. In just one night, Jacob learned that when we finally get honest, God will restore relationships that we thought were so fragmented and broken they could never be put back together.

THE HUMBLING

When the two brothers finally faced each other after all those years, Jacob decided to humble himself and repent while putting himself at Esau's mercy—come what may. Because of this act of contrition, the two men wept and hugged each other as long-lost brothers should. Though they agreed to merge their tribes during their reconciliation talks, Jacob was still conflicted about how to proceed. Pondering what to do next, he got alone and sat under a tree, where God soon came to him. The Bible says he wrestled with God all night long. Can you imagine wrestling with God for even a few seconds, let alone all night long? You would think God would pin him to the mat and ding, ding, ding! That would be it. But God was intentionally driving Jacob to the point of total exhaustion.

God wanted him mentally, physically, emotionally, and spiritually exhausted because He was planning to break Jacob of himself. Jacob's entire life had been about getting what Jacob wanted, and God was teaching him a lesson we all must learn. When you are ready to get right with God, He will bring you to the end of yourself just as He did with Jacob, and it will be the best thing that could happen for you and your family.

WHAT IS YOUR NAME?

Through this epic night-long struggle, God exhausted Jacob and wrapped it up by dislocating his hip, leaving him limping for the rest of his life. But before God cut him loose, Jacob clung to Him tightly and begged the Lord to bless him. To that, God basically said, "Okay, under one condition. Tell Me, what is your name?" (See Genesis 32:27.) That's a powerfully penetrating question. God wasn't asking as if He didn't know or was waiting to hear him spell it out: J-a-c-o-b. No, God had just called his name two and a half verses earlier. He knew Jacob's name even before Jacob did, and the name itself wasn't the point of this extraordinary question.

God required Jacob to be honest about his name before He would bless him because its meaning revealed his true identity. The name Jacob in the Bible means to supplant, circumvent, and overreach. If your name is Jacob, don't let that stress you out. As we see in the Word of God, your name is redeemed. Jacob originally meant the deceptive one or child of deceitfulness, and that's exactly how Jacob lived his life for decades. He was as crooked as a dog's hind leg and lower than a snake's navel in a wagon track. This guy made straight As through school because he was a cheater. God looked at him and said, in effect, "I'll bless under one condition." He didn't sing a little song, do a little dance, say a little prayer, request a bunch of money to be in the offering, or do anything you might see done in a church service today. The Lord had come to Jacob as a man to make him free in a most intimate fashion. With Jacob clinging to Him tightly, He said, in effect, "I have one piercing question for you, Jacob. What is your name?" That was one of the heaviest moments in the history of our faith.

THE BREAKING AND THE REBIRTH

Why did God ask Jacob that question? Because the last time Jacob sought a spiritual blessing and was asked for his name, he lied. His father, Isaac (the son of Abraham), asked him that question years earlier, on the day Jacob stole Esau's birthright blessing. Isaac was a very old man on his deathbed that day, and he could barely see, so Jacob tied goatskins onto his arms to make him feel hairy like his brother Esau. During the deception, Isaac asked Jacob, "Who are you, my son?" Jacob answered, "My name is Esau."

All those years later, Jacob had finally humbled himself to his brother for this betrayal, and God decided it was time for his breaking. Jacob had finally faced his lies and true identity before God, but everyone else had swept it all under the rug. Even Esau (surprisingly) decided to let it go and forget about it, but not God—and not Jacob, either.

On that historic morning, God backed Jacob against a tree and broke his hip to ensure he couldn't escape the truth of this divine moment. I don't believe for one second that Jacob was confused by God's question. He knew what God was really asking. So, he answered, "My name is Jacob." My name is supplanter. I'm a deceiver. I'm crooked. I'm a thief. I'm a liar. He finally broke down and came clean before God. And God said, in effect, "Ding! Ding! Ding! Winner, winner, chicken dinner!" God chose this moment following

Jacob's humbling to properly give Jacob the blessing he tried to steal all those years earlier, but first, He had to deal with Jacob's integrity.

After many decades of family struggles, it was finally time for Jacob and his family to step into their destiny as the children of God. Jacob was finally ready to stand on the truth through it all. Notice that Jacob's relationship with God was corrected only after Jacob was broken in repentance. Once Jacob embraced the truth through his brokenness, God renamed him Israel. I well up with tears every time I consider the beauty of that moment.

That morning, Jacob was basically reborn as Israel, which means God contends, God wrestles, and God is victorious. From that day forward, no longer called Jacob, but Israel, the great patriarch, and his sons went on to birth the twelve tribes that became the nation of Israel—His chosen people to this day. Jacob had to swallow his pride and embrace his brokenness on that amazing day, and in doing so, he changed the world.

AN HONEST BLESSING

If God anointed His chosen people and established His chosen nation through brokenness and repentance, what might He plan to do for you and yours once you come clean with Him? If you are living in any form of deception, you should feel compelled to throw yourself at the feet of the Lord and embrace the process. Do that, and He will contend for you as you work it out before Him— with Him—and He will be the victory for you and your family just as He was for Jacob and his, no matter how jacked up your past has been. Once you come clean about all things with God, He will empower you through your battles and give you renewed hope and a beautiful new vision for your future, grounded in the truth. Right now, God is asking you, "Who are you really? What is your real name? What is the dark identity that is keeping you from your blessing?"

If you're thinking, "Well, you know, Pastor, it's just a bad season in my life. Don't worry about it. I'll get through it." My answer is, "You won't get through it until you get honest about it." Men, I can't apologize for singling you out. To whom much is given, much is expected, and God has given us a lot of authority and influence in this world, so man up when I speak to our uniquely masculine struggles. Far too many men justify pornography in their lives, and since they won't come clean about it, their dishonesty will block their paths to victory and render the armor of God useless in their hands. If this is you, please be encouraged and consider Jacob's bittersweet story. I'm not saying it won't hurt a bit, and there will surely be some weeping, but no matter the cost, it will be worth it all.

Some of you get on your knees and pray, "Lord, bless me, give me the power of the Holy Spirit, do great things in my marriage, and do great things with my kids!" And God wants to, wants to, wants to! But you're kinking up the hose. You're blocking the flow of His power because of your dishonesty. In a message like this, I've learned I don't even have to get specific for many of you to feel torn up with conviction while reading this. That's the power of honest Bible teaching. It always finds its target (Heb. 4:12).

DON'T BE DECEIVED

No matter how well things can seem to be going for stretches of time, even while living in deception, your dishonesty will ultimately lead to defeat 100 percent of the time. The devil punishes us with temporary counterfeit success, peace, and love. It never lasts, and it always leads to death and defeat. You can't fight evil while being evil. You simply cannot fight falsehood with more falsehood, no matter how skilled you've become at hiding the truth. In a few chapters, we're going to see that one reason we need the shield of faith is its ability to quench the fiery darts of the wicked.

Lies and slanders are going to come at you and come around you, and you cannot fight these lies with denials or more lies or other blame-shifting tactics like blowing up with the spirit of offense. These are all schemes of the enemy. They're examples of the evil imaginations and lofty arguments that exalt themselves "against the knowledge of God" (2 Cor. 10:5), so do not practice them.

Some of you know exactly what I'm saying, so don't miss this chance to take hold of the way out of that vicious, destructive cycle. There is a reason that firefighters use water rather than gasoline to fight a fire, right? In Ephesians 5:26, Paul wrote that the Word of God is like water that washes us and sanctifies us. You cannot keep lying to yourself and expect God to reveal the truth of His Word and the life of His Son in you.

The demonic Adolf Hitler, whose name is now synonymous with evil, believed that if you tell a lie loud enough and often enough, the people will believe it. He was right, and if you tell your lies loud enough and long enough (and tack an out-of-context Bible verse to it), you'll also start believing your own lies. You'll be guilty of speaking lies in hypocrisy, with your conscience seared with a hot iron (1 Tim. 4:2). God knows we've seen that sort of evil brainwashing played out in the corrupt government and their partners in the media to unprecedented degrees during these dark days, but we're also seeing it in the church like never before.

On the personal level, you can get to a place in church life so steeped in deception that you might even start to believe that your dishonesty is some sort of spiritual gift. There is never a time in your life that God will ever justify or condone deception or dishonesty. There are no little white lies—just lies. We are commanded to tell the truth no matter the cost and trust the Lord to handle the fallout, come what may. Aren't you ready to end the worrying, paranoia, hypocrisy, and constant scheming required to maintain the evil in your lifestyle? Isn't it exhausting? There can be no peace in a life filled with dark secrets, so put on the belt of truth and free your conscience from the devil's grip.

PRIDE BY ANY OTHER NAME

My Bible says if you don't get born again, you'll remain in deception because you come forth of your mother's womb "speaking lies" (Ps. 58:3). No one has to teach you to lie, because lying comes naturally to everyone, and it always creates a false (temporary) sense of security. It's the prideful self-preservation mode for those who aren't born again. You can't be righteous while practicing unrighteousness, and you can't be full of light when you live in darkness (2 Cor. 6:14). Some say, "Well, I just can't make myself vulnerable to my family or my friends." You'd better, or you'll be destroyed. That's just wicked pride being used as an unrighteous hiding place. You'd better clean it up, you'd better confess it, you'd better deal with it, and you'd better pay it back. Whatever *it* is, you'd better humble yourself and repent.

Speaking of paying it back, I believe in restitution, but restitution is not salvation—it's a product of salvation. It's like the man who got born again after years of cheating the government, so he mailed them a check. In the cover letter he wrote, "I'm sending you a check for $5,000 because I got born again, and God convicted me." And at the end of the letter he wrote, "P.S.: If God keeps convicting me, I'll also send you the other $5,000 that I owe you."

Some people want to half-step with God, but you cannot correct falsehood with more falsehood or even shades of falsehood mixed with partial truths. It's either all the truth, or it's not the truth at all. If you don't deal with it in full honesty and continued accountability, you will stay in that addiction, you will stay in that habit, you will stay in that bondage, and you will stay in that dead-end relationship. You will have no freedom, you won't be able to pray, and you won't be able to move forward. The only thing that puts out the fire of a lie is God's honest truth and nothing else.

> Lying lips are abomination to the LORD: but they that deal truly are his delight.
>
> —PROVERBS 12:22

CHAPTER EIGHT

Belt of Truth: Part 2

Better is the poor that walketh in his integrity, than
he that is perverse in his lips, and is a fool.
—PROVERBS 19:1

NOW THAT WE know the belt of truth serves as the central piece of armor, let's look at its purpose as the protector of our midsection, the spot we commonly call our gut. Your gut represents the core of your very being and what you're really made of—your integrity or lack thereof—and not just how you like to perceive yourself. If your gut isn't honest, you fall on the wrong side of Proverbs 19 (above), and all you'll ever know is confusion, deception, and fear.

We commonly say that truly bold people have a lot of guts. They're gutsy, or in more recent terminology, "they have intestinal fortitude," a term that points directly to the armoring nature of the belt. When people say, "I felt it in my gut," that's what the Bible is pointing to with this aspect of the belt. Your gut is fortified and protected by the belt.

As a caveat, I'm not trying to overgeneralize or rebuke all folks who aren't bold. I know some people are just born timid and shy. I get it. But for the most part, if you meet a Christian whose entire life is marked with timidity and hesitation and fear, you can be sure they've got something to hide—even when people around them can clearly see they lack integrity in this area. If you're born again and walking in the truth, it will give you the capacity to get crazy bold and gutsy *when needed*—as led by the Holy Spirit within. It will make you bold in your home. It will make you bold with your kids. It will make you bold at school. It will make you bold in your workplace and in your community. It will make you bold wherever you go. You'll have the guts to face all the enemy throws at you.

When you are born again, you are girded with truth at your core, and you can feel the truth deep in your gut. From there, everything else works together for your good in life because you know that you are walking in truth with Christ—girded up in His belt of truth. That's a powerful place to live. It's the only place to live. What's sad is that far too many believers don't want to live there because pride or fear keeps them from getting real, so they won't get right with God about what's going wrong in their lives. In essence, they're running from the command to be born again.

WORD FROM A WATCHMAN ON THE WALL

We all have some struggles in our lives, so let's put away the shame once and for all. If we're serious about putting on the whole armor of God and standing firm in this spiritual war with urgency, we will come clean with God and immediately get some accountability in our lives. For those of you who cannot stop blaming others for what you lack and deflect all your problems with a victim mentality, I have news for you: You are not a victim! You're a victor! Jesus didn't die for you so that you can walk around like a permanent victim. Jesus died for you so that you can have the way, the truth, and the life—and life more abundantly!

NO SECRET IS SECRET

Did you know that the devil dwells in your secrecy? He thrives on it. If you're living in the sort of denial that nobody knows, it's time to wake up. The devil knows, you know, and God knows. That's more than enough. If you cling to your secrecy, you will develop a dependency upon your lies, right? The old adage tells us that a liar must have a great memory, and that's a fact. If you are a liar, you've got to remember what you told this one so that you can tell that one, and you can tell this one, and you can tell that one, and it's like lining up dominoes that you know can't stay lined up nor stand up forever.

Once you start telling lies, you'll eventually begin to believe your own lies because you will have seared them into your conscience through all the time spent rehearsing and rehashing your maze of dominoes, and the enemy will keep you imprisoned in this wicked maze until the end of time—until you break free. Taking that first big step into the light can be daunting, I know, but if you're serious about being born again and putting on the whole armor of God, it's a step you must take. With a little bit of faith, an ounce of intestinal fortitude, and the spiritual accountability necessary to stay the course, you can uproot that mountain of lies and toss it into the sea where it can never haunt you again (Matt. 17:20).

GETTING RIGHT WITH GOD

He that covereth his sins shall not prosper: but whoso confesseth and forsaketh them shall have mercy.

—PROVERBS 28:13

Maybe you think you have victory but don't see any evidence of it because you're still addicted to perversion or pornography or abusing prescription medication. You may need the help of a deliverance ministry to address spiritual sources of your addictive behaviors. Seeking deliverance for your addiction can help you identify and dismantle any spiritual strongholds, generational curses, or demonic influences that may be at work. Through repentance, renunciation of sinful behaviors, and the authority of Jesus Christ, you can experience true breakthrough and lasting victory.

But the first step is admitting you have a problem. Maybe you're an addict who knows the truth and knows that God knows the truth, but nobody else does, so you feel paralyzed under the burden of your secret life. Unless you get honest about it, you'll never break free. Coming clean with the truth is the only process that can deliver you from deception, and that typically requires you to get to a state of desperation, which is, in effect, a gift.

Some of you married folks have an unbelievably disconnected relationship with your spouse because your marriage lacks honesty at some level. There are things that you have hidden from your spouse, and vice versa, and you've been deceived into believing you can *never* bring it up because you fear confession will be the very thing that destroys your marriage. In reality, it will be the very thing that saves you. The truth does that.

The secrets and the lies will do the destroying, so please deal with them before it's too late. You should have no secrets whatsoever in a marital relationship. It's a horribly sinful way to live. The problem hides within the self-deception that we can somehow be successful while being dishonest. Despite

77

the false peace you may experience for a short time, you will never know victory in deception, especially not in spiritual matters.

CASE STUDY: SKIPPING JOHN

I want to share a fifty-thousand-foot flyover synopsis of something that happened to me many years ago when I was a much younger man traveling as an evangelist. This very true story is a powerful illustration of the vital importance of personal truth and integrity. The events get a bit bizarre at times, so I hope it triggers a few chuckles after such a heavy study on honesty. I've learned a lot about the Holy Spirit and the supernatural since my early days as an Independent Baptist evangelist, praise God. So though I'm well-equipped to handle this sort of situation if it happened today, I believe these events and my own gut reactions helped propel me to where I am now.

Years ago, a pastor in Memphis called and asked me to speak at a revival meeting at his church on a date that I had already booked for a revival meeting near Chicago. To my surprise, he said he was going to pray that God would cancel my schedule so that I could be there, and I was thinking, "Thanks, sir, but it's my schedule, not yours. What gives?" Just two days later, the previous booking called to say they had accidentally booked two evangelists for that same week and asked what I thought they should do. I told them to bring in the other guy because I was heading to Memphis just as the pastor in Memphis had prayed.

I called the man of God, and he was elated. In fact, it seemed like he knew something I didn't. If you've heard a lot of my preaching, there are several illustrations I frequently draw from my experiences in revival meetings at this man's church, so you might remember me mentioning him a time or two. He was a tiny older guy with a big old family-sized Bible—all duct-taped together—and a big black cane with duct tape all over it as well. That dude could really get fired up, but somehow, he was the only person who would ever get excited in his tiny church. Even when he was jumping around and banging his cane on the floor, his congregation remained stoic, lifeless, and—yes—colder than a mother-in-law's kiss.

VERY SMALL AND VERY BROKE

This church was dry and dead, but while I was preaching, the pastor would get excited every thirty-five seconds. He would hold that Bible up in one hand and hold that staff up in the other and yell, "Amen, little buddy! Amen, little buddy!" This guy was genuinely excited. However, he seemed to be more than just a little reluctant when he got his first look at me. If you think I look younger than my age now, you should have seen me back in those early days. I used to show up, and people would be like, "Hey, let's give this little guy a love offering and a pack of Pampers!" Others would ask, "Does your mother know you're this far from home?"

This pastor was clearly reluctant to hand his grumpy old church over to me, but thank God we hit it off rather quickly. The pastor had this gravelly, growling voice that now reminds me of that little, yellow, squishy woman in the movie *Monsters, Inc.* Do you know the character? (Don't judge me, I know most of you have seen it too!) So, Pastor-squishy-Monsters, Inc., in his gravelly voice, was like, "Brother Greg, I don't think you're gonna want to stay at my church this whole week for our revival because I've got two massive problems. We are very, very small, and we are very, very broke."

So I said, "Praise God, birds of a feather flock together. I'm very, very small and very, very broke too, so we're going to get along just fine!"

When I started preaching on Sunday morning, that little church had twenty-two people in it. You could tell no one had been saved in that building in a very long time because when I gave the invitation, a lone fifteen-year-old boy walked the aisle, and you would have thought somebody got shot in the building. Their eyes bugged out of their heads, and their necks were swiveling around in shock. They could not believe somebody got saved in the church.

So I told the congregation, "If you come back tonight at six o'clock, we'll see it again." I'm telling you, that whole week, people got saved and baptized like crazy. The meetings got bigger and bigger every night. We started with twenty-two people, and by the time Friday night rolled around, the crowd had grown to a hundred and fifty-seven people, all packed in this little bitty building.

The preacher came to me and said, "Brother Locke, God told me to tell you to cancel next week's revival meeting where you're supposed to be and stay here seven more nights."

To that, I thought, "You have already jacked up my schedule two times, little man, but let's see what I can do."

I called the previously booked pastor, and he was like, "Look, we're a brand-new church, and we can change the tickets, so that's fine. You stay in Memphis and see what God's doing." So I stayed seven more nights, making it a fourteen-day revival meeting—something that is almost unheard of these days.

JOHN THE SINNER

During the second week, the Holy Spirit was moving strong, and I was preaching in a big way. I believe it was Wednesday night when this guy suddenly came walking in the back door. I had not yet met him, but I knew his name because the pastor had earlier told me, "We've been praying for this guy named John. He's thirty-eight years old, hates God, and hates his family. He is on every drug you can imagine, and he is growing whatever he can grow and selling it around town. This guy is crazy as can be, but he's promised to come to church. You'll know when you see him because he'll be super late, and he'll be covered in grease because he's a mechanic."

Sure enough, about halfway through my message, a guy came walking in through the back door covered in grease, so I figured John had arrived. He came sliding in and sat down beside his soon-to-be-ex-wife and his father. I say soon-to-be because they had already filed for divorce. John had been unfaithful and was using all kinds of drugs and was involved in all kinds of wickedness and deviance. He was filled to the brim with sin, but I didn't care. I was just glad he was at church. I don't exactly remember what I was preaching that night, but I was getting into the heat of the message. If you're familiar with my preaching, you've noticed that sometimes I get so stirred up that I can't even help myself. This was one of those nights.

I was on fire, jumping around all over the place. I remember I was having the time of my life and was in the process of loosening my tie when I looked over at John and noticed his face had turned red as a rose. I've never seen a man's face turn so red. I thought this guy was mad as a hornet, but he wasn't mad at all. It turns out he had Crohn's disease and had driven directly from work, so he hadn't taken his medication and was about to have a spell. I didn't realize that at the time, so I did my best to keep from being distracted by his bright red face.

I just kept on preaching with fire, and when I reared back and slapped the pulpit with my big class ring, the very millisecond that my ring rang against that wooden pulpit, *BAM*! John fell over and passed out on the floor. When it was starting to look like a medical issue, I just threw on the Jake brakes. I'm not the sort of preacher who just stops right in the middle of a sermon, so it wasn't easy to change gears so fast. It felt like I was trying to stop a 747 during takeoff.

This was new territory for me, and no one seemed to be taking any action, so all I could do was down-shift and get busy praying for this guy. At that point, all I knew was that his name was John, his life was a wreck, and he was passed out on the floor. That's all I had to work with. As I prayed, I was hoping someone was calling 911 to get this guy to a hospital as soon as possible.

Some of their folks finally got busy attending to him, so I continued leading the congregation in prayer, and I couldn't help but watch what was going on with flopping John. I told the congregation to bow their heads and close their eyes, but not me! I kept one eye open to watch what happened next with old John. Jesus said, "watch and pray," and there's some stuff in church you just don't want to miss! They eventually carried him out and took him to the hospital as we finished the service.

PUTTING OFF YOUR GRAVECLOTHES

After that little scare, I assumed I'd never see John again. But guess who showed up the next night? Old John—but check this out. This time John had his hair slicked back, gold wire-rimmed glasses, black shoes, black pants, white shirt, red tie, black jacket, and a Bible under his arm. The dude showed up looking like a grease monkey the first night and came back the second night looking like a missionary fresh off the plane, but he wasn't even saved— not yet.

He came in, slipped through the crowd, and sat in the same exact spot near the outer edge of a back row. I was thinking, "Oh, that's a bad spot, dude. Scoot over a little bit to a seat with a little less history, would you?"

I'll never forget that I was preaching on the raising of Lazarus from the dead. Ironic, right? When I got to the end of the message, where Jesus says to loose him and let him go, I brought it home by explaining that there are some things you need to set loose and other things you need to intentionally get rid of. I told that packed house that you can't claim to be born again and still look and act like the same person you used to be. I remember shouting, "You've been resurrected from the dead, so you've got to change your graveclothes. Put them off, put them off! PUT THEM OFF!"

It was one of those sermons where I just let the wheels come off and shot-gunned the Word of God all over the room. "Get rid of the graveclothes! Get rid of the graveclothes! Put them off!"

When I got to the invitation, I said what Billy Graham always used to say. "All stand, heads bowed, eyes closed. Band, come and play 'Have Thine Own Way,'" etcetera. Maybe you know the drill. As soon as that woman began to hit the piano keys—I mean the very second she hit the first chord—old John jumped up and said, "Excuse me, pardon me, excuse me, excuse me, pardon me," as he made his way to the center aisle where everyone could clearly see him. The guy could have just told his dad to get out of the way so he could more quickly come down the side aisle, but I guess he had seen enough people come down the center aisle that he wanted to do it like everybody else.

What he did next was entirely unexpected. Until then, I'd seen people get to an altar by every means possible—except skip. Old John skipped. Don't forget, we're talking about a quiet, little, nestled-down country Baptist church, and for the second night in a row, skipping John had them tore up from the floor up.

All I said was, "If God spoke to your heart, would you come?" and John got all revved up and started skipping down the middle aisle of a Baptist church in Memphis, Tennessee. And I thought, "Oh man, it's about to get on, Lord! It's about to get good!"

GET THIS MAN A PILLOW

I'm telling you the gospel truth. They had a pulpit and a platform stage about three feet high, and this cat came sliding in on his knees like a Babe Ruth baseball player coming home. It was an exciting moment until it got weird.

To my absolute shock, John tilted back and started beating his forehead on the wooden part of the floor in that little Baptist church. At that point, I was thinking, "Either this dude is cracked out of his mind, or he's demon-possessed—one of the two, if not both—somebody please get this man a pillow and help him in the name of God!"

But no one was doing anything. It was crickets aside from the sound of John's head hammering the wooden floor, and the folks were just standing around dumbfounded. I realized I was going to have to help this man because nobody else was moving a muscle, and I didn't blame them one bit. It was a dramatic scene. So I took my little Bible, walked over, and got where I could sort of look him in the eye, and all I said was, "John, can I help you?"

If you think he spooked me the first night, that was nothing. When he finally stopped banging his head to look up at me, this cat shot back up on his knees like a rocket. His eyes were bugged out of his head all bloodshot, and I could almost sense the hair standing up on the back of his neck. He didn't need a microphone, and I'm glad he didn't have one. I'm also glad he didn't know anything about me before he got started because this guy—for the next thirty or forty seconds—said things out loud that most folks wouldn't even tell their pastor in private. I mean, this guy let the cat out of *everybody's* bag.

I didn't have time to stop him, I promise you, and here's how he started his public confession. "Oh God... I'm a fornicator!" Can you imagine? Gum was falling out of people's mouths, small children were hiding behind their grandparents, and everyone was like, "Whaaaaat did he just say? Little old ladies were looking at me as if to say, "Did he say—?" And I was looking back at them like, "Yep, he said it!"

JUST GETTING WARMED UP

Before anyone could respond to his verbal outburst, old John started beating his chest. Then he reached into his pocket and pulled out a pack of Marlboro cigarettes, wadded them up, and threw them on the floor. He then reached into his other pocket, pulled out another pack, and tossed them out too. At this point, I'm thinking to myself (here's my carnality), "That is great. I admire that. But if you've got hand grenades and switchblades in your pockets, leave them in there, sir! Do not mess up what God is doing in this service!"

I'm telling you, this guy was dead earnest, weeping and squalling, and no one had any idea what to do. In Bible college, they taught us that when something happened that we didn't know how to handle while serving as an evangelist at someone else's church, we were supposed to hand it over to the guy in charge—praise God! So I was like, "P-p-pastor... can you help this guy?"

The pastor finally came waddling over, and he got down on his knees and just started talking to John, who was still wailing away. After a few moments, the pastor started praying a simple childlike faith-filled prayer. About that time, people started coming forward in response to the invitation, and the pastor suddenly got up and yelled with his gravelly, growling voice, "Stop the music, stop the music!"

So they stopped the music, and it got dead quiet in that building. Then he said, "We've been praying for this man for a lot of years to get born again, old John here, thirty-eight years old. And tonight, he got born again by the grace of God!"

Let me tell you, that little Baptist church got lit up! They started clapping, whistling, and shouting, and even the people who had been sitting down all week stood on their feet and joined in the celebration. If you were raised Baptist, you know how out-of-order that scene must have been in that sleepy, little church. This place was on fire like they got hit by lightning! So I figured we were going to eventually start hugging necks and shaking hands as we prepared to go home. Oh, how wrong I was.

It Sure Does Feel Good

Once it quieted down, John looked up at me and said, "Hey preacher, you reckon I can come up in that box and say something to the church?"

And I thought, "If he's going to say all that down there without a microphone, what's he gonna say when they stick a booming mic right in the man's mouth?" I had every reason to believe this guy was about to air out everybody's laundry, so I said, "Whatever the preacher wants."

Then the pastor said to John, "Just keep it to the point, son. Keep it to the point."

So John came up with one of those old hardback songbooks, and he started repeatedly hitting it against that hard, wooden pulpit. I began thinking I was going to have to interpret for this guy because there was no way he was going to be able to talk coherently in his current state. He was just banging that book and hitting the microphone and clearing his throat, and everyone was holding their breath, thinking there was no way this guy had a testimony to share. But then God showed up. You don't need to have seminary training to know when God shows up, and it can't be manufactured.

John put that book down, straightened up that little tie of his, fixed the microphone, and then looked out at that room and said, "I don't know a lot about this church business. I don't know about this God stuff y'all are talking about. But I'll tell you fine people one thing. It sure does feel good to come clean with God. It sure does feel good to come clean with God."

Getting Honest

That was a long time ago, but as you can tell, I'll never forget that night. I'm not saying you have to have the same experience. I'm not a Catholic priest, so I don't have to know the fine details of your junk. I'm not saying you'll ever have to jump up and grab a microphone at a church and tell everything you've ever done to the world. But whatever it looks like for you, you'd better have a come clean with God moment if you want to live the born-again life and make use of the armor of God. You'd better have a moment where you get honest with God, yourself, your spouse, your kids, and everybody around you because dishonesty and lack of integrity will never ever lead to victory.

Before the rest of the armor can work, before the whole armor of God can ensure continued victory through the battles that currently surround you and the battles that await you, you've got to put off your graveclothes and put on that belt of truth. You've got to wrap it around your midsection. You've got to pull it tight. And you've got to commit to becoming a person of integrity at the core of your being—in your gut—not just from your mouth.

The devil does all he can to convince you that people won't understand, and they'll reject you if they ever learn of your lies and secret sins, so you've got to realize there is no temptation overtaking you but that which is common to man (1 Cor. 10:13). You are not alone. We all have our junk to confess, and we all have to make this decision, so don't ever think you are alone in this regard.

I believe that private sin calls for a private confession, and I believe that a public sin calls for a public confession. I also believe that there are people around you who can love you through this crucial crossroads into the born-again life. Once you do the right thing, God will provide the people to help you remain accountable, to help keep your feet on the ground, and to help you continue to fight from a place of victory. But you have to be honest, and you have to want it.

Let's bring an end to the secrets. No more shady deals. No more exaggerations of fact. No more living a lie. We've been made free by the truth of the gospel. Don't let this moment pass without taking those first steps. It may hurt a little for a little while, but in time, you'll never regret it. Freedom in Christ is worth the cost.

> Then said Jesus to those Jews which believed on him, If ye continue in my word, then are ye my disciples indeed; and ye shall know the truth, and the truth shall make you free.
>
> —JOHN 8:31–32

CHAPTER NINE

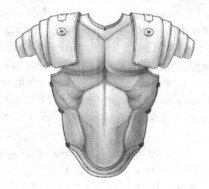

Breastplate of Righteousness

*Stand therefore, having your loins girt about with truth,
and having on the breastplate of righteousness.*
—EPHESIANS 6:14

I
N THE PREVIOUS chapters, we discussed the front end of our key verse and learned that to put on the whole armor of God, we must first tighten the belt of truth. If we don't live a life of truthfulness and integrity, the rest of the revelatory discourse on the armor of God is futile. In that same verse, Paul also introduces the breastplate of righteousness. I believe the Lord led Paul to couple these two pieces together for very good reasons. The breastplate of righteousness—right doing—is a foundational message found in every book of the Bible. If the concept of righteousness has evaded you, or if you've been misled into believing it is not a biblical command, let's look at a few key verses and passages to get you fired up for some personal study.

WHAT EXACTLY IS RIGHTEOUSNESS?

Some may immediately look to the Ten Commandments to define right doing (Exod. 20:2–17), and that is indeed a solid starting point, but obedience to the law and the prophets falls short of Jesus' path to righteousness (Matt. 5:19–20).

Paul wrote that if righteousness were possible through the law, then Jesus would have died in vain (Gal. 2:21). Righteousness cannot be attained through what is known as legalism, which is the effort to achieve God's approval through strict obedience to the many laws and traditions that the Levitical priests of the Old Testament called commands. Most scholars agree there are 613 of them, so if you want to live under the old covenant like an Orthodox Jew, good luck with that!

The New Testament makes it perfectly clear that legalism is antithetical to the gospel (Rom. 3:28). None of us can attain righteousness through our good behavior alone (Rom. 3:10), so don't ever make the mistake of thinking righteousness—right doing—has anything to do with human perfectionism, which is impossible. This, of course, is truly good news, which is the definition of the word *gospel*.

Righteousness is made possible only through the indwelling of the Holy Spirit, which comes only through faith in Jesus as our risen Lord and Savior. It is the product of the life-transforming belief in the gospel of Jesus Christ that marks those of us who are born again (John 3:1–21; Rom. 1:17; 1 John 2:29, 5:18). This is a central truth in the new covenant with God in Jesus. From this, we know righteousness is far more a matter of our motives and desires at the heart of us, certainly not our ability to obey 613 rules. In His Sermon on the Mount, Jesus put it this way:

> Blessed are they which do hunger and thirst after righteousness: for they shall be filled.
>
> —JESUS (MATTHEW 5:6)

Jesus is telling us that when we sincerely desire and pursue right doing as He defines it, He will fill us with His righteousness on the inside (Matt. 6:33). This is the indwelling of the Holy Spirit that powers the whole armor of God, as discussed earlier. Though you will endure stumbles in your walk with Him (Rom. 3:21–26), it is the condition of your heart, mind, soul, and spirit that will determine whether you get back up and stand in *His* righteousness—to do the right thing in obedience to His Word. This is the substance and purpose of the breastplate. All that said, if you are born again, you will put all your heart into abiding in Him and His righteousness, living in His ways, His truth, and His life so consistently that it will become your nature to produce the fruit of righteousness (John 14:6, 15:1–11).

For this, though we know we cannot work *for* righteousness, we do, in fact, work *from* righteousness, and in both cases, the righteousness is His, not our own. So don't make the tragic mistake of believing you can live however you please and still claim to be born again just because you said a prayer or jumped in a baptismal tub. Those are beautiful acts for a saved believer, but let's be honest—anyone can go through the motions.

A FALSE SENSE OF SECURITY?

James, the brother of Jesus, made sure we could never escape the fact that real faith always produces good works and right attitudes. In the Book of James, we see that "faith without works is dead." I trust you realize that dead faith is fake faith (Jas. 2:14–26). In this well-known yet seldom-taught passage, James is not saying that the faith that saves us can be obtained through our works and good deeds but that anyone who is truly saved and born again will produce the fruit of right doing as a natural outgrowth of their walk with Christ.

In other words, doing good works will never save you, but the saved will always do good works. This truth can be best proven through Jesus' Sermon on the Mount (Matt. 5–7), which is His single longest discourse on righteousness. It's no coincidence that this is the first sermon of Jesus that we're given in the New Testament. In His closing statements from this most famous of all sermons, Jesus hammers home the crucial role of righteousness:

> Wherefore by their fruits ye shall know them. Not every one that saith unto me, Lord, Lord, shall enter into the kingdom of heaven; but he that doeth the will of my Father which is in heaven....Therefore whosoever heareth these sayings of mine, and doeth them, I will liken him unto a wise man, which built his house upon a rock: And the rain descended, and the floods came, and the winds blew, and beat upon that house; and it fell not: for it was founded upon a rock. And every one that heareth these sayings of mine, and doeth them not, shall be likened unto a foolish man, which built his house upon the sand: And the rain descended, and the floods came, and the winds blew, and beat upon that house; and it fell: and great was the fall of it.
> —JESUS (MATTHEW 7:20–27)

Jesus is telling us that anyone who is truly saved and born again will produce a life of righteousness in Him (on the "rock"). He's also telling us that our public confessions of His Lordship eventually prove worthless unless we build this life of right-doing solely upon His teachings. For this, we know the breastplate of righteousness is rendered powerless in the hands of the foolish who do not thirst and hunger to know and obey the whole Bible.

If you take a moment to read each of the verses I noted through this brief exploration of righteousness, especially the Sermon on the Mount, you'll see what I mean when I say that the workings of each piece of the armor of God—truth, righteousness, faith, Gospel peace, salvation, the Word of God, and prayer—is interconnected and entirely interdependent. In the Spirit, the armor is one suit, and it's supernaturally invincible. I also like to visualize the armor as being made of the same hardened steel found in the sword of the Spirit, as that points to the fact that the Word spoke all the armor into existence.

These perspectives underscore the fact that you can't pick and choose among the armor. Our Lord is the all-or-nothing God (Mark 12:30). Though you may feel temporary worldly benefits and warm fuzzies through the selective or occasional use of each piece of the armor, it really is all or nothing. In fact, if you're not fully armored up, it will be easier for the devil to destroy and kill you because of your false sense of security.

We see that sad reality playing out in these last days like never before, as so many leaders betray their high calling while swearing that they're born again and heaven bound with the hammer down. They think they're safe because they carry the sword once in a while and proudly wear the helmet, sort of, and they sample the other pieces in times of crisis or on special occasions. It's not for me to question their faith or salvation, but it's too easy for them to study and speak the Word of God only when it's convenient. Recall Jesus' closing statements from the Sermon on the Mount.

When someone lacks the desire to obey the full counsel of the Bible (with hunger and thirst), their churches and personal lives are doomed to collapse. They have built their houses on the shifting sands of convenience, selfish desires, and worldly fears, so they cannot put on the whole armor of God and are rendered defenseless.

The same concern is true for every one of us, so don't get puffed up or complacent just because you're in a good place right now. Our purpose, our families, and the spiritual lives we are building on earth and in heaven are under attack, and just in case you haven't noticed, it's a never-ending, increasingly intense attack. If you don't stand on the rock of Christ's righteousness with hunger and thirst for more, when the furious storms begin to rage, great will be your fall, says the Lord.

THE HEART OF THE MATTER

Remember, in Paul's day, the people would have easily understood his symbolic use of armor because they were all very familiar with the dress of Roman soldiers and their citizen draftees. They realized that a Roman soldier would never go into a battle without his breastplate firmly secured, as they knew it was the armor that covered most of his vital organs.

The breastplate of that era covered his heart, his lungs, his stomach, and many other highly vulnerable organs. If you get punctured in the heart or lungs during a fight, you are done for. A soldier couldn't fight after suffering what was typically a mortal wound to the chest in the days of Paul. Soldiers had to wear that breastplate—that bulletproof Kevlar vest, as it were—to cover up these vital areas. So when Paul wrote this to the first-century Christians, they understood exactly what he was saying.

When the Bible talks about the heart, you must understand it's not always referring to that pulsating, blood-pumping organ within our chest (though the Lord lets us know in context when it is). The physical heart, in the context of the armor, is metaphorical for the inner recesses of our being—our true heart, mind, soul, and spirit. Before you jump up and say, "Wait a minute, doesn't the helmet cover our mind?" the answer is unequivocally yes, and we'll dive deep into the helmet soon enough. Just remember that every piece is interconnected and interdependent, so when we discuss the mind in the context of the armor of God, you'll soon realize why the Lord provided so much cover for it.

In the context of the breastplate, we're referring to the framework of how we think, how we feel, what we desire, what motivates us, and who we really are at the very heart of who we are, including our delicate emotions—all of which are issues of our spiritual heart. Proverbs 23:7 tells us that as a man "thinketh in his heart, so is he."

Proverbs 4:23 says, "Keep thy heart with all diligence; for out of it are the issues of life." Because of this, the enemy will always aim first to strike us at the heart, the very essence of who we are. You must keep your heart—who you are inwardly—fully protected with all diligence because out of it flow all the issues of life.

Sometimes we hear parents say to a daughter, "Don't give your heart away to the wrong man." They're obviously referring to her spiritual heart, not the blood-pumping organ. John Calvin, the great preacher of yesteryear, famously said the heart is "a perpetual factory of idols."[1] The history of mankind proves him right, but never has he been more right than in these last days.

THE IDOL FACTORY

The devil knows that if he can strike at the very essence of who you are—if he can get inside you and attack your heart, mind, soul, and spirit—he will easily manifest his dark power and work through your outer actions. In doing so, he will render the breastplate of righteousness useless in your life. The battle for your soul is indeed an inward battle. (If you're from Tennessee like me, you might call it an "innards" battle.) The enemy will come against your heart with all that he has. He will use every diabolical device in his little bag of magic tricks to ensure you worship idols. He'll throw things at you that will captivate your heart. He'll use money, fame, family, friends, your repetitive sins, your past failures, and your addictions. He'll use whatever works.

He knows far too well what will pierce your heart because he knows who you really are at the heart of you. He's been studying mankind like a snake in the grass since the days of Adam and Eve, and he's been studying you and me. He knows all your weak spots, and he knows all your temptations. He knows all the chinks in your armor, and he knows which pieces of armor you fail to put on. In most cases, the enemy knows you better than you know yourself.

He also knows the Lord has a hope and a future planned for your life (Jer. 29:11), so he and his minions have paid very close attention to your words and actions while waiting for the most opportune time to strike. He did it to Jesus, and he'll do the same to everyone who is saved and born again.

When the devil has your heart, he has your treasure and your dreams, he has your marriage and your kids, and he has your soul and your spirit. So you must protect and cover your inner being, the essence of who you really are in Christ. That's why truth and integrity are prerequisites to the breastplate. You have to know the truth about who you really are before you can ever protect who you were created to be.

SHAME AND GUILT

In ancient days, the Roman soldiers would march triumphantly into battle despite knowing many would die. Their courage and discipline were unrivaled in their day because they believed in their cause and fought with the conviction that victory was theirs. That confidence was their secret weapon that conquered the ancient world. They weren't worried, they weren't afraid, and there was no doubt, anxiety, or paranoia because they knew they were better armored and better trained than the enemy. They trusted that when a sword finally came at their heart, their breastplate would deflect it.

Most of us don't know true courage in our safety-first, highly pampered culture, so we don't naturally walk in that assurance. For that, many live their entire lives mortally wounded. They are alive but cut to the core; they're bleeding out. They live as if they are already defeated and dying, and they spend more time thinking of death than eternity because the devil has destroyed them at the very heart of who they are.

When the devil strikes at your heart and finds his mark, he can take away your victorious calling and deceive you into believing you were never good enough or courageous enough to be called by God in the first place. That's why he's called the accuser of the brethren. If he can get to your heart, you will live in shame and guilt for the rest of your life, and it will crush your spirit.

Don't ever forget what I tell you next. God Almighty will *never* use shame and guilt on His children. *Not ever.* If there are Christians in your life who throw these knives at you, stay clear of them (and get them to read this book). God is a loving Father who will only use conviction through the Holy Spirit to correct, train, rebuke, chasten, and transform His children.

Meanwhile, the enemy, your flesh, and the world will use condemnation, guilt, and shame at every opportunity, repeatedly screaming in your face, "Look at what you did! Look at what you said! You'll never live that down! We told you this would happen! Everyone knows! Now you've lost everything!"

The gospel never mocks us or jeers at us with "I told you so." The grace and mercy of God will never beat you down like that. Shame and guilt are the dark weapons that the enemy uses to cripple the body of Christ.

You might be thinking, "Pastor Locke, you don't know who I am, and you don't know what I've done." But as a pastor and a born-again sinner, I do know. I may not know all He has rescued you from, but I know all I need to know. I know that all have sinned and fallen short of the glory of God (Rom. 3:23). All we can do is repent, seek His kingdom and His righteousness, and get back up fully armored to stand.

BEWARE SELF-DEFINED IDENTITY

Never forget who you are in Jesus Christ. You are not your sin. You are not your rebellion. You are not your addictions. We are bought with the precious, red, royal blood of Jesus Christ. We are seated with Christ in heavenly places. I know I'm adopted into the family of God. I know I'm accepted into the beloved. If you don't like me, that's okay. Jesus thinks I'm to die for! Don't lose who you are (or can become) in Jesus.

Some people get their identity from their profession, and others from their external relationships. When a man loses his job (in most cases that I've observed), his identity fades with it because his entire life is wrapped up in how he makes his living. The lesson is obvious. You should never allow anything in this world to determine your identity—not even your spouse, your children, or your career. God knows who you are, and that's all that matters. He's the one who made you that way.

Meanwhile, the enemy will always identify you with your sin. Recall from the previous chapter how the devil was able to torment Jacob with his sinful identity all those years. But our Father will always call you by your true name— your true identity. He didn't say, "Jacob, what is your sin?" He said, "Jacob, what is your name?" This is where the belt of truth and the breastplate of righteousness connect and work together. You'll never rightly deal with your sin until you get right with God and understand who you really are at the heart of you—at the essence of your identity in Christ—as defined by the gospel.

KEEP YOUR HEART

No matter what it costs, no matter what you have to sacrifice, you've got to keep your heart covered by God. The issue of the heart is the heart of the issue (Prov. 4:23). When your heart is jacked up, your whole life is jacked up. I often hear people say that when we have a tough decision to make, we just need to trust our hearts. If that's you, you'd better quit watching all those Hallmark movies.

God said that the heart is desperately wicked and deceitful above all things, and only He can rightly search it (Jer. 17:9). If you trust your heart over the counsel of the Holy Spirit, you'll be a mess. It's the armor of *God*, not the armor of *you*, so you must never depend on your own strength and wisdom. That's like trusting tin foil to stop a sword.

Don't ever be deceived into trusting in your own personal power and your own personal identity. Those are, in effect, the stuff of self-righteousness, ungodliness, and there is no power in any of it. Trust only in the heart of God revealed in His Word through the counsel of the Holy Spirit and act accordingly, and you'll be living in righteousness. Therein you'll find the protective power of His breastplate in the whole armor of God.

> No weapon that is formed against thee shall prosper; and every tongue
> that shall rise against thee in judgment thou shalt condemn. This is the
> heritage of the servants of the LORD, and their righteousness is of me,
> saith the LORD.
>
> —ISAIAH 54:17

CHAPTER TEN

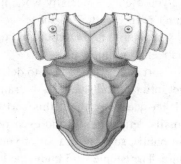

Breastplate of Righteousness: Part 2

And the LORD God formed man of the dust of the ground, and breathed into his nostrils the breath of life; and man became a living soul.
—GENESIS 2:7

CONSIDER MORE DEEPLY what we see in the symbolism of the breastplate of righteousness. To me, it sounds powerful and impenetrable. As I was studying in preparation for this teaching, I found a thousand applications for each one of the pieces in the whole armor of God, but especially the breastplate, because it covers the most vital organs. Now that we've considered the heart of the matter let's remember that it's not just your heart that the devil is trying to destroy. He's also trying to pierce your lungs to choke the breath of life out of you. If your lungs get punctured during battle, it's game over. If you can't breathe, you can't fight.

People in the UFC (Ultimate Fighting Championship) league know that if their opponent can't breathe, they can't fight back. If they hit their counterpart in the right place, they can knock the wind right out of them, and they won't be able to function, fight back, or defend themselves. If they can't breathe, they lose both their offense and their defense. In short order, they're little more than Jell-O on the mat.

The devil knows that's also true of you and me. When your defenses are down, while he's already at work attacking your heart, he also finds ways to knock the wind out of you and take your breath away. Have you noticed that when something bothers you deeply, especially when it blindsides you, it can start to feel like you can't even breathe? In those moments, you can't even begin to fight back. All you want to do is roll up in a tight little fetal position and give up. I know this feeling all too well.

To further explore this sort of attack and how to defend against it, I believe the Lord wants me to get intimate and shamelessly transparent about my own battles in this regard. I get questions about this sort of attack all the time through phone calls, emails, letters, texts, and even people approaching me in the church and out in public, so I know a lot of you will be able to relate to what I'm about to share. The people who know me best have no doubt that I'd fight a buzz-saw barehanded if God wanted me to. If it were necessary in order for me to preach the gospel, I'd fight a grizzly bear with a switch.

I believe even the casual social media followers, my haters included, realize I'm always ready to fight the good fight on the front line of the battle. That's who I am when I'm teaching the kingdom of God and His righteousness in the public domain. That's the "blue checkmark" Greg Locke. That's the "grab a microphone and set fire to the stage" or "throw out a rant video on social media where everyone is fair game" preacher who loads the old gospel Gatling gun and *pow! Pow! Pow! POW*—just goes after it.

All of that is indeed true at the very heart and soul of me. But when I'm off the stage or away from social media—off the platforms I was called by God to speak from with passion and fire—I'm a relatively reserved guy. I'm sure some of you picture me jumping up on my dining room table during an impassioned discussion with my family, but that's never happened once—not yet anyway!

CRYING IN THE WILDERNESS

When we look at John the Baptist, we see that even the most fiery, offensive, and politically incorrect preacher in the Bible (aside from Jesus) was rather subdued when he wasn't preaching. In fact, when he was thrown into the dungeon and fell into a weakened state, he was even prone to doubt and probably a good bit of anxiety as well (Matt. 11:3, Luke 7:19). I'd love to explore John's outrageously courageous life (along with the earlier prophets like him) right here in this book, but I'll have to save that for a future text. My point is once we're born again, our complexities do not instantaneously go away (some should never go away), and the enemy is going to attack us where we prove to be most vulnerable.

Though I embrace being a voice crying out in the wilderness like John—all to make Jesus known to the world before His return—I'm relatively meek when I'm not in that wheelhouse, so to speak. When atheists, people in the LGBT community, and even the demon-controlled folks at Planned Parenthood sit down to talk with me at a coffee shop, their typical takeaway is that I'm not nearly the jerk they thought I was. And it's true. I'm not really that big of a jerk—*that* being the operative word.

Nonetheless, all bold folks are a bit jerkish at times, and as John the Baptist proved, that's exactly how God wired some of us. But again, that's not my persona around town or at home with my family. That sort of fire is simply not required, nor is it beneficial in most of those settings. That said, I feel the Lord compelling me to be wide-open with you concerning the subject at hand—breathing while the enemy is trying to choke us out—and you may be surprised by what I share next.

MY FIGHT AGAINST ANXIETY

In the seasons leading up to the chaos of 2020, I had just come through two years of intense breaking, persecution, and growth, so things were going beautifully in my life. It was "the good old days" of 2019, and our church was growing again. Our building was going through an expansion and was being put back together in an amazing way. Things couldn't have been better between me and my wonderfully red-hot, God-fearing wife. Our six kids were growing up fast and acting crazy—mostly in a good way. All was going relatively well in my world, faster than I could have expected after all we had endured together. But behind the scenes, I was still feeling the enemy's attacks against my peace of mind, and sometimes it felt like I couldn't breathe.

There were times that I felt like an emotional wreck, and as good as things were going in my life, it just didn't make sense to me. I could literally break into tears watching a dog food commercial, and I'm not even a dog man! I could be driving down the road and hear something on K-Love and just start squalling and hyperventilating like a little baby. It was crazy, and it just wasn't adding up.

If you're a member of Global Vision or if you've already read *This Means War,* you know I have a special tree off the beaten path where I go to spend time alone with the Lord. Jesus had His mountain; I have my tree. My dear brother, Buford, calls it my burning bush. At about one a.m. on a particular morning, there I was, at my tree, crying out to God. Even in a season of beauty where I was fighting hell head-on without an ounce of fear or worry, there were nights I couldn't sleep a wink—not even for an hour at a time.

THE GIFT OF WISE COUNSEL

Throughout the Bible, we are commanded not to fear, not to worry, and not to be anxious. In King James English, these are often translated as "take no thought" or "care not" about the things we can't control or shouldn't ever try to control (Matt. 6:25–34). These very unhealthy aspects of our fleshly humanity are, in effect, sinful, but like most issues of the flesh, many of us have to journey through intense breaking and healing to overcome them. This is why the enemy is always trying to pierce our lungs and steal our breath. He's trying to choke the life out of us by using our most easily accessible sins and the weakest chinks in our armor—fear and worry.

If you can relate because you also deal with anxiety, do a quick inventory to see if any of these spiritual issues could be the underlying cause:

1. Is the enemy whispering lies in an attempt to get you to doubt God's provision, control, or faithfulness in an attempt to steal your peace, joy, and trust in God?

2. Do you have unresolved guilt or unconfessed sin that is weighing heavily on your spirit? Feeling unworthy or distant from God can be the source of anxious thoughts or feelings.

3. Do you need to strengthen your spiritual foundation or under-standing of God's love and grace? Without a strong under-standing of your identity in Christ or God's love for you, it is easier for the enemy to deceive you, leading to feelings of insecurity and anxiety.

4. Do you have any past experiences with the occult, false teach-ings, or unhealthy spiritual influences? These influences can create confusion, fear, and spiritual unrest.

Seeking deliverance and diving into the Word of God to better understand who He is and who you are in Him can set you free and put your mind and spirit at rest.

During my season of anxiety leading up to 2020, I reflected deeply on all the Lord teaches about this issue in His Word, so I went straight to the Lord in prayer without ceasing, I tirelessly pored through the Bible, and I sought the wisdom of the wise counsel in my life—starting with my wife, Tai. Each of these beloved folks knew me intimately, and each assured me that I was indeed pursuing the kingdom in my life with greater passion than ever before. Having already come through my season of intense breaking and healing, I knew I had developed an unquenchable hunger and thirst for His righteousness, and I also knew I was actively casting off the worldly concerns that the hypocrites pursue. This combination of godly counsel and a growing prayer life began to fine-tune my mind in times of rest (much more on the mind and prayer later in this book).

Since that point, whenever something triggers anxiety in me, God's peace begins to wash over me and through me. In these stressful moments, I'm reminded that the Holy Spirit is guarding my heart and mind with peace that surpasses understanding—steadily breathing life into me—despite the temporary emotional distress.

> And the peace of God, which passeth all understanding, shall keep
> your hearts and minds through Christ Jesus.
> —PHILIPPIANS 4:7

IT COMES WITH THE TERRITORY

I have come to recognize that it wasn't worry or fear or anxiety that was wrecking my emotions but the realization that we were, in fact, heading into the last of the last days when persecution would exceed anything we have ever experienced. My soul and spirit were crying out in the heavenly realm in a way that was brand new to me, and the Holy Spirit was revealing what was coming in 2020, and I *knew* these visions weren't the product of too much Dunkin' or Red Bull. Of course my emotions were going to be wrecked! I'm still just a man who makes my share of mistakes that can momentarily beat me down, but that doesn't mean the breastplate isn't actively protecting my lungs and the essence of who I am in Christ.

Like so many men and women of God before us and every preacher and prophet in the Bible, if we are called to stand against the devil on the front lines of the battle, we will have moments where we wrestle through our emotions and find it difficult to breathe. There will be times when we endure weeping for a night that has nothing to do with the sins of worldly fear or worry. We will have our share of restless nights in our garden or at our tree. And if the pending assault by the enemy is especially daunting, we may even travail to the point of sweating blood, just like Jesus in the Garden of Gethsemane (Luke 22:44).

Knowing all of this, when I now find myself emotionally wrecked by a prophetic vision or dream of the storms that currently surround us or are soon to strike, I just trust the Lord and let it be. If I struggle to sleep or burst into tears, I don't exacerbate it by worrying about what's wrong with me. I don't let it turn into the sort of anxiety that sucks the breath out of me because I know that's a dart from the enemy that the Lord won't allow to strike my lungs. I just let it be and wait for His peace to wash over me and through me.

If you know you're seeking the Lord and giving your all to do the right thing but still lose sleep over issues of the heart, the Lord will ensure you get all the rest you need. So just trust Him, and let it be. I'm not quoting the Beatles; I'm quoting the Bible.

If ever there was a time in history when someone received news that should have wrecked them, it was when the Angel Gabriel told young Mary she was soon to give birth to Jesus. She knew she would face severe persecution and doubt, even from Joseph, whom she had not yet married, and she knew the religious crowd would call for her to be stoned to death for adultery. But she trusted God and said, in effect, "Let it be unto me according to God's Word." (See Luke 1:38.)

BE STILL AND KNOW

I know that many of you can relate to where I'm going with this. There are times when nothing is wrong. You can be preaching Jesus, reading the Bible, giving generously, loving your spouse, raising up your kids, and doing everything you're supposed to be doing, yet somehow, you feel like someone parked a truck on your chest. That was me not so long ago. If you are currently struggling with the sort of intense anxiety that I lived through in 2019, don't you ever let the devil tell you it's because you're wicked.

Recall our discussion of shame and guilt. Reject them. We all need deliverance from those demons. If you have a calling from God to fight on the front lines of the battle in these last days, just trust that these attacks come with the territory and let God's peace carry you through it. Once you recognize the calling the Lord has placed on your life, there will be times you feel emotionally burdened, even when everything is going right. But through it all, you can still breathe, and your heart, mind, soul, and spirit will be well protected against everything the enemy throws at you. Like Mary, simply trust God and His Word. He's got you. In these high-anxiety moments, "be still," let it be, and prayerfully seek His kingdom and His righteousness no matter how wrecked you may feel in your emotions. Do this, and you will be protected by God's breastplate when the enemy attacks, and He will be glorified in you.

> Be still, and know that I am God: I will be exalted among the heathen, I will be exalted in the earth.
>
> —PSALM 46:10

WHEN YOU'RE ON THE VERGE

Regardless of your ministry or profession, some of you struggle with worry and anxiety for good reason—you've yet to get honest about who you are and have yet to come clean with the Lord. The devil knows when you're on the verge of your breakthrough, so he will do all he can to seize your heart and knock the wind out of you before you can get there. He knows when the Lord is in the process of transforming you, so he'll do all he can to keep you thinking it's too late for you, and he'll tear your nerves to shreds in the process.

Some of you are in his crosshairs because the devil knows you're on the verge of getting born again, and some of you are on his hit list because he knows you're getting ready to lead others to Christ or become a threat to him in some other way. I attended seminary and earned my degrees through a denomination that ridiculed the supernatural gifts of the Spirit in modern times, especially the prophetic. In 2019, I was still struggling with it, and the enemy took a lot of shots at me because of my study into this subject, so I wavered a bit—but not anymore.

Maybe you're in that same transitional season in your spiritual life. Maybe the Holy Spirit—God within you—is trying to wake you up to spiritual gifts and miracle-working power that the enemy has tricked you into denying most of your life. The devil knows that if you ever get a grip on your anxiety and start to stand in God's righteousness, you'll turn your circles of influence and your piece of the world upside down for Jesus—even if you're armed with little more than a squirt gun. I've been there. Maybe the devil is trying to make some of you think you lack the power to save your marriage, or maybe he's using shame or unforgiveness to suck the breath out of you. Maybe you're consumed with the thought that your prodigal is never coming home, and all the while, the enemy is piercing your heart. Some of you are watching the news every night or stuck on social media all day, and it has you fretting and worrying about whatever dark plan is coming around the next corner.

Many of you are just drowning in fear about money issues while your mind is being racked by one hypothetical after another—even those that you know, deep inside, will never happen. And some of you are hyperventilating over all the above, tripping into another panic attack while the enemy pierces your lungs and takes away your ability to breathe. If so, stay the course and take the Word of God to heart.

DO NOT WORRY

Jesus commanded us not to worry in its most life-applicable and beautifully poetic form right in the middle of His Sermon on the Mount (Matt. 6:25–34). Most of the contemporary versions of the Bible add headings like "Do Not Worry" or "Don't Be Anxious" to this passage. As noted earlier, wherever you see the words "take no thought" in the King James, you can translate it to "do not worry, nor be anxious."

If you don't surrender your thought life to the Holy Spirit, you will never overcome your worldly fears and never truly trust (or fear) the Lord. You'll become consumed with attacks that can "kill the body" while ignoring the antidote that saves your soul from hell. In the following passage of the Sermon on the Mount, Jesus details our most common sources of worry, all of which have to do with fears concerning our long-term well-being, comforts, or finances in this dimension. Then He delivers the bulletproof solution with inescapable clarity:

> Therefore take no thought, saying, What shall we eat? or, What shall we drink? or, Wherewithal shall we be clothed? (For after all these things do the Gentiles seek:) for your heavenly Father knoweth that ye have need of all these things. But seek ye first the kingdom of God, and his righteousness; and all these things shall be added unto you.
> —JESUS (MATTHEW 6:31–33)

In the final verse in this passage, Jesus gives us the antidote. Rather than allowing your mind to be consumed with "all these things," seek first (be consumed with, thirst and hunger for) the kingdom of God and His righteousness. This points to the breastplate of righteousness in its most supercharged form. If you are struggling with anxiety, please take this most beautiful command of Christ to heart. You may remember that I cited Matthew 6:33 in the previous chapter when I stressed that we cannot produce righteousness in and of ourselves, for it is *His* righteousness that we are to thirst and hunger for. It is His righteousness alone that fills us through the Holy Spirit to empower the breastplate for the protection of our spiritual heart and lungs. As discussed in detail in chapters 1 and 2, His indwelling is the source of that power, and He's ready to be that source as soon as you seek Him.

GOD IS STILL GOD

Nothing brought the schemes of the devil and his desperation to light more effectively than the train wreck that was 2020, and 2023 offers little promise of things getting better any time soon. In fact, you're right to expect that things will get worse and worse and worse. But fear not! God still parts waters. He still raises the dead. He still heals diseases. He can still turn the water into wine, and He can still walk on water. He can still walk out to the rickety raft of your life and iron out the wrinkles in those waves and say, "Peace! Be still!" The wind and waves still obey Him. He can still beat addiction. He can still put homes back together. He can still bring back your wayward child. He can still revive your church. He can still drive the demons and the rulers of darkness to their knees. He can still do what He's always done because He's always been God, and God does not change!

The key to unlocking the revelations of spiritual warfare comes not through your own wisdom, Dr. Wigglejaw's wisdom, Sister Bottlestopper's wisdom, or even Dr. Phil's wisdom. It comes through your ability to take control of every thought in your mind, to take every anxious and worrisome thought captive, and obey all of Jesus' commands—especially His commands not to worry and not to succumb to fear. It comes through knowing you are born again and committing your heart, mind, soul, and spirit to become more like Jesus—hungering and thirsting for His ways, His truth, and His life. And it comes through committing to seek first His kingdom and His righteousness through His Word.

> For God hath not given us the spirit of fear; but of power, and of love, and of a sound mind.
>
> —2 TIMOTHY 1:7

FEAR GOD ALONE

In Joshua 1:9 and Isaiah 41:10, the Lord echoes the command to *never* be afraid or dismayed. I could go on and on citing literally hundreds of passages that repeat this core message of the Bible—more than 365 times by most counts. The Lord assures us that He has provided us with the antidote to fear: trusting in Him and fearing Him alone. Jesus said, "And fear not them which kill the body, but are not able to kill the soul: but rather fear him which is able to destroy both soul and body in hell" (Matt. 10:28). That's a sobering truth for a lukewarm believer or anyone who is struggling with fear and anxiety.

If you're not yet born-again, I hope you start to see the beauty and tragedy in the reality of heaven and hell, just as God intends it. It is His perfect will that none of us would perish in hell (2 Pet. 3:9), so if that warning has escaped you all your life, maybe you should fall on your knees right now to repent for your fear and fully embrace your newfound courage. Before you can even begin to stand against the devil's attacks, you've got to get your breath back and put on the breastplate of righteousness by walking out of your anxiety and standing in His righteousness. You must regain control of your breathing because if you can't breathe, you can't fight!

Quit letting depression keep you in bed. Quit letting fear, worry, and anxiety wreck your spirit for weeks on end. It's time to get up and breathe again before the devil kills, steals, and destroys you and your destiny. You cannot fight spiritual battles with carnal weapons, so you've got to stop fighting in your flesh through fear and worry. "For though we walk in the flesh, we do not war after the flesh" (2 Cor. 10:3).

OBEDIENCE TO THE AUTHOR

Though he were a Son, yet learned he obedience by the things which he suffered; And being made perfect, he became the author of eternal salvation unto all them that obey him.

—HEBREWS 5:8–9

In this exploration of the breastplate of righteousness, I'm confident you recognized that the righteousness of Christ, for which it stands, boils down to a simple yet challenging word—*obedience*. Not only is obedience necessary to protect ourselves from the attacks of the enemy, but as we see in the passage above from the Book of Hebrews, it's also tied directly to our salvation.

Recall our discussion of the connection between salvation and obedience in the previous chapter. It's an irrefutable biblical truth. If you're bound to a denomination that teaches otherwise, that may seem like a tough pill to swallow, but swallow you must. That's not the word of Greg; it's the Word of God, so you ignore it at your own peril. Never forget Jesus' piercing question: "Why do you call Me Lord but do not do what I say?" (See Luke 6:46.)

This mirrors the key verse in His closing statements from the Sermon on the Mount, where He stated in no uncertain terms, "Not every one that saith unto me, Lord, Lord, shall enter into the kingdom of heaven; but he that doeth the will of my Father which is in heaven" (Matt. 7:21). To put it in layman's terms: if you refuse to obey the Word of God, you can't claim to be saved and born-again.

Rather than think of obedience as a burden, you should see it for what it really is, a blessing that assures we spend eternity in heaven with the Father, Son, and Holy Spirit—with God—the Author and finisher of our faith. As we proceed, I will write under the assumption that you fully realize that it is His righteousness in you that you work from to produce your right doing—and not your own perfection or your own ability to adhere to the laws and traditions that burdened the Hebrews (the Jews) before the days of Christ.

Jesus purchased your salvation with His death on the cross, and all He asks in return is that you receive the gift of His righteousness through your obedience to His written Word. Once you do, He will protect your heart, restore your breath, and give you all the rest you need to stand and fight in battle. So put on His breastplate and stand against the enemy to receive all the Author has written into the story of your life on earth and in heaven. Amen!

> Come unto me, all ye that labour and are heavy laden, and I will give you rest. Take my yoke upon you, and learn of me; for I am meek and lowly in heart: and ye shall find rest unto your souls. For my yoke is easy, and my burden is light.
>
> —JESUS (MATTHEW 11:28–30)

CHAPTER ELEVEN

Shoes of the Gospel of Peace

And this gospel of the kingdom shall be preached in all the world
for a witness unto all nations; and then shall the end come.
—JESUS (MATTHEW 24:14)

E ARLIER IN THE book, I mentioned that every single piece of the armor of God is designed for the front of the believer because God's soldiers aren't equipped to run and hide in the high country. In a spiritual war, we can't back up, pack up, slack up, or shut up until we've been taken up into heaven. True believers are going to take the fight to the enemy. Jesus told us not even the gates of hell can prevail against the local church of Jesus Christ that withstands and stands against the enemy (Matt. 16:18). And we absolutely cannot retreat when a battle starts up. Paul wrote that we ought to be in a good fight (1 Tim. 6:12), and for those who obey this command, he also wrote:

> Henceforth there is laid up for me a crown of righteousness, which the Lord, the righteous judge, shall give me at that day: and not to me only, but unto all them also that love his appearing.
>
> —2 TIMOTHY 4:8

WHAT IS THE GOSPEL OF PEACE?

In the previous chapters in our study of the *whole armor of God* recorded by Paul in the sixth chapter of his letter to the Ephesians, we learned we must first put on the belt of truth, because without honesty and personal integrity, the rest of the armor simply won't work for us. Then we discussed the breastplate of righteousness and learned that the enemy comes directly after our hearts and our ability to breathe the breath of life. As we continue with Paul's discourse, we find the most misunderstood piece of the armor in our next key verse:

> And your feet shod with the preparation of the gospel of peace.
> —EPHESIANS 6:15

The Bible talks about the gospel of peace, the gospel of God, the gospel of the kingdom, the gospel of the grace of God, the gospel of Jesus Christ, and— most specifically—simply, the gospel. They're interchangeable terms that talk about one message, so it's important that you realize there is no difference in the meaning of each, regardless of which term is used.

The gospel of peace is the gospel of Jesus, which is simply the gospel. I've heard some teachers try to make a delineation here as if Paul is stating we should walk like pacifists while armored up or make "peace on earth" the primary message of the gospel. That's not only silly, but as I noted earlier, it's dead wrong and can verge on heresy, so let me dispel that here. In Paul's discourse on the armor of God, the word *peace* is used interchangeably with the name of Jesus, as He indeed is the Prince of Peace (Isa. 9:6).

JESUS HIMSELF IS OUR PEACE

In the context of Paul's teachings in his letter to the Ephesians, we see that he had already established the biblical meaning of the word *peace* earlier in chapter 2. In this beautiful chapter, Paul plainly states that Jesus is our peace (v. 14) and fully explains that the peace of Jesus is the unification and reconciliation of the Jews and non-Jews to God, "that he might reconcile both unto God in one body by the cross, having slain the enmity thereby" (Eph. 2:16). That, of course, is a powerful prophetic truth of the gospel message. Furthermore, Jesus Himself told us that the peace He gives us is not the same peace that the world gives (John 14:27), which is a godless, passive (or pacifist), tolerant, self-medicating peace.

Jesus also stated in no uncertain terms:

> Think not that I am come to send peace on earth: I came not to send peace, but a sword.
>
> —JESUS (MATTHEW 10:34)

In this famous verse, Jesus is pointing directly to the most powerful piece of His armor, the sword of the Spirit, which is the Word of God. We will, of course, fully discuss the sword of the Spirit later in this book. Like the word *love*, the word *peace* has multiple applications. Recall our discussion in the previous chapter of God's peace that protects our "heart and mind" from fear and worry (Phil. 4:7). Even in this context, God's peace has nothing to do with pacifism. On the contrary, God's peace enables us to stand and withstand in the face of the enemy's attacks, not to run and hide or surrender to the enemy for the sake of worldly peace. Even in the face of tremendous opposition from the enemy and his minions, God promises peace that surpasses all understanding—through Christ Jesus—for all who stand and withstand while contending for the faith.

WHAT IS THE GOSPEL?

In Romans 1:16, Paul wrote, "I am not ashamed of the gospel of Christ: for it is the power of God unto salvation to every one that believeth." Our church isn't the power of God that saves. My preaching isn't the power of God that saves. Our singing isn't the power of God that saves. Money in the offering plate and social media followers are not the power of God that saves. In the kingdom age in which we live, the gospel alone is the power of God that saves. So the question then becomes, what is the gospel? It's the *good news* of the substitutionary death, the burial, and the resurrection of our Lord Jesus Christ. To add anything to that is a perversion. To take anything away from that is heresy. The resurrection of Jesus Christ is the most celebrated mystery in the history of humanity. It is the good news (glad tidings) unto salvation for all who truly believe it. Jesus is God, and He lives. That fact *is* our peace.

> Surely he hath borne our griefs, and carried our sorrows: yet we did esteem him stricken, smitten of God, and afflicted. But he was wounded for our transgressions, he was bruised for our iniquities: the chastisement of our peace was upon him; and with his stripes we are healed.
>
> —ISAIAH 53:4–5

The Bible says that Jesus was seen by more than five hundred credible witnesses after He walked out of the grave. Now, I may not be the smartest, but I'm not going to concede that I'm stupidest, either. Did you know that in a court of law, it only takes one witness to put your tail under the jail? Of course, under the corrupt court systems we see today, all of that comes undone, and even the testimony of thousands can be dismissed. But according to the actual law and Constitution of the United States, one credible witness is considered enough evidence, so let's work from that truth.

Can you imagine five hundred people all credibly saying they saw Jesus alive and well after His resurrection? There simply was no doubt of this fact among these early disciples and the thousands who endorsed their credibility. It's the only reason they were willing to die horrific deaths simply to do all He instructed them to do. He's alive. He's alive. He's ALIVE! This is the truth that saves. If you truly believe this and truly love others—if you are saved and born-again—you'll risk all to make it known, just like every single one of these first disciples, just as we are commanded.

> For God so loved the world, that he gave his only begotten Son, that whosoever believeth in him should not perish, but have everlasting life. For God sent not his Son into the world to condemn the world; but that the world through him might be saved.
>
> —JESUS (JOHN 3:16–17)

TIME-OUT: A QUESTION FOR ATHEISTS

Do you know the real reason atheists deny the deity of Jesus and the concept of a Judeo-Christian God? It's not that they don't believe in higher powers or alternate dimensions. Most of them believe in both. However, if you acknowledge the existence of God, you also have to acknowledge accountability to Him and His teachings. Atheists simply don't want accountability, and they certainly don't want to risk their lives for any cause higher than their own, so they deny the existence of God altogether. By doing so, they also skirt the reality of the afterlife in heaven and hell. Yet at the end of their lives, they are going to face God whether they believe in Him or not, and their spirits are going to spend eternity *somewhere*. Denying the existence of hell won't make it one degree cooler if you find yourself entering through its gates when you die.

Hell is a very real dimension, and it's still there no matter what you believe. You can deny you're sitting in a chair all you want, but if you're sitting in one, it's still there no matter what you believe. So, here's a light science question you can ask the next time you're confronted by an unbeliever. Even atheists know that our unique lives (what they may call our life force) consist of pure *energy.* Our lives are not comprised of the particles of matter that give us form in this dimension. Anyone who agrees with this is just one degree of enlightenment away from realizing they are spirit/soul and not merely a mass of dust and open space held together by energy fields like every other object we see. In physics, there is an accepted truth called the law of conservation of energy. This law states that energy can neither be created nor destroyed but simply moves from one state to another.

Like so many scientific laws, this was a mysterious biblical concept long before modern scientists caught on. With this in mind, ask your atheist and agnostic friends *where* exactly they think their energy (the invisible substance of their spirit/soul) came from. Then ask them *where* exactly they think it's going when they die. I know many will dodge the real question by shifting the discussion to some rudimentary, new-age nonsense, but deep inside, they know the energy that makes them a unique life form with character, reason, and self-awareness is far more than electricity.

I can promise you that this discussion will lower their guard a bit when they truly consider it, even if they scream you out of the room when you first raise it. This isn't a book on apologetics or a study of spirit and soul, so I'll have to reserve further discussions of this sort for future texts. At the very least, I hope this serves well as food for thought—both for your atheist friends and for yourself in times of doubt. Don't be mistaken; hell is very real, and no one wants to risk their soul being cast into the lake of fire for all eternity after they die. This is why it can be said that we're all in the business of winning souls for Jesus.

THE MEANING OF "SHOD"

Reflecting on our key verse, Ephesians 6:15, we see that we are commanded to walk in and through the gospel of peace and "shod" our feet with the preparation of the gospel. The Old English word *shod* is the past tense of the verb to shoe, which in modern English is the word *shoed.* This is simply the condition of your feet once you have covered them with shoes, or in the case of the Roman soldiers of Paul's day, with special sandals designed for battle.

You probably realize that your Nikes, your Pumas, your church kicks, your line-dancing boots—whatever you're wearing—can be deadly if used for that purpose. But you probably don't know that if you deliberately stomped someone on the ground and were charged with assault, the court documents will say that your victim has been *shod*, and they'll identify your shoe as the deadly weapon. The same was true of Roman soldiers. Their battle shoes weren't just defensive armor but were often used as a weapon in battle through the act of kicking or stomping. So there are times you will undoubtedly use these metaphorical shoes to kick through some doors and other strongholds established by the devil, but that's still not the primary weaponized power they hold.

Once you've been shod with the preparation of the gospel of peace, your walk becomes the most effortless offensive weapon in your arsenal. In fact, if shod properly, your walk should prove effective in warfare, even when running on autopilot. We know our worship and our prayers are weapons, and we know the Word of God, the sword of the Spirit, is the most powerful weapon, but you probably never considered that your walk is a weapon. So, in a practical sense, you need to realize that if you say one thing and do another—if you live in hypocrisy—you have no power in your walk and, therefore, have no power in your fight.

CHRISTIAN CHAMELEONS

The biggest problem with most churchgoers is that they act one way when they walk into the church but live another when they walk out of the church. They're pretenders. Being a chameleon is amazing if you're a lizard, but it stinks if you're a Christian. We have evangelical believers all over America who attend churches of all sizes—small, medium, and large—that lift the name of Jesus and shout His praises on Sunday but return to pouting on Monday. They're not powerful, they don't have a testimony, and they don't realize that their walk is hurting them and hindering them in their battles against darkness. But if you walk in truth and His righteousness shod with the gospel of peace, your walk is a weapon.

Your personal testimony is invaluable. At the end of your life, it's all you really have. No one cares how much money you have if you're a fake. No one cares how successful you are if you're a hypocrite. Jesus showed up at the temple and told the churchgoing crowd, "You draw near unto me with your mouth, and honor me with your lips, but your hearts are far from me." (See Matthew 15:8.)

Sadly, the world doesn't take us seriously anymore because they can see that we don't practice what we preach or walk what we talk. They can see that we do nearly all the same unrighteous things that they do, and most of them don't even believe in God. When we walk as the world walks, we live with a lack of integrity, and we live in unrighteousness.

The Bible says you've got to strap on that belt of truth, you've got to strap on that breastplate of righteousness, and you'd better get yourself some of those glorified shoes. You'd better be shod because we are using our testimony to the power and the glory of Jesus Christ. You may not know how to give a theological discourse, but you can walk in a way that's worthy of the gospel of Jesus Christ. It's a shame that so many people live their entire lives without their immediate sphere of influence ever knowing they're a believer. I've performed funerals for people where somebody would show up and say, "Well, my goodness, I didn't even know they were a Christian." What would people say of you?

YOUR WALK IS A WEAPON

Your talk talks, and your walk talks, but your walk talks louder than your talk talks. If you are saying one thing and doing another, you are not a powerful believer—if you're even a believer at all. Regardless, if that's you, you're a miserable individual. No one expects you to be perfect, least of all God, but do not think you can tell Him and your family that you're going to do one thing and then live for your worldly concerns or chase after the things of this world (Mark 4:19). Who can stand hypocrisy? Certainly not God.

Of the top ten reasons why people don't attend church, number one is that they can't stand hypocrites. Let me interject a mini time-out. If that is your reason for not attending a local church, you need to know it's a lousy excuse. Skipping out on church because there are hypocrites in the house is like canceling your Planet Fitness membership because of all the overweight people on the treadmills. Ridiculous, right? You're not going to the gym to lose *their* weight; you're going there to lose *yours*. Likewise, you're not going to church because it helps others; you're going to church for what it can do for you. There are going to be hypocrites everywhere you go, and I'd rather go to *church* with hypocrites than go to hell with them. Amen?

Your walk is indeed a weapon, and we need to be shod with the preparation of the gospel of peace to weaponize it in service to God and not the enemy. Do not say you're a believer on Sunday if you live like a heathen the rest of the week. When you do, you're hurting the cause of Christ, and you're doing exactly what the devil wants you to do. You're giving a black eye to your local church and to the whole body of Christians. Gandhi, who was raised in the Hindu religion, famously said he might have become a Christian if it weren't for the Christians. We should be especially sensitive to how we represent Jesus among unbelievers. Sometimes we are our own worst billboard. Your walk is a weapon—for the cause of good or for the cause of evil.

PREPARATION

Notice that our key verse emphasizes that our feet must be shod with the *preparation* of the gospel. The Bible is saying that if we're not preparing to win, our armor is compromised, and once the enemy sees this, we've already lost. People often say we can "fall into sin," but there's no such thing. We walk into it. We don't slip and fall into anything. Sin is always a choice.

When you're driving down a highway, it's seldom a sudden blowout that leaves you flat on the side of the road. It's the slow leak that leads to the blown tire, so you're immobilized over time. We need to lose this "fell into sin" slang from our vernacular. We walk right into it with our eyes wide open. Compromise happens when you fail to prepare. It happens when you fail to make up your mind *not* to give in to temptation *before* the situation arises. It's not the temptation that is the problem; it's the lack of preparation, the lack of commitment beforehand. Jesus said temptation would come (Luke 17:1), so there's no avoiding it. The problem is when temptation meets an opportunity through our compromise.

When you're spiritually prepared, you acknowledge that temptation is coming so that *when* the opportunity finally presents itself, you're ready to overcome the temptation and avoid walking into it. Waiting until you're in the heat of a moment of temptation seldom works, if ever. Don't do it. This disastrous approach to temptation stems from a lack of spiritual preparation.

If you have ever come out of active addiction, or if you're in it right now, you've got to make up your mind to prepare. In this case, the best way to do that is to seek help from fellow believers before the temptation comes on Friday night. We've helped many who battle these demons, so if you have no one to turn to, please reach out to us at Global Vision, but please don't try to face it alone. Otherwise, when the enemy puts the temptation in your lap, you'll be like a puppet in his hands with no one there to help you break free, and there's no telling what the devil will do to you or use you to do to others.

I know breaking free of addiction is a massive challenge, but don't ever doubt that there is hope and help for you if you're prepared to humble your-self and ask for it. Many who are fighting addiction approach temptation with an "I'll cross that bridge when I get to it" mentality, but you already know you'd better burn that bridge before you get to it! If you're not prepared to win that battle, you've already lost. This goes for every type of repetitive sin. Addiction isn't only about drugs, alcohol, and perversion. The enemy knows everyone's favorite sins, yours included, and he's doing all he can to destroy you with them.

EXHORTING THE CHURCH

I say it a lot, and I'll continue to echo it until it's no longer true. American Christianity is far too American and not nearly enough Christian. It's weak and anemic, our spiritual eyes are sunk back in our heads, and our little bellies are swollen from spiritual malnutrition. The American church, in general, is too consumed by the cares of the world and the deceitfulness of riches to invest in spiritual preparation, let alone hunger for the gospel and the whole Word of God (Matt. 13:22). In most cases, what is true of your local church is also true of you. If you are content in a spiritually dying church, you are spiritually dying right along with it.

At the time of writing this book, I've preached in sixteen countries, and I could probably preach in seventy more in a month if God sent me. Hungry, impassioned ministries around the world are always calling and writing, fully expecting revival and just pleading for fire starters to bring their sparks to their nations. They're spiritually on fire because they're spiritually prepared and hungry for more of the gospel. But here in America, most ministries are as dead as a hammer and as dry as a bird's nest. Spiritually speaking, the average unchurched believer is in an even worse condition than the church.

When I go to nations in Africa, they beg me for Bibles. When I go to the Philippine Islands, they beg me for Bibles. When I go to Asia and Australia, they beg me for Bibles. Even when I go to Europe, where they're dryer than cracker juice, they also beg me for Bibles. Yet here in America, where we are rich in worldly comforts and typically have several dusty Bibles tucked away in our homes, we're not preparing for the gospel; we're preparing for our churches to die. It seems like some are thinking, "Well, everyone keeps saying Jesus is coming again sometime soon, so we might as well just roll up the doors and be done with it, right?" Jesus is indeed coming again soon, but we'd better work while it's yet day because the night comes when no man can work (John 9:4). Do not ignore this exhortation. We will be judged harshly if we just curl up and sleep or hide away in "safety" while we wait for His return.

> And let us consider one another to provoke unto love and to good works:
> Not forsaking the assembling of ourselves together, as the manner of
> some is; but exhorting one another: and so much the more, as ye see
> the day approaching.
> —HEBREWS 10:24–25

WALKING AWAY

Few phrases are more beautiful than *the gospel of peace*. Do you remember the angels who showed themselves to the shepherds on the night of Jesus' birth? They said God is going to bring *peace* to all the earth, along with *good tidings*—the gospel—to all men (Luke 2:13–14). The Bible tells us that Jesus obtained this peace through the blood of His cross—thus, the gospel of peace (Col. 1:20).

As noted earlier, Jesus tells us that He didn't come to bring worldly peace but a sword (Matt. 10:34), referring to the Word of God and its often-cutting message when presented to those who reject the gospel. By saying this, Jesus made sure we realized that we all have to cut some stuff out of our lives; we all have to do some spiritual surgery. There are people in your life that don't want peace *with* you; they want a piece *of* you. The sooner you cut those toxic, ungodly people out of your life, the better. Let them have their chaos and Facebook fun. Just walk away from that nonsense. They're trying to pull you into their poison. Don't let them.

> Make no friendship with an angry man; and with a furious man thou
> shalt not go: Lest thou learn his ways, and get a snare to thy soul.
> —PROVERBS 22:24–25

THE GOD-SHAPED HOLE

The Bible says that once we are saved and born again—once we're in God's school of preparation—we're shod to deliver the gospel of peace. There's only one message in the world that can bring about real hope, real security, real redemption, and real peace. That's the gospel of the Prince of Peace—Jesus Christ.

You can tell people about all the best self-help books in the world. You can send them to the best motivational gurus. You can encourage them to try hypnotherapy (I don't recommend it). You can encourage them to take part in all sorts of Christian counseling, and I'll never minimize that. But before any other approach could make a difference, you first have to realize you have a vacuum system in your soul that is cycling and sucking through everything in the world while you strive to find something that will fill what's lacking inside. Many of you self-medicate your way through your problems, and addiction is upon you. Until you get the peace of God that surpasses all understanding, you'll keep drinking it, you'll keep smoking it, you'll keep eating it, you'll keep snorting it, you'll keep taking it, you'll keep shooting it, you'll keep looking for it, you'll keep holding it, you'll keep handling it, you'll keep sleeping with it, and you'll keep going and going and going—until it destroys you. There's a God-shaped hole inside you that only God can fill—with the gospel of peace. Once we're filled, our mission is clear.

Go into all the world and proclaim the gospel to the whole creation.
—JESUS (MARK 16:15, ESV)

CHAPTER TWELVE

Shoes of the Gospel of Peace: Part 2

All power is given unto me in heaven and in earth. Go ye there-
fore, and teach all nations, baptizing them in the name of the
Father, and of the Son, and of the Holy Ghost: Teaching them to
observe all things whatsoever I have commanded you: and, lo, I
am with you always, even unto the end of the world. Amen.
—JESUS (MATTHEW 28:18–20)

THE BIBLE SAYS we are to be prepared *in*—filled with—the gospel of peace. Once filled with it, we are then called to deliver it through our walk. Like a vessel, we're called to carry the world's most impor-tant message to everyone we can touch. That's it. Nothing bombastic, nothing crazy, and nothing outlandish. Just the gospel. It's that simple. When we go to Kroger, we are to carry the gospel. When we go to Chick-fil-A, we are to carry the gospel. When we go to Walmart, we are to carry the gospel. When we go to church, we are to carry the gospel. When we go to work, we are to carry the gospel.

Everywhere we go, we are to carry the amazing, life-changing, reconciling, heaven-granting gospel of peace. Do that, and you will marvel at the power and the peace you will receive in return—weaponized armor to carry the gospel boldly through the battlefields in this spiritual war. This is the primary reason Paul links the shoes to the gospel.

Five times in the New Testament (in Matthew, Mark, Luke, John, and Acts), we are imperatively commanded by Jesus to carry the message that we have received to a world that has yet to receive it. It's called the Great Commission for a reason. I'm sorry if you didn't know this, but it's not a mere suggestion or job description for missionaries. Read the passage above from Matthew again, but this time read it slowly, and take in the weight and urgency in every word. Then be reminded of the gravity of the moment. Jesus said this just before He lifted Himself into the heavens to sit at the right hand of the Father with many credible witnesses present. Imagine the prophetic power in that commission and recognize how it has changed the world. Surely, you'll agree that sharing your faith is not optional, right? It's a command from the very mouth of God.

YOUR PERSONAL STORY

Some folks may be better at sharing than others, but all you really have to do is tell people what God is doing in your life. Tell them how God is answering your prayers and what God has done to change you. You may say, "Well, I just can't explain the Romans Road, or the Ten Commandments, or John's Highway." And that's all right. Those are religious terms, anyway. In time, you'll get all the theology you feel you need if you're serious about your life in Christ—if you're sincerely born again. In the meantime, just start telling folks what happened the day you got born again, even if today is that day.

Tell them what happened when God came alive in you. Tell them how God cleaned up your sorry carcass and put you on the straight and narrow. Tell them what Jesus now means to *you*. That's all they really want to hear. A lost person doesn't want a theology lesson from you, and they certainly don't want your religion. They simply want to believe that if the gospel really works in you, maybe it can work in them, too.

I know that some of you get extraordinarily nervous when it comes to talking to someone about your faith. I get it. I really do. Sometimes you feel insecure and nervous because you realize your walk hasn't been an effective weapon in this war against evil in the world. You're afraid to open your mouth, and you don't want to be viewed as a hypocrite. It reminds me of Abraham's nephew, Lot. In Genesis chapter 13, Lot moved to the infamous city of Sodom. Then, in chapter 19, we learn he had lived there for thirteen years working for them and getting a paycheck every Friday, when the angels of God warned him to flee the city. They told him Sodom's destruction was imminent, so he immediately told his kids, "We've got to get out of here! God's gonna destroy this place, so we've got to get out now!"

To that, his sons-in-law said, "Who do you think you are, Billy Bible?" That's not exactly what they said, but I'm sure you get the gist. They were like, "Oh, you've been telling the same jokes we tell, you've been looking at the same junk on the internet as us, you've been using the same coarse language and going to the same clubs and other sordid places and putting up with the same ungodly nonsense, and now you're gonna come in and get all spiritual on us and start telling us how spiritual we need to be? *Au contraire, mon frère!*" They laughed him out the door, and then they died in the fiery flames because his testimony was rotten.

OVERCOMING INSECURITY

Sometimes we don't share the gospel because our lives haven't been backing it up. Sometimes we don't share the gospel because we use lousy excuses that we believe come from the Bible. People say things like, "Well, you know, you've got to be careful telling people about your faith because you might scare them away." If that's you, let me ask you a question. Where exactly are they going if you scare them away? Hell number two? They're already lost! It's not like there's a secondary place to go, right? It's not like you can put them in a worse place than they already are!

When someone is headed for hell, they can't be any more turned away than they already are. Worrying that you might "scare them off" is just an excuse, and you need to get over it if you ever want the whole armor of God to work in your life. Don't ever forget that you can't pick and choose which pieces to wear. If you're not walking in those gospel shoes, you're armorless. You wear it all or none at all, so put it all on and let it shine!

> Let your light so shine before men, that they may see your good works, and glorify your Father which is in heaven.
>
> —JESUS (MATTHEW 5:16)

TIME-OUT: WHEN THE GOSPEL ISN'T PREACHED

There are people all over the world who don't even have a church building, so they're literally meeting in caves. I know people who are standing on the side of a river right now preaching the gospel, and they have more power than I will ever imagine or pray to have a day in my life, yet they don't even have a tent to cover their heads. They don't have cushy chairs, they don't have air conditioning, and they don't have high-tech redneck video screens and live streams.

In America these days, you can't get a quartet to sing in a phone booth without a microphone and an elaborate sound system, yet most preachers in nations experiencing revival don't even have a bullhorn. They just stand up on the side of the river and start preaching the gospel, and people start getting born again by the droves. Why? Because the power of God is in the simplicity of the gospel, not in our technology and certainly not in our comforts.

Before the lockdowns started, we were hearing people proudly boasting that the church in America is a powerhouse. Really? How so? As we've learned over the past few years, the church in America has become a total joke on the historic landscape—a mockery of the biblical model—and most churches are led by compromising hypocrites who are destroying their testimony, if they ever had one.

I don't care how many letters I get from angry pastors for telling the truth and calling them out. If you recall our discussion of Jude in chapter 1, I'm simply obeying the Word of God. I'm contending for the faith in the body of Christ. These delinquent pastors seldom preached the gospel even when they were still gathering. Even among those that have reopened, most are operating with a greater degree of cowardice than they exhibited before the tyrants took over America.

They seldom, if ever, invite souls to be saved, and most don't ever seek and serve the lost—they just *say* they do. They talk it, but they don't walk it. Their churches are socially distanced coffee clubs that peddle fear rather than contend for the faith or preach the gospel. Their altars are off-limits, and their baptismal tub—if they even have one—is typically boarded up or used to store their Christmas decorations. Why? Because most pastors don't really fear God. They just say they do. For that, they seldom preach the gospel, and they're ignoring the Great Commission where it's needed most, right here in America where the lost live right next door.

The Holy Spirit showed Paul that this day was coming. That's why he exhorted us to have the process of preparation going on without ceasing while going to every nation, including our own, to fearlessly preach and teach the gospel. Shodding our feet with the preparation of the gospel of peace takes effort, and it takes obedience and devotion to the one who saves.

LOVE BIBLICAL TRUTH, FEAR GOD

The fear of the LORD is the beginning of knowledge: but fools despise wisdom and instruction.

—PROVERBS 1:7

Even before the mass godlessness of 2020, the church in America was accepting sinful nonsense it should have never even entertained as a possibility; stuff the Bible clearly calls wickedness, perversion, lawlessness, and abomination. It begs the question, "Does anyone really fear God anymore?" Evidently, not many. In most corners of America, the church is openly accepting godlessness, and when someone like me armors up and speaks out against it, we're called xenophobes, racist bigots, homophobes, and transphobes (whatever the heck that's supposed to mean), and now we're even being called insurrectionists and terrorists, just because we put on the shoes of the gospel and go where most fear to go. Of course, none of these accusations are true, but this is what happens when you walk boldly in the gospel and truly fear the Lord enough to obey the Great Commission. The world is beginning to hate us, and that's okay.

The Word of God commands the church to be lit up and on fire for gatherings where the full gospel is preached, no matter the cost. We have the only book in the entire world that was written and sanctioned by God, yet most pastors act like we have no freedom or authority to gather freely and take it to the streets to push back against tyranny and perversion. Most are simply refusing to stand against the wiles of the devil, and for that, they're complicit in his schemes. Church, we'd better get busy preaching the gospel for the sake of the gospel, or millions of souls may be lost to eternity in hell.

We will all be held accountable for what we do with the good news in these dark days, but no one will have to answer more severely than your pastors, Greg Locke included (Jas. 3:1). I'm commanded to contend for the faith to the very end, so I have no choice but to stand and push back today—in the church, in the streets, at conferences, and even in the halls of government if necessary. I desperately love God, and I sincerely fear God. I'll risk my life on earth before I risk eternity with Jesus. I pray the same becomes true of your pastor before it's too late.

And ye shall be hated of all men for my name's sake: but he that endureth to the end shall be saved.

—JESUS (MATTHEW 10:22)

BEAUTIFUL FEET

The Book of Revelation tells us that, even in the end times, an angel will fly through the heavenlies and all through the atmosphere proclaiming the gospel (Rev. 14:6). All the way up to judgment day, the Lord is going to commission men and angels to do all we can to help the lost find Him. We're not just here to receive it; we're also here to share it. Paul wrote that the only way people can hear the gospel is if someone tells them (Rom. 10:14). Paul also wrote, "How beautiful are the feet of them that preach the gospel of peace" (Rom. 10:15).

Let's just be honest. Feet are ugly, right? Think about that. There is only one pair of feet on the planet that I care anything about, and they aren't mine. I'm telling you; I have some long nasty toes on some "swing from the monkey bars" kind of feet. If I ever lose a finger or two, I'll have plenty of replacement parts for the surgeon to work with. Do you know what I'm saying? I just don't like looking at feet, and mine are ugly. How on earth some people work full-time on other people's feet, I'll never know. They don't make enough money as far as I'm concerned.

Yet the Bible says if you'll deliver the gospel of peace, God thinks you have beautiful feet. It doesn't even matter how gnarled up those old toenails are. You can wear a size five, or you can wear a size fifteen. It doesn't make any difference. You can wear boat-sized shoes, or you can be like my wife, Tai, and have little-bitty Smurfette-sized feet (the only feet I care about). It just doesn't matter to the Lord what your feet look like. If you share the gospel, He loves your feet, calluses, bunions, and all.

PAUL, SILAS, AND THE JAILER

When was the last time you used your feet to deliver the message? I'm not trying to guilt you, I promise. I'm just telling you that you ought to win somebody to Christ once a year, just by accident. I mean, every now and again, someone ought to say, "Wow, you've got something a little different from what I've got going on in my life. What's doing that in your marriage? How did you beat that addiction? Why do you always have that glow about you?" Consider Paul and Silas. Those cats were in jail at midnight, beaten and stripped naked. They were hurting, broken, bloody, bruised, raw, and shamed in front of many.

The jail was filled, and all the other prisoners were griping, crying, and moaning—as prisoners surely did in the unimaginably harsh dungeons of those days—but do you know what Paul and Silas did? Even though it was after midnight, they prayed and sang praises unto God. The prisoners heard them, and so did their Philippian jailer. While everyone else was fussing, cussing, and complaining about their rights, the jailer heard Paul and Silas worshiping God, and suddenly an earthquake rocked the whole prison and busted the doors open. God shook the whole jail, so make sure you know that *Jailhouse Rock* was around a long time before Elvis ever rolled out of Memphis, praise God.

Once the earthquake subsided, the jailer came running in, fell on his knees, and asked Paul and Silas what he must do to have in him what they had, pleading, "What must I do to be saved?" (Acts 16:30). They didn't have to go through a long theological discourse. They didn't have to deliver a ten-point sermon or ask the man to confess every sin he had committed since high school. Paul said, "Believe on the Lord Jesus Christ, and thou shalt be saved..." (Acts 16:31).

That jailer was ripe for the picking. He saw how they walked, and he saw how they lived—in spite of the intense persecution of their current situation. You see, when you walk the talk with consistency, your walk does most of the talking. Paul and Silas had clearly put on the whole armor of God, and this historic event is a perfect example of the defensive and offensive power we receive when we are shod with the preparation of the gospel of peace.

Do you know why they were arrested, beaten, and imprisoned? Yes, they were preaching the gospel, but that's not why they were imprisoned on that occasion. They had been arrested because Paul confronted the wickedness and deception he witnessed in the public square—all of which had been widely accepted by the authorities. Paul spoke out against it for all to hear with no fear of the consequences.

When you see me and others like me calling out the wickedness in the public square or the pastors who are bowing to these dark forces rather than confronting them head-on, remember Paul and Silas—and remember their jailer. Spiritual warfare can indeed be dangerous, but when we're fully armored up, we can trust that God will have His way in and through us, and only God knows how many will be saved when we stand and contend for the faith—"how beautiful are the feet."

DIVINE CHAIN REACTION

When you read the entirety of this story as recorded in the Book of Acts, you'll see all the ways the enemy attacked Paul and Silas, persecuted them, falsely accused them, and beat them, even before he placed them in chains deep in the dungeon of a pagan nation. If ever there was a time to be overcome with fear that is intense enough to shut a man's mouth and stop his walk, you would think this would be it. But not for Paul, and not his student Silas either.

They put on the whole armor of God, they walked in the gospel of peace, they boldly exposed the works of darkness, and when persecution came, they didn't cower; they lifted the name of Jesus in praise! They continued walking their talk even while shackled in stocks and chained to a prison wall. Many were led to Christ by their testimony in prison that night, and many more were reconciled to God as the jailer, in turn, led his family to Christ. Eventually, like a divine chain reaction, many who heard of their transformation began to ask, "How do I get the peace and the power they have?" Praise God that we know. Beautiful are the feet that are shod in the preparation of the gospel of peace.

IT GETS EASIER

If you're asking why people don't want what you have, the first question is, do *you* want what you have? It's sort of like a fat man selling diet pills. Who is going to buy diet pills from a dude that shows no evidence that they work? Why does anyone want a Jesus that you claim works in your life when they can't see any evidence that it's true? I'm not saying you're going to be perfect, but you should be noticeably different from who you were before being born again.

The fact that your walk is a weapon requires you to be in the process of preparing for battle every single day. If not, you've already conceded. You and I have the most powerfully anointed message on the planet to carry to the world—the gospel of peace. If you deliver the message, people may reject you, but God will reward you. People may cuss at you, but God will exalt and praise you. I know some of you are bolder than others and that some of you are better equipped than others. Some folks can talk to a doorknob. I get it. But we're all called to reveal it in our walk. Do that, and the sharing will get easier and easier over time.

HE'LL BE THE JUDGE OF THAT

Ultimately, it doesn't matter what we think we're capable of or even what we believe about who and what we are in the sight of God. Jesus alone will be the judge of that (John 5:22). We'll discuss salvation at great lengths in later chapters, and as you'll see, if you're saved and born again, your salvation is indeed assured. Praise God! But Jesus leaves no doubt about this: we must be ready, in season and out of season (2 Tim. 4:2).

Our walk must reflect the preparation of the gospel of peace wherever we go, and we must stand up and go, or we place ourselves in great peril on the day of His long-awaited return—no matter what we say we believe. These aren't the words of Greg; they're the words of Jesus. Read the parable of the virgins, the parable of the talents, and the parable of the sheep and goats from His Olivet Discourse to see how serious Jesus is concerning our preparation and actions during these last days—and how tragic the consequences will be for those who don't obey Him. (See Matthew 25.) Jesus commanded us to go, to preach and teach the gospel to all creation, and to teach all nations to obey everything He commanded us (Matt. 28:16–20). In His closing statements from the Olivet Discourse, Jesus left us with a sobering message.

> Then shall he answer them, saying, Verily I say unto you, Inasmuch as ye did it not to one of the least of these, ye did it not to me. And these shall go away into everlasting punishment: but the righteous into life eternal.
>
> —JESUS (MATTHEW 25:45–46)

I tell preachers all over this nation that I don't care about the style of their church. It's not the style but the content of the preaching—the Word of God—that grows us as individuals and as the body of Christ. That's my greatest commitment through my preaching and my writings. I'm excited about all that we have covered in the previous chapters of this book; I've grown through it, and I trust you've grown through it too. That said, I hope you're ready for the beautiful promises and challenging revelations we'll discuss in the coming chapters. The Lord always saves the best for last. It's true of the Bible, and I believe it will prove true of this study of the Bible as well.

> But grow in grace, and in the knowledge of our Lord and Saviour Jesus Christ. To him be glory both now and for ever. Amen.
>
> —2 PETER 3:18

CHAPTER THIRTEEN

Shield of Faith

Above all, taking the shield of faith, wherewith ye shall be
able to quench all the fiery darts of the wicked.
—EPHESIANS 6:16

A S WE MOVE on to discuss the shield of faith, the Lord makes a some-
what shocking, typically overlooked statement, so you don't want to
miss it. The first two words He uses to introduce the helmet reveal
a fascinating truth about faith: "Above all." Most folks sweep over qualifier
words like that as if they're in there just for flow or poetic purposes, but you'd
better pay attention when God gives you an important detail like "above all."

Let's look at what the Lord means by "above all." In the context of our key
verse, the words *above all* tell us that the shield is more important than all the
other pieces combined. If you don't have the shield of faith, all others will fail,
even if you wear them with perfection.

If that confuses you, we can crystallize it down to this: Faith in God is
above all. Without the shield—without faith—the belt won't fit. The breastplate won't work. The shoes won't effectively carry you anywhere. The sword

will be dull. And the helmet won't protect you. In fact, if you don't have faith, even your prayers will prove empty. We must learn to emphasize and prioritize according to God's teaching and slow down long enough to see the true meaning of His qualifying statements in the Bible. Every word matters, so be careful when using modernized verses that ignore that rule.

Consider how many folks call themselves Christians without ever claiming to be born again or having a single born-again experience. Everyone is in a hurry to take the badge of honor and the gift of eternity through simple mental assent, but far too many ignore the actions and behaviors that the Lord made prerequisite for this matchless treasure.

Have you ever noticed how we live for such small things in American Christianity? Such tiny little dainty things that don't even matter. We live for man-made machines that God might turn into a bucket of bolts at the next stoplight. We live for houses, fame, fortune, accolades, and relationships that could burn to the ground tonight. We live for all sorts of stuff in this world, but we ought to live *above all* for the things that matter to God—the things that He said truly count toward eternity with Him—and the highest among these is faith.

When you stand before God, the amount of money you had in the bank will not be questioned. The car you drove will not matter. All the things you accomplished in the systems of this world will be of no consequence. God couldn't give two flips of a wooden nickel how many friends we made or how many Facebook followers we have. None of that matters to God.

THE METAPHOR OF THE SHIELD

When we think about a shield, we have some great illustrations to work with. Personally, from a movie-goer's perspective, I love *Captain America*. I identify with that cat. Who wouldn't like to be *Pastor America*, right? I love what that character stood for. If you ever want to get me something to put up in my office, find me one of those Captain America shields. I'd take it, praise God. But don't get me one of those plastic ones. I want the real one made from that indestructible metal, which doesn't really exist (or else I wouldn't be asking). In all seriousness, when we picture the shield of faith, we need to erase any images of a round Captain America sort of shield. In the armor of God discourse, we need to picture the shield used by the first-century Roman army that Paul and the early church were familiar with. It was a four-foot-tall, three-foot-wide, rectangular, mostly wooden shield called a scutum. When a soldier got behind this slightly curved shield and hunkered down, it covered his whole body, so the shield of faith isn't just a secondary protector of our vital areas. It protects *every* part of us and can work in concert with the shields of others to create a shield wall that can increase the defensive strength when outnumbered in an enemy attack.

That's what faith can do—but only for mature believers. I must make that distinction because, in this context, Paul is not talking to lost people about the faith that saves (Eph. 2:8–9); he's talking to God's people about the faith that grows within us and eventually overrides every other concern, desire, or belief.

WHAT IS FAITH?

Now faith is the substance of things hoped for, the evidence of things not seen.

—HEBREWS 11:1

It's a shameful, horrible disgrace that in the church in America, we believe God can save us from hell, but we don't believe God can pay our bills. We don't believe God can help our kids. We don't believe God can defend us from traitors in our government. And we don't believe God will heal us and work everything together for our good. Let me propose something that may be unsettling, but you need to hear it. If you say you have faith in God—faith in the Father, faith in Jesus the Son, and faith in the Holy Spirit—but do not have the growing, ever-increasing faith to trust His promises and believe that His commands are requirements and not mere suggestions, maybe you're not yet a believer. Maybe you've made a mental transaction, but you're still seeking to believe what you've bought into.

The word *believe* is, in effect, a verb form of the noun *faith*, so though they're not interchangeable in a sentence, they have the same meaning. The same goes for the nouns *belief* and *trust*. As you've surely noticed, we loosely use the root words *believe, faith,* and *trust* in modern English. You can believe or trust it will rain today, but you're not saying that you *know* it will rain. You can have faith or belief in your favorite sports team, but that doesn't mean you'd bet your life on their ability to win.

The biblical meaning of faith is more closely defined as a supernatural knowing with full confidence, and this confidence overcomes all doubts—by definition. To believe, trust, or have faith in Jesus is to *know* He is God and His Word is true. In biblical terms, *believing* in Jesus equals *knowing* Jesus (John 3:16), not merely believing He exists. Even the devil and his minions believe that, but they don't know Him, don't have *faith* in Him, and are certainly not saved or born again.

131

FAITH THAT GROWS

And the apostles said unto the Lord, Increase our faith.
—LUKE 17:5

When you have genuine faith, you are in the process of becoming a new creation and are indeed born again. Praise God! If you still have doubts, don't beat yourself up, and never condemn yourself or allow anyone else to speak condemnation over you. Not everyone gets struck by metaphorical lightning when they first accept Christ. This is why our faith *must* grow.

If ye have faith as a grain of mustard seed, ye shall say unto this mountain, Remove hence to yonder place; and it shall remove; and nothing shall be impossible unto you.
—JESUS (MATTHEW 17:20)

It's normal to start your journey with a few doubts, but if you have the faith that saves, you will begin to hunger and thirst for a genuine heart-to-heart relationship with Jesus that drives you to study His Word out of sheer desire to know Him better. You grow your faith. Jesus taught that faith can be like a tiny mustard seed. Despite its small beginning, it has the potential to move mountains and work miracles. Jesus also taught that once a mustard seed is planted in good soil, it will grow to become a tree so great that the birds of the air make their homes in its branches (Matt. 13:32). This is a beautiful picture of His kingdom and the potential of both the faith that saves *and* the faith that grows. Not only does it empower you, but it blesses all those around you.

THE ONLY GOD

Ye are my witnesses, saith the LORD, and my servant whom I have chosen: that ye may know and believe me, and understand that I am he: before me there was no God formed, neither shall there be after me.
—ISAIAH 43:10

People can believe that Jesus is a great man of history but never really believe He is God, nor believe He's omniscient (all-knowing), omnipresent (present in all places at all times), and omnipotent (all-powerful). As discussed in the introduction, Jesus is without question the Author of all, as are the Father and the Holy Spirit—our Triune God. The reality of God is a profound mystery that we can fully witness but can never fully explain on this side of heaven.

But know this: besides our God, there is no other (Isa. 45:5). Many false religions exist, and thousands of false gods have been written into existence by men through mythological literature and philosophical texts, but all are folly compared to God and His Word. Many traditions and literary stories mirror the Judeo-Christian record; some falsely claim to predate the Bible. But you can rest assured that none predate the living Word of God.

> In the beginning was the Word, and the Word was with God, and the Word was God. The same was in the beginning with God. All things were made by him; and without him was not any thing made that was made.
>
> —JOHN 1:1–3

From Adam and Eve to the Jews and Christians who are grafted into His family through Christ, we have always been the only true people of God. Modern-day Israel is still the Israel of antiquity, the Jews are still the Jews, and we are still the saints and disciples of Jesus—the children of the living God. I could dive deep into a study of apologetics that prove His existence through science and logic, and maybe someday I will. I could talk endlessly about His amazing supernatural acts throughout history, including those I've witnessed in my own life, and sometimes I do. Jesus is my life, and I pray the same is true for you.

HE IS WORTHY

> But ye are a chosen generation, a royal priesthood, an holy nation, a peculiar people; that ye should shew forth the praises of him who hath called you out of darkness into his marvellous light.
>
> —1 PETER 2:9

How often do you *marvel* at your place in this riveting story of His people—the people of the Bible? How often do you thank Him for calling you into this chosen generation, this royal priesthood, this holy nation of peculiar people, written into His Book to praise Him and tell of His glory—the only God who calls us out of darkness into His marvelous light? He is your Father, and He is for you! Jesus is your Savior, and He loves you! The Holy Spirit is your counselor and comforter, and He wants to dwell *in* you!

God is not a figment of man's imagination; we are a figment of His, brought to life in these earthen vessels to fulfill a specific purpose (2 Cor. 4:7). Right this moment, He is calling you to a deeper place in Him—to grow your faith.

Find more opportunities to fall on your knees in humility and gratitude for Him. This wide-open recognition of His living presence will unquestionably grow your faith.

MORE ON THE "ALL" FACTOR

Sometimes people try to caution me. They say that if I continue talking about my all-consuming love for God like this, I'll be labeled as some kind of Jesus freak. I'm counting on it! He calls us to be peculiar people who love Him with all our heart, soul, strength, and mind (Luke 10:27). Never forget, all means all. Jesus is the all-or-nothing God, so it's impossible to be too obsessed with Him.

The core problem in Christianity is that we don't love God enough, so most don't fear disobeying Him. Loving Him with our *all* is the only biblically correct response to how He first loved us (1 John 4:19), and this sort of ongoing recognition of the overwhelming love and ever-present reality of God will supercharge your armor for the battles at hand. That's why I started writing books. My only obsession is to express my love and devotion to Jesus in every way possible.

He is worthy. He is God. Don't ever forget why we're here and why you're reading this. If you want more power to fight the good fight and stand against the enemy in victory, plant your faith in good soil (a 100-percent devoted heart) and grow it to thirty, sixty, or one hundred times its current reach, just as Jesus promises for all who truly believe and obey Him (Matt. 13:23).

GROWING LIKE DAVID

I believe the sort of faith that grows starts by becoming more deeply in love and more sincerely in awe of God. Do that, and you will start overflowing with His strength in times of need. Faith that grows will erase all doubts and, in time, supernaturally transforms you. It is the faith of one who is born again. Without it, Jesus said we can't even see the kingdom of God (John 3:3), much less enter it or receive the supernatural power that manifests as the armor of God. Quite simply, if you don't really believe in God, you will neither receive nor believe in His armor. Let's be honest about that. But as the Bible teaches, we walk by faith, not by sight (2 Cor. 5:7), so hang in there. Keep seeking Him in spirit and in truth, and He will respond in kind.

> The LORD is my strength and my shield; my heart trusted in him, and I am helped: therefore my heart greatly rejoiceth; and with my song will I praise him.
>
> —PSALM 28:7

Few men in history accessed the power of God in times of battle more effectively than David. He's the most famous warrior in world history and the most prolific worshiper in the Bible. He was also a master of stringed instruments and penned most of the Psalms. David proved when your heart truly trusts in Him, rejoices in Him, praises Him, and obeys Him, He becomes your strength—and your shield. Do that, and like David, you'll grow your faith.

But before he was ever a warrior or a king, David was first a worshiper. Worship is any act of reverent obedience to God, and it all stems from the depth of your faith and your genuine love and gratitude for all He has done. Singing "psalms and hymns and spiritual songs" is among the simplest ways to exhibit and grow your faith in the living God (Eph. 5:19–21).

If you've been shy about singing His praises in a time of praise and worship during a church service, just let it go. It's time to let down your guard and just lift your voice to Him, for Him. Like your water baptism, praise is a beautiful public display of your faith, but in this case, you can do it every day, no matter where you are, not just on Sundays and Wednesdays in your local church. If you're cringing right now, I get it.

I came out of a denomination that discouraged wide-open, Spirit-filled worship. You don't have to sing at the top of your lungs or dance as David danced—though sometimes I do even when I'm preaching, praise God. Just remind yourself that your voice matters to Him, even in public worship. He really wants your praise in song, especially in gatherings, even if you can't carry a tune—even if it's simply a melody in your heart that washes over you and through you enough to make some joyful noise. The Bible tells us He inhabits our praise (Ps. 22:3), so you know He wants it, and so should we. Don't you want Him to inhabit your environment everywhere you go? Of course you do! Consider it one more way to train up for greater boldness! Besides, when we sincerely praise Him, He always blesses us, just as He blessed David.

Listening to praise and worship music or Christian music radio in your car and at home can help immensely. Listening to the modern psalms of Christian music is a beautiful way to grow your faith. When I'm driving, which I do a lot, there's nothing else I'll put on the radio. It always uplifts me, especially in contrast to the alternatives.

OUR GREATEST DEFENSE MECHANISM

If you're confident in your faith, remember that faith does not stop growing when you are born again. Your faith initiates and introduces itself when you first get born again, and then it continues to get bigger and bigger and bigger. I want to be bigger in my faith in God by this time next year, far bigger in faith than I am right now, and so should you. If you continue growing your faith, one day at a time, all the biblical teachings that seem vague or hard to see today will eventually become clear (1 Cor. 13:12). A growing faith is our greatest defense mechanism. That's not a Greg Locke-ism; it's in the Bible.

A growing faith is greater than all the other pieces of armor combined. As we learn from Psalm 28, the Lord Himself becomes our shield of faith when we pursue God with all our hearts. No wonder He puts the shield "Above all." Who doesn't want God to be their shield through battle? Talk about a no-brainer. When your faith is growing, the devil cannot get to you. You can stand against the wiles of the devil because your faith protects you from all the fiery darts of the evil one. I will explain that in biblical and historical context in the next chapter.

> Whom having not seen, ye love; in whom, though now ye see him
> not, yet believing, ye rejoice with joy unspeakable and full of glory:
> Receiving the end of your faith, even the salvation of your souls.
>
> —1 PETER 1:8–9

DOUBTING GOD

Knowing all this, we must ask why our faith is so terribly weak. Too often, we talk about faith like atheists talk about faith. We say, "I want to believe in God, I really do want to believe, but at the end of the day, He's just gonna have to prove Himself to me." If God hasn't already proven Himself to you, I'll eat my dirty socks. He has proven Himself to you repeatedly. Your very existence is proof. In all the Bible, God never lied. You might have been disappointed because you had a false expectation, but God has never shown Himself to be wrong about your life. He has never lied to you. He has never deceived you. He has never stopped helping you for one natural day since the moment you were born again, and He never will.

No matter what you do, God will not leave you, and He will never forsake you. If you don't believe that, you don't believe a thimbleful of the Bible. If you still don't believe this, make sure you share your concerns with fellow believers, pastors, and trusted Christian counselors that have the confidence you want and the spiritual maturity you need. We're not designed to walk this out alone. Do that, and your faith will undoubtedly grow. You will know beyond a shadow of a doubt that God will never abandon you but will become your shield of faith—your divine defense mechanism.

> And Jesus answering saith unto them, Have faith in God.
> —MARK 11:22

OPTIMIZING YOUR GROWTH

Many popular songs and hymns remind us that worship is indeed a weapon. It's not a piece of armor in and of itself but is a means to grow our faith and strengthen our grasp of the shield of faith. So when we sing lyrics like, "This is how we fight our battles," we're literally weaponizing the shield for defensive and offensive maneuvers through our battles. That said, worship through song is just one of the spiritual acts that grow our faith. As you have probably surmised through our recognition of the interdependent interconnectedness of the whole armor of God, the putting on of each piece will indeed grow your faith.

Many sing their hearts out in church but never grow in faith because they have not put on the whole armor of God or they don't even have the Holy Spirit actively empowering them. Your faith will not grow if you don't remain in the Word of God or walk in the gospel. Your faith will not grow if you know nothing about prayer, truth, righteousness, or salvation. Your faith will not grow if you're not yet born again. So, springing from your increased understanding of these concepts, you've got to recognize that your faith will not grow if you only go to church when you feel like it. Your faith will not grow if you don't surround yourself with people who also have a growing faith. And it certainly won't grow if you're surrounded by worldly unbelievers or religious hypocrites. I want to be surrounded by God and His people. Those are *my* people.

I'm not filling my life with worldly drama. Are you? I want to surround my life and my family with people who are making a difference for the kingdom of God. Birds of a feather flock together, and there is only strength in numbers when the numbers are equally yoked. I don't get into fear-based speculations or gossip, and I don't waste my time with people who do. I'm not hanging out with people who are always down in the doldrums or always cussing and fussing.

I want to be around folks that read the Bible and walk it out. I want to be around people that love the house of God and show up to worship Him. I want to be around people who love lots of Bible preaching, and not just mine. I want to be around people who are growing in their faith, because it makes me want to grow in my faith. It makes me want to do more, be more, go more, and say more for the sake of the gospel. It makes me want to have a better defense mechanism. Yet, more now than ever, the faith we see exhibited by the church is shrinking when it should be growing. It's time to grow up, church!

> Jesus saith unto him, Thomas, because thou hast seen me, thou hast believed: blessed are they that have not seen, and yet have believed.
> —JOHN 20:29

CHAPTER FOURTEEN

Shield of Faith: Part 2

*But without faith it is impossible to please him: for he
that cometh to God must believe that he is, and that he
is a rewarder of them that diligently seek him.*
—HEBREWS 11:6

WITHOUT FAITH, IT is impossible to please God. That's a verse
we should all memorize. As we learned earlier from our look
at Hebrews 11:1, faith is the substance of things hoped for and
the evidence of things not seen. No matter what we face, we can never stop
hoping and knowing that God is going to do it, even when we can't see how
He is going to do it. All is futile if we don't, and God leaves us no room or
reason to justify lacking it. Those with real faith seek Him for all we need
because we truly believe He is God and believe He desires to reward and
bless us. This kind of faith pleases Him (Heb. 11:6).

If you believe you're facing too much tragedy or poverty to grow this type
of faith, you need to read Hebrews 11. Do that, and you'll realize you have
no real reason to doubt that He can do exceedingly abundantly more than we
could ever ask or think (Eph. 3:20). You'll be reminded of the many faithful
believers of old who faced every horrible challenge you can imagine. He talks

about David, Jephthah, and Rahab. He talks about Zacharias, Moses, and Noah. He talks about all these great heroes of our faith from the Old and New Testaments. All these people had massive odds against them. Yet, because they had a growing faith that they put into action, God moved in and through their lives to do the unimaginable.

FAITH ON OFFENSE

We talk a lot about David and Goliath in the church, going back to our Vacation Bible School days. Most of us grew up thinking, "Oh, look at David taking out that giant. He must have been such a well-trained, powerful warrior." No, he was still just a kid at the time of his coming-out party against Goliath. He was a fifteen-year-old shepherd boy who had yet to receive training with the sword, spear, or any tangible armor of a warrior. All he had was his trusty slingshot. The King James Bible says three times that he was "ruddy." He was just a ruddy little kid. He didn't have bulging biceps with a training regimen that would put Planet Fitness to shame.

David was just a little kid, closer to an eyes-sunk-in-his-head, anemic, oversized-shorts-in-gym-class weakling of a teen. This kid was not trained to fight anybody, much less the biggest, baddest dude in the Philistine army.

When Goliath came out and saw David, he said, "I'm gonna kill you, kid." And David was like, "What do you mean you're gonna kill me?"

And Goliath was like, "I've been eating punks like you since I had my prison sentence. Whatever, whatever, whatever!"

Everyone who witnessed this historic scene laughed at David—on both sides of the battle. They said, "David, this guy is too big for you to kill!"

And David was like, "Have you seen him? He's too big for me to miss!"

Now, you believe what you want to, and you can dismiss this if you want, but I believe David could have sat down cross-legged, turned around backward, put a hand over his eyes, and flicked that little rock like a heat-seeking Holy Ghost missile. I believe that little stone would have gone where it needed to go no matter how David flung it. In fact, I believe he could have yelled, "Boo!" and the giant would have fallen over dead. You see, it wasn't the stone, and it wasn't David's skill. His faith in God caused the giant to fall dead to the ground.

David's greatest weapon was his faith, and he knew it. Faith was his defense mechanism *and* his offense mechanism. That's why he could walk out and say, "Okay, I'm not just gonna kill you. You've got four brothers, so I'll get five smooth stones and kill your whole wicked family all at once!" I like ambitious people who aren't afraid to bite off more than they can chew. I like people who are bold enough to put themselves in situations where they're sunk if God doesn't bail them out.

If you're serious about engaging in this spiritual war, you should find yourself praying and simply jumping out there with such faith that if God doesn't save you, you're done. If God doesn't pay it, you're done. If God doesn't do it, you're done. That's what David did. He just walked out and said, "I come to you in the name of the Lord."

The Philistine's response was, "You cannot win this battle," and the Israelites agreed.

So David said, in effect, "You're right because the battle is the Lord's." (See 1 Samuel 17:47.) This historic battle isn't recorded in the Bible to entertain our children. It's there to teach us what a growing faith can do. So get your face out of Facebook, put your face in *the Book*, the Bible, and let your faith grow.

HOW THE SHIELD WORKS FOR US

In our key verse, Ephesians 6:16, God said, "Above all, taking the shield of faith, wherewith ye shall be able to quench all the fiery darts [arrows] of the wicked." From this, we know that trusting God enables us to absorb the impact of the arrows and the rush of the enemy's attack intent on destroying us. Do you know what the shield did for a real-world warrior in biblical times? It withstood the full brunt of the enemy, no matter the weapon he used. It took the arrows and fiery darts, it took the spears, it took the shoving, it took the fists, and it took the press of the surging hordes. It took the impact intended to destroy the warrior and everyone else he was protecting behind him. Sometimes folks say, "Oh man, this is going to destroy me!" If that's you, and if you keep that up, you're probably right. This attitude places your faith in the bad reports instead of almighty God, and that will destroy you. When we think our problems are bigger than God, we are defeated before we ever get started.

Sometimes we think that—because we cannot see the forest for the trees—the problem is bigger than God. Do you realize that when Jesus walked into a town, He always left people better off than when He found them? And do you realize that Jesus performed miracles because of a serious and evident problem that needed His divine intervention?

We know from the Gospel of John that Jesus' first public miracle was turning water into wine. Do you know why? Because they ran out of it way too soon, and in a wedding celebration that typically lasted several days, that was a problem. Sure, there's a lot to unpack that made this first miracle prophetic and extraordinarily beautiful, but don't miss the simple fact that there was a real problem—and He simply solved it. Yes, He knew the timely miracle would grow the faith of His disciples, but don't ever forget that Jesus also wants to solve our problems! In keeping with this stream of thought, why do you think Jesus raised Lazarus from the dead? Because he died, and that was a problem! Jesus healed people because they were sick, diseased, and disabled.

These were very real and present problems for the people Jesus healed. There is always a problem before God works a miracle. So in most cases, our tragic error is that we have all our faith in our problems and none of our faith in God's miracle-working power. When we are suffering with this sort of misplaced faith, all we see is the raging Red Sea. Yet when Moses faced the raging sea with Pharaoh's army bearing down on him, he told the Israelites to stand still and go forward (Exod. 14).

With that in mind, how can we stand still and go forward in the face of our own problems? We must stop thinking as the world thinks and start to see what no one else sees—in faith. We must see beyond the nonsense. We must see beyond the smoke and mirrors of the devil's schemes. When the world says seeing is believing, God says believing is seeing.

SIMPLE FAITH

In these days of the Holy Spirit's indwelling, God will never work a miracle for a skeptic. I've heard people say they would believe in Noah's ark if someone could produce physical evidence from the ark itself. That sort of person wouldn't believe it even if they took a slip-and-slide vacation cruise on the ark. If you don't believe what the Bible says—through faith alone— you won't believe the ark existed even if you time-traveled onto the boat and smelled the animals. You'd more readily believe it was a psychotic event or an alien abduction than attribute the experience to the living God.

Have you ever cut your head open, pulled your brain out, and played with it? No, but you know it's in there. You don't need to see or fully understand how it works. Jesus tells us the wind blows where it wishes, and you can hear its sound but can't tell where it came from or where it's going. This is true of everyone who is born again of the Spirit (John 3:8). You can't see the wind, but you see the effects of the wind. You can't see God, but the heavens declare His glory, and the whole universe shows His handiwork. To deny God is the most foolish decision a person could ever make. Grow your faith, and you will eventually see all you need to see and receive all you really need.

We've all allowed problems to destroy us, and when we did, it was because we failed to take up the shield of faith "above all." We didn't trust God to do it. Instead of believing God, we believed what the boss said, what the lawyer said, what the doctor said, what a family member said, or what a misguided preacher said.

You'll continue in this destructive pattern until you establish your beliefs and convictions based on the Word of God and nothing more. If you're not careful, you will become dismayed, disheartened, depressed, and discouraged by what you see in the natural. You must look past what you see with your natural eyes to invisibly know God is in heaven *and in you*. He has plans that are in your best interests for His glory. Trust Him.

TRUSTING GOD COMPLETELY

> Every word of God is pure: he is a shield unto them that put their trust in him.
>
> —PROVERBS 30:5

Your human body is not built to withstand some of the pressures you allow it to withstand. If your faith isn't growing, these pressures will destroy you. You must allow the shield of faith to absorb pressures in your marriage, finances, body, church, workplace, and nation. Faith that grows will absorb it all, even when it would have otherwise destroyed you.

I've been told that I can seem insensitive in the face of the craziness around us. Depending on your perspective, you might see me as just the opposite, but those who see me daily or weekly generally think I'm a bit cavalier about all the chaos. The truth is, I'm neither. I've learned that the craziness around me has no control over what will happen next, as only God controls all these things. I'm sensitive to all of it, but I don't let any of it freak me out—not anymore.

Once and for all, I have embraced the fact that God can do exceedingly abundantly more than we could ever ask or imagine (Eph. 3:20). Winston Churchill is often credited with saying, "If you're going through hell, keep going." So when all hell breaks loose, so to speak, don't stop, don't take pictures, don't take samples, just keep going. You've got to get to a place where you say, "I am not going to allow this stuff to destroy me. I'm just gonna believe God and let Him deal with it!"

Just be still and let it be as the Holy Spirit leads, in accordance with the Word of God. Yes, that can feel like a very wheels-off way to live, but it's time to grow our faith so large that we boldly tear off the training wheels. We must trust God to work all things together for our good (Rom. 8:28).

EXTINGUISHING THE FIERY DARTS

In our key verse, the Lord tells us that the shield of faith will be able to quench all the fiery darts of the wicked. There are two key takeaways from this verse that I don't want you to miss. First, it recognizes that more than one dart will be fired at you. At times, there are going to be bundles of them raining down. Second, it informs us that the piercing force of an arrow isn't its only threat, as it can spread like fire even if it isn't a direct hit.

Historically, when the enemy army was trying to destroy an entire city, the frontline soldiers that took a defensive posture would be attacked first by bowmen. These archers would often light their arrows on fire, and they would rain their arrows down upon them. By doing this, even when they were unable to strike one of the soldiers, they would still strike their wooden shields, potentially setting them on fire and making them useless.

When the defending force anticipated this sort of fiery attack, they would coat their shields with an absorbent tar or pitch. That way, when a fiery dart penetrated a shield, it would be extinguished by the tar and rendered harmless. Through this imagery, the Bible tells us that the shield of faith can protect us even from the most incendiary attacks when we stand firm and remain engaged in the process of increasing the defensive power of our faith.

WHAT ARE THE FIERY DARTS?

I could list hundreds of devices the enemy uses as fiery darts to destroy you, including lies, deception, temptation, discouragement, doubt, division, discord, fear, and anxiety. Virtually anything can be twisted by the enemy and turned into a dart to pierce your heart. The devil knows your weaknesses, your soft spots, your difficult realities, and your most vulnerable temptations, and he aims his darts accordingly. This is why we must be transparently open with God about our struggles (recall our discussion of the belt of truth), but we also need to be transparent and open with other brothers and sisters in the Lord who can hold us accountable.

The devil's metaphorical fiery darts burn more intensely in the dark, so we must bring our struggles to light before God and the accountability partners we have locked shields with. Do that, and when a fiery dart finds its mark, you can extinguish the destructive fire. As you read this, you might be completely crippled in your spiritual walk because you've been trying to hide your struggles from God, even though He already knows all. Keep in mind that when you come clean with God, it's not for His benefit but for yours. You cannot hide your sin from God, and you can't outrun His judgment. So get right with Him now and quench that sin before it burns you and your relationships to the ground.

The Bible tells us to confess our sins because God is faithful and just. We are guaranteed that He will forgive us and purify us (1 John 1:9). Confessing sin is a vital first step to deliverance, and there are several reasons why:

1. It's an acknowledgment that we have been ensnared by sinful behavior, thoughts, or attitudes that may have opened doors to spiritual bondage. It is recognizing that we need deliverance from these strongholds in order to experience freedom and restoration.

2. It is one of the most powerful spiritual weapons for breaking the power of the enemy. By openly admitting and confessing our sins, we bring them into the light, stripping the devil of his ability to hold them over us in secrecy and shame. Confession dismantles the stronghold the enemy has established and weakens his influence over our lives.

3. Confession requires humility and genuine repentance, which are essential in spiritual warfare. When we recognize our need for God's forgiveness and turn away from sinful behavior, we align our hearts with His truth and righteousness. We position ourselves to receive God's deliverance and victory over the enemy.

4. Confession opens the door for God's cleansing and renewal in our lives. As we confess our sins, God's forgiveness and mercy are poured out upon us, allowing us to experience the transformative power of God's love and grace, bringing healing to areas that have been affected by spiritual bondage.

5. Confession is an act of reclaiming our authority in Christ. By confessing our sins, we assert our identity as forgiven and redeemed children of God. This strengthens our position in spiritual warfare, enabling us to stand firm against the enemy's attacks and claim the victory that Christ has already won for us.

Confession is part of a broader process of deliverance and spiritual warfare, but it is one of your most effective spiritual weapons in snuffing out the fiery darts of the enemy. In case you're still unsure what constitutes a fiery dart, I'll give a few examples. A fiery dart might be your temper, and the devil expertly aims each arrow to push your buttons until you explode. A fiery dart might be lust, and the enemy's shot becomes a destructive fire that you alone keep burning for lack of faithfulness. Maybe your fiery dart is an ungodly relationship that you know should not exist, yet it keeps burning up your life. Your most destructive fiery dart could be your pride or simply your thought life. For many, the most dangerous fiery dart is the love of money—materialism.

All these sinful fires start as darts that enter our minds through our senses, and most of you leave your senses wide open to the enemy's attacks (more on this in the next chapter). This should serve as a reminder that you must put on the whole armor of God. The shield helps the breastplate and the helmet protect your heart and mind, but God won't cover you if you're ignoring or taking the other pieces of His armor for granted. Doing so is evidence that you lack faith, so the shield won't even work.

NOT ALWAYS A SIN

Before we close this chapter, it's important to realize that some fiery darts aren't necessarily *sins* until you let them start to burn down your life. Some of these darts are fast-moving distractions you can readily deflect or easily duck when you see them coming. For some of you, your fiery dart may be that you don't really want to get out of your depression because you've become so comfortable with it. It has become all you know.

Depression is more than manageable and not at all sinful when properly dealt with. Spiritual deliverance from the grip of demonic influences affecting your mental and emotional well-being includes a few key steps: 1. Identify and renounce any ungodly beliefs and repent of any sin. 2. Search your heart for any unforgiveness. The release of forgiving others can be an important step toward healing and freedom. It opens doors to God's grace and allows for a fresh start. 3. Renew your mind by meditating on God's Word to combat negative, depressive thought patterns and infuse your mind with hope and encouragement.

As I shared earlier, one of my fiery darts is anxiety. Is anxiety a sin in my life? No, not as long as I take measures to ensure it doesn't burn my life to the ground. Some people start to accept destructive behavior for the rest of their lives, rationalizing that it's just part of who they are. If that's you, don't lose heart. By the time you finish this book, I believe you'll be growing in your faith like never before, and you'll be fully equipped to ensure the fiery darts always miss their mark when the enemy fires them at you.

THE POWER OF COLLECTIVE FAITH

Every one of us has the potential to develop faith that is potent, redemptive, liberating, forgiving, and outright invaluable to ourselves and our immediate families. The faith you possess as an individual could even change the world, and we've seen many Christians accomplish that feat since the days Jesus walked the earth as a man. One person fully armored and armed with the Word of God and prayer can do anything. That said, while individual faith is indeed powerful, collective faith is unstoppable.

When an entire church of people locks shields and comes together as a unified force, far greater things can be done. You've probably seen a few historical films or binge-watched a TV series based on old-world warfare that depicted a shield's importance in large battles.

Before the era of modern warfare, shield-carrying warriors would come together and place their shields side by side, interlocking them into a shield wall and often even a shield ceiling of sorts. Some armies even had hooks on one side of their shields and eyelets on the other to truly lock their shields together. After doing this, they would simply lean into their shields and position their swords through the gaps to create a barrier that could stop an attacking army in its tracks, often protecting an entire city behind them.

When the enemy hordes attempted to break the line, the defending army thrust their swords between the shields with devastating effect. Here's what the Bible is teaching in this context: You can deflect and absorb much of what the enemy throws at you by standing alone with your shield. But when the enemy truly unloads on you from all sides, you'll need fellow soldiers who are well-trained in the Word of God to lock shields with you. This is why the Bible instructs us to surround ourselves with a local church family comprised of people who share our beliefs and genuinely want to fight the good fight with us. God is building an army for this spiritual war we're in, and He intends for you to find your tribe and intercede in battle for each of them, as each of them intercedes for you.

AN UNBREAKABLE FORCE

When you have a local church family in a passionate Bible-believing church that realizes all that is at stake in these dark days, you're surrounded by people who genuinely love you and support you and get behind you and encourage you and uplift you and even bear your burdens for you when they're too tough to bear. When you're in a church family that locks shields to fight a good fight, there's nothing you can't overcome.

A church that leans into its shields, fully armored up and undivided, is an unbreakable force that can repel anything the enemy fires at it. Not even the gates of hell can prevail against it (Matt. 16:18). Napoleon was considered a great military genius. Though a short, little, unassuming man, he tore the Western World to shreds. He became one of the most powerful emperors in Europe through one simple strategy: divide and conquer. I'm sure he was well aware that Jesus said, "Every kingdom divided against itself is brought to desolation; and every city or house divided against itself shall not stand" (Matt. 12:25).

Likewise, a divided church cannot stand and will not be able to withstand or absorb the fiery darts of the enemy. When a church body comes together and believes together and worships together and serves together and gives together and prays together and fasts together and grows together—when they interlock their shields of faith to fight together—they create a barrier that can protect an entire community, not just their own homes.

God designed the church to be leaders, not blind sheep: the head, not the tail. We're to be the very force that holds a community—or a nation—firmly and fruitfully together (Deut. 28:13). Most mature adults have come to understand the destruction that results when a house is divided. If we ever hope to see the Lord heal our nation, we must grow our faith as one body—one church—that obeys the Word of God, not the commands of a tyrannical government nor the whims of a godless culture. Judgment doesn't come first to the White House, the crack house, or the jailhouse. Judgment comes first to God's house—the church (1 Pet. 4:17).

THE LOCAL CHURCH IN THE VERY LAST DAYS

When the rapture finally happens, all hell will break loose on the earth. The few local churches that stood for Christ and interlocked their shields will get snatched up and rescued out of here by God, and His power will be snatched up with us. At that time, the devil will take full control of all the people and stuff left behind, and the tribulation of those days will be brutally dark. Knowing this, while we still have time, we've got to get busy locking our shields at the local level.

Suppose you're not part of one of the few living churches that stand in defiance of the enemy's schemes. In that case, you need to find other born-again believers to walk, pray, fast, love, and serve with—others serious about fighting the good fight in this war against evil. From there, individual local churches must begin to unite and erase the superficial denominational, cultural, and racial lines. It's not too late for the remnant to rise and lead the whole world into the light, but it would require an unprecedented degree of love, unity, respect, perseverance, understanding, and—*above all*—faith. We'll also have to be prepared to humbly lock shields with some knuckle-headed peculiar people, just like us.

NO PERFECT CHURCHES

So if you are looking for a perfect church body filled with perfect people, please don't visit Global Vision or any other Bible-teaching churches. At Global Vision, we have a slogan. We're a church "where broken people find new meaning to life." That's who we are, what we do, and what we'll always be. For anyone hoping to be born again, brokenness is a blessing, for the Lord attends to the brokenhearted and saves the crushed in spirit (Ps. 34:18).

I believe many of you are reading this book because your pastors have bowed down to the golden calves of this world and refuse to contend for the faith (1 Tim. 6:11–12). If your pastor is among the cowering delinquents, before you give up on him, do all you can to breathe life into that dead man's bones! Confront him as Nathan confronted David, and maybe he will repent for his disobedience and sin (2 Sam. 12:1–13).

If your pastor is among the remnant who are pushing back, standing firm, and risking all to keep your church open and fight for the least among you, be sure to lock shields with your church family and surround that man of God! Your pastor needs you as much as your family needs him. Lock your shields, church, and watch what God will do through the power of your collective faith.

The collective church doesn't stand a chance unless the local churches get right with God. It starts with each of us boldly lifting our shields against the enemy, but we also must lock shields with other believers right where we live—or we'd better get up and go where there is a body with life.

WHEN YOU LACK FAITH

If you're struggling with your faith, it's no wonder you're a mess. No wonder your emotions are all over the place. No wonder people can't stand being around you. No wonder you're a crabapple all the time. You're absorbing the enemy's fiery darts through attacks that your heart, body, and mind shouldn't have to endure.

Without a growing faith, you can't control it, you can't handle it, and you can't even mentally process it. But if you can sincerely and boldly say, "God's got this," you'll be, in effect, holding up the shield of faith, and your faith will absorb every dart the enemy fires at you. You'll be able to withstand it all, you'll be able to stand firm in the battle no matter how bad things get, and your faith will grow stronger. But if you're not carrying your shield of faith and locking in with a local body, don't complain to God that you don't feel protected when the fiery arrows come flying in from all directions.

God has never promised to protect you if you live in disobedience. Likewise, if you won't submit to an authority that you *can* see in a local church body, it's unlikely you'll ever submit to an invisible God that you *cannot* see. The enemy wants to burn this nation, your church, your job, your family, and your life to the ground. He aims to burn the whole world to the ground.

This isn't fiction. It's not even religion. It's the Word of the living God, creator of space and time. The greatest minds in world history and every legitimate born-again believer can attest to the Bible's absolute veracity. The devil wants to devour you. Doubting that fact can destroy you, so get sober and vigilant, especially where the airwaves are concerned!

FROM THIS MOMENT FORWARD

Either you believe in God, or you don't. There is no gray area. If you don't truly believe, it's no wonder your life has been riddled with arrows, bullets, and fiery darts. No wonder anxiety is tearing you to shreds. No wonder your depression and discouragement are growing worse. No wonder you feel like your job will always be a dead end. No wonder things are going amuck and awry in your life. No wonder! The fiery darts are coming against you, and they're finding their mark.

The assumed truth of the text is that you will get shot at, and there is no avoiding that. The enemy wants to destroy you; no one can escape this fact. God doesn't try to excuse, denounce it, or erase it. In this life, we all must pass through this trial by fire (1 Pet. 1:7). Life in Christ is like being in the streets of inner-city Chicago at night. If you're out there, you'll have to dodge many bullets! There is no doubt about that.

If you are going to live as a believer, the devil is going to hate you. We simply must believe in God more than we believe in our problems. Promise yourself that you will start believing that God is bigger, better, and greater than the darts and temptations you will face from this moment forward. Then, when the fiery darts come, if you feel your shield is dropping, remind yourself that you have committed to growing your faith and locking shields with your local church family. Do that, and your little mustard seed of faith will take root deep in your heart and grow for the glory of God!

> That the trial of your faith, being much more precious than of gold that perisheth, though it be tried with fire, might be found unto praise and honour and glory at the appearing of Jesus Christ.
>
> —1 PETER 1:7

CHAPTER FIFTEEN

Helmet of Salvation

And take the helmet of salvation, and the sword
of the Spirit, which is the word of God.
—EPHESIANS 6:17

E'LL SOON DIVE deep into the message of the sword, deeper than any of the other weapons, but we have a lot to unpack concerning the helmet before we get there. Notice a very important word used in the context—the word *take*. This tells us that God doesn't hand your salvation to you, He doesn't put it on you, nor will He allow anyone else to put it on you. If you don't take hold of it and put it on by a decision of your own—if you don't take it—it doesn't get appropriated into your life. Some of you need to quit blaming everybody for your own negligence. No more saying, "It's my spouse's fault, it's my dog's fault, it's the preacher's fault, it's the government's fault, it's my boss's fault." Quit it! If you don't put it on, it's your fault alone.

We've already discussed that God will hold pastors responsible for any negligent leadership, but that doesn't in any way exonerate you—especially not in a culture where the Bible is as close as your cell phone. In our key verse, God said to *take* the helmet of salvation. These pieces of armor are God's gifts. He makes them available to us, but He won't force us to wear them. We must decide to do that because real spirituality is a choice. Salvation is a choice, and you're as close to God as you want to be. That's as cut and dry as it gets.

For those who feel like you're a million miles away from Him, I say, "Turn around!" Quit blaming everybody else. No more excuses, no more exclusions, no more exceptions. He said we have to *take* the helmet. If you don't protect your mind, none of the armor matters because it all begins right here in the mind. The helmet is designed to protect your brain, eyes, and other sensory organs wired into your head. In a real physical battle of biblical times, when a soldier took a shot to the head, he was mortally wounded. He was done; he was dead or soon to die, and the rest of his armor did not matter one lick. Even today, you could walk into battle looking like Iron Man, but if your head isn't covered, you're an easy target.

> Because the carnal mind is enmity against God: for it is not subject to the law of God, neither indeed can be.
>
> —ROMANS 8:7

THE HEAD OF THE MATTER

If the enemy gets a clean shot at your head, you're going down for the count. This is why the church in America is such an easy target. The culture of this wicked, perverted world has corrupted our minds. I'll admit that if I were writing the text of our key verse, I would have said something different. Recall that in our discussion of the breastplate of righteousness, we learned that it protected the heart, mind, soul, and spirit, the essence of our being— collectively referred to as our heart. For that, I would have assumed that salvation was connected to the breastplate, wouldn't you?

This, of course, points to the interconnected interdependence of the whole armor, but the helmet is *uniquely* critical for the most beautiful reason. God says righteousness comes out of the issues of our hearts, but salvation starts in our heads. There's a saying, "He missed heaven by eighteen inches, the distance from his brain to his heart." You can have a mental assent to knowing who Jesus is, but even the devils know who Jesus is. Even the devils know that Jesus is the *only* way to heaven. Even the devils know God's Word—far better than any of us.

The devil and his demons know all of this. They readily confess it and tremble at the thought (Jas. 2:19). Yet not one demon has ever been regenerated by the grace of the gospel. They can't have it, so they're out to destroy those of us who can. We know that salvation is not just a matter of head knowledge, but you will never get the gospel into your heart until you first appropriate it in your mind. This is why the devil wants your brain scrambled up and uninformed. He wants to ensure you can't think straight. How evident has that strategy become in these dark days? The devil doesn't care what you believe as long as you don't believe the truth. Because the truth will make you free (John 8:32).

BRIDGING THE HEART-BRAIN GAP

Salvation will never reach your heart until it first crosses your mind. In the Bible, the heart and the mind are used interchangeably. He talks about the heart, the inner recesses of man, what we think about, and what we muse over. As previously discussed, the Bible says the issues of life flow out of the heart (Prov. 4:23), so we know we must protect it well. Absent salvation, the heart is desperately wicked. It's deceitful above all things. You can't trust your heart.

The Bible teaches us that whatever a man thinks in his heart, "so is he" (Prov. 23:7). Your heart doesn't do the thinking; that's your brain's job. But your brain sends the message to the heart (heart, mind, soul, and spirit), where it takes root, and your heart responds to the brain and, in turn, directs the brain. I'm not trying to speak scientifically here. I'm not a doctor or a nurse, and I certainly don't play one on TV. I'm just telling you what the Bible says: salvation will never take hold of your heart if it doesn't first take hold in your head.

In this context, we see that people come to church where they hear the Bible taught through sermons, but they don't automatically believe it. It doesn't get into their hearts because they never really ruminate on the Bible's truth or truly let it cross their mind until they truly believe it. Meanwhile, they believe what the liberal professor taught them, what the creation-denying scientist taught them, what Planned Parenthood taught them, and what the corrupt media taught them. Sadly, that misinformation takes root in their hearts, even when it's a bald-faced lie.

MIND GAMES

If the devil can get you to the place where you doubt the Word of God and all it teaches, he's got you exactly where he wants you. Some of his biggest mind games are to get you to question the accuracy, relevance, or reliability of God's Word. He is always trying to shake your faith and make you doubt the truthfulness of Scripture. He'll use social standards, secular philosophies, and popular beliefs to shape cultural narratives that contradict or undermine biblical truth. By promoting alternative worldviews and values, he aims to subtly erode confidence in the Word of God and make it seem outdated or irrelevant. Why? Because faith comes by hearing, and hearing by the Word of God (Rom. 10:17).

When the Word of God is spoken, the devil's next tactic is distraction. He doesn't want you thinking about it, so he trips you into thinking about that pot roast that you left in the slow cooker at the house, getting to the buffet on time, getting your oil changed, the promises you made to the kids, or getting to the lake. Or "Did I feed the dog? Did I leave the oven on? Is the toaster still plugged in from breakfast this morning?" Or he'll nudge you to check Facebook or your text threads from the friends you'll be meeting up with later. He'll use every worldly concern imaginable to confuse the processes of your mind so that you are not hearing and absorbing what the preacher is saying. For that, many people come to church and listen, but they don't really hear what is said.

Have you noticed that most men are marvelous at listening without hearing? I can look someone square in their two God-given eyeballs while they're talking, and I'll be saying, "Yep, yep, yep, yep," and all the while, I'm mentally saying, "Please don't ask me what you just said because I didn't catch a single word of that!" Some of you wives reading this at home just turned to your husband and said, "What do you know, Pastor Locke's got the same problem as you, honey." Right? I know some ladies have this same issue, but it's prevalent among men. When we're not intently focused on what is being said, we can listen, but we don't hear. That's what happens in the church and the Evangelical world. We listen and listen to preaching, but we never appropriate it because we don't really hear or grasp what's being said. Our minds are too cluttered. We're thinking about twenty-five thousand different things, and none of them are what's being said by the preacher.

PROTECTING YOUR THOUGHTS

I could preach the same sermon two Sundays in a row, and hardly anyone would say anything about it. But no one would ever forget if I wore the same outfit two weeks in a row. The people on Twitter would never let me live it down. I could preach the same stories, verses, and principles, and 90 percent of the people in the church would not even realize that I repeated myself because they're *listening*, but they're not *hearing*.

If you saw me jump up on the platform wearing the same thing I wore the week before, you'd be like, "Oh, my goodness, doesn't that boy have any clean clothes at home? Don't they own an iron? Bless his heart; he had to wear the same thing two weeks in a row!" We hear what we want to hear. We see what we want to see. We listen to what we want to listen to, leading us to believe what we want to believe. That's a formula for destruction and a curse from the enemy that must be broken.

If salvation is ever going to get into your heart, it must truly cross your mind while it is clear and receptive. The Bible says to take (pick up, appropriate, choose) the helmet of salvation. Knowing all that, here's the nitty-gritty of what I'm driving at. You *must* always protect your thoughts. If you're already wearing the helmet, you have the assumed truth that you're born again, right? You have salvation. It crossed your mind, and then the cross entered your heart. So know this: once you are born again, you become a targeted playing field for the devil, and he and his minions begin to wait for opportune times to start playing a higher level of head games with you.

An idle mind is indeed the devil's workshop. As you might have already picked up through our study on spiritual warfare, your mind is the preeminent battlefield where Satan makes his moves, and your heart is the prize. If you lose the battle for your mind, it will not be very long before you lose the battle for your heart, body, and soul—the essence of who you are.

Have you noticed that you can only think about something for so long before you'll get involved in it? It doesn't even matter whether you initially wanted it. Everything you have ever done—righteous and unrighteous—started in your mind. Every bit of it. It happened when the Lord delivered the Israelites from Egyptian slavery. Once they were free in the wilderness, many were tempted, and thousands were slain because they murmured, cussed, fussed, and complained.

For that, we see the Lord made them wander through desert wastelands for forty long years despite the fact that the Promised Land was just two weeks away geographically. Because of all the ungodly things they got involved with and because of their persistent unbelief, they were forced to wander in the wilderness; many of them for the remainder of their lives. In that same context, we see today that most people are bombarded with temptations to practice adultery, idolatry, wickedness, and even witchcraft, and a large percentage are taken prisoner by the enemy.

TAKING EVERY THOUGHT CAPTIVE

> For though we walk in the flesh, we do not war after the flesh: (For the weapons of our warfare are not carnal, but mighty through God to the pulling down of strong holds;) Casting down imaginations, and every high thing that exalteth itself against the knowledge of God, and bringing into captivity every thought to the obedience of Christ; And having in a readiness to revenge all disobedience, when your obedience is fulfilled.
>
> —2 CORINTHIANS 10:3–6

By now I hope you're becoming familiar with this amazing scripture. It's the passage that provides the title of this book, and I've already referenced it several times, but let's take a deeper, more reverent look at it. When I repeat a verse or passage in my books, it's for a very good reason. I'd like you to read it aloud so you can hear and digest it.

Maybe you can make 2 Corinthians 10:3–6 a memory passage from this day forward. It is prophetic for these last days and is such a crucial instruction in the battle for your mind (and thereby your heart, body, and soul) that you should remind yourself as often as possible throughout each day. It is, in effect, the key to the integrity of the helmet. Taking every thought captive is a practical and powerful strategy that involves managing your thought life, discerning between truth and lies, renewing your mind with God's Word, exercising spiritual authority, and guarding against spiritual attacks. If ever there was a scripture that identified your mind as the frontline battlefield between God and the devil, this is it.

God is saying that if you don't take every thought captive, the devil will use your thoughts to take *you* captive. Watch your thoughts as closely as you would watch dangerous prisoners, or they'll make a prisoner of you. If you're like most people, there's a good chance you are a prisoner to your thought life. You're a prisoner to the things that you think about, and you know it. How did this happen? you ask. It's simple. You thought about dark things so often that you started looking at them, and once you started looking *at* them, you started looking *for* them, and in very short order, you started acting them out.

TIME-OUT: THE ENEMY'S AIR GAME

Be careful what you let into your ears and your eyes. Be very careful. If you find yourself wondering how the enemy can so easily attack your mind and your heart, always remember that he is "the prince of the power of the air, the spirit that is now at work in the sons of disobedience" (Eph. 2:2, ESV). I discussed this in *This Means War,* and it's a subject worthy of its own book, so I won't dive too deep into it here. Just be sure you *always* remember that the devil controls most media and entertainment, and most of you let him fly right into your hearts, minds, and homes on the airwaves—through your digital devices, radios, and TV, every day. He'll use these devices to destroy you if you're not armored up.

It doesn't even have to be as overt as pornography or occultic material. Watching content that promotes immorality, violence, sexual impurity, or other ungodly behaviors can desensitize us to sin and erode our moral compass. It can create a fertile ground for the enemy to tempt us and lead us away from God's commands. Constant exposure to negative influences can breed fear, anxiety, and hopelessness, weakening our spiritual defenses and opening us up to spiritual attack.

Don't fall for this trick of the enemy. It is not something we can take lightly. Regular exposure to media that portrays characters with worldly values can shape our beliefs, attitudes, and behaviors in ways that contradict God's truth, leading us to compromise our faith and adopt the values of the world. The enemy can use what we watch to sneak into our hearts and minds and influence our thoughts, attitudes, and actions. By presenting distorted images of pleasure, success, and fulfillment, media can tempt us to pursue worldly desires at the expense of our relationship with God. This can lead to spiritual bondage and hinder our ability to experience the fullness of God's plan for our lives.

You must gain control of what you and your kids allow into your eyes and ears. The devil has been attacking us through our senses since we were born, so we must be very careful about the media and visuals we allow our children and even our babies to consume. One of the most rewarding ways to do that is through replacement strategies. Read more Bible. Consume more Christian and conservative media and entertainment. Listen to more Christian music. Spend more time playing board games or adventuring outdoors!

When it comes to what you allow into your temple (1 Cor. 6:19–20), you are either worshiping at the altar of God or the high places and principalities of Satan's domain. To put it another way, either you're glorifying God or you're glorifying Satan. You're killing your flesh, or you're feeding it. And your flesh is where the devil has room to operate in your life. Don't fall for the lie that it's harmless; it's not. It's good versus evil. Choose wisely.

Being mindful of the influences we expose ourselves to is crucial. This includes the media we consume, the company we keep, the entertainment we engage in, and the belief systems we entertain. Every outside influence we open the door to is riding the airwaves of Satan's domain, so each must be filtered and controlled. This involves making intentional choices to avoid situations, environments, or activities that may lead us into sin or compromise our faith. The Bible warns that the prince of the power of the air (and the airwaves) is "at work in the sons of disobedience," so you do not want to be counted among that crowd. In these last days, it's becoming very easy to see who these "sons of disobedience" are, and when we search out how they fell into the devil's trap, it doesn't take long to connect the dots directly to the media and the entertainment they consume. Garbage in, garbage out. They're being brainwashed, and born-again believers cannot risk suffering their fate.

I know it's a huge challenge in this media-driven world. But this is the enemy's most powerful inroad, so be always on guard, or he'll consume you and your family before you even know it. The various media represent the fighter jets in his air attack, and those aircraft drop smart bombs on us. That's why I engage in media battlefields with such fiery resolve. We *must* keep watch, push back, and call it out, or the devil will fly right in and devour us (1 Pet. 5:8). We must armor up, lift our shields, and stop letting the enemy fly in through our senses.

YOUR SIN WILL OUT YOU

God loves you too much to let you get away with sin. Once you start acting out the darkness you allowed into your mind through your senses, you'll invariably do all you can to cover it up, but the Bible says your sin will eventually out you. It says, "Your sin will find you out" (Num. 32:23). That means that your sin will uncover itself no matter what you do to hide it. You'll leave something behind, you'll leave a trace, you'll talk in your sleep, or someone will say something that starts unraveling your web of lies. You must protect your mind by taking every thought captive to the obedience of Christ—the gospel—because everything wicked that you've ever done began within the disobedient rattlings of your head. We must protect our thoughts. I believe that is the number one problem with every single person on earth.

Once we recognize that the mind is a battlefield, we also must realize that our weaponized thoughts aren't always going to be evil, wicked, deviant, perverted pornographic things. Sometimes your mind just plays tricks on you, and you've got to take hold of that reality. There are two types of thoughts that I want to discuss in this context. These are the two most tempting thought patterns you must take captive and put away for good. First are dirty thoughts. No one wants them initially, but dirty thoughts are triggered by virtually everything we see in our modern media-driven culture.

Once seen or heard, these dirty thoughts metastasize into perverse and stupid words. Ephesians 4:29 tells us not to speak any form of corrupt communication, but only that which is good for edifying godliness, so that it may minister grace to the hearers. Do you know why you say stupid stuff? Because you think stupid stuff. Do you know why you say righteous stuff? Because you think righteous stuff. Why are these true? Because Luke 6:45 says the mouth speaks out of the abundance of the heart (heart, mind, soul, and spirit). So whatever you think, you'll eventually act out unless you can control your thought life.

You might think, "Well, when I'm thinking dirty thoughts or looking at dirty things, I'm not hurting anybody but myself." If that's you, wake up! You're hurting everybody around you, including yourself! Your thought life will eventually erode your character and hurt everyone you care about. There is not one person—me included—who would sign up to have their deepest thoughts published to the internet or projected up to a big screen during a church service.

Not one of us would say, "Pick me! Pick me!" Not one of us would want to go through such nonsense because there's something about the inner recesses of your mind that you believe to be harmless if you can just keep it hidden in there. But you can't. I'm sorry. God's bigger and more omniscient than any of us can grasp, and I believe Him when He says it can't be hidden for long. Either you will confess it in obedience to Christ, or it will eventually out itself—and take you down with it.

AN UNLIKELY SOURCE

I don't intend to glorify evil, wicked people, so bear with me as I draw an illustration. Some time ago, we watched a documentary that was so graphic and unbearably dark that we had to shut it off about halfway through. It was about the mass murderer Ted Bundy, a demonically possessed rapist, torturer, and killer. The documentary played samples from Ted Bundy's confession tapes that revealed how the devil was able to gradually possess him throughout his life. Can you guess what he repeatedly talks about? Pornography, his thought life, and how it all started so benign. In the tapes, he would say that the power of pornography would grip him, and it got worse when he was eleven and even worse when he was fifteen, twenty-two, and thirty-five. The older he got, the tighter the grip on his heart.

Because pornography promotes sexual immorality, objectification, and lustful desires, which are contrary to God's design for human sexuality, watching it creates a rift between a person and God, and the enemy can take advantage of this vacuum to manipulate that person into some very deep, dark bondage. It leads to addictive behaviors and obsessive thoughts, creating a fertile ground for the enemy to torment folks mentally and emotionally, intensifying their bondage and further isolating them from healthy relationships and God's love. The person's ability to resist temptation plummets, and the enemy now has free range to influence and control their thoughts, desires, and actions.

Bundy said the more he thought about pornography, the easier it became to act it out and force it on unsuspecting women if they didn't willingly participate. Many lost their lives, and the ones who survived lost their dignity and more, all because one man could not control his thought life—he could not "take every thought captive." So erase any notion that dirty thoughts are harmless. They're devastating.

Maybe envy and covetousness are your dirty thoughts. Maybe they're revenge or self-righteousness. Whatever dirt manifests from the sin in your heart, if you lose the battle in your mind, it's only a matter of time before you do the devil's bidding. Whatever you think is secret today, someday, everyone will know. It will be shouted from the housetops. It will be shouted from the courtrooms. It will eventually come out, so please start controlling your thoughts.

YOU ARE VICTORIOUS!

The second category of thought patterns that I want to help you get free from are those that make you believe you are defeated. Do you know why some of you never do anything for God? It's because the devil told you that you can't. "You aren't worthy enough. You aren't big enough. You aren't spiritual enough. You aren't educated enough." Yada, yada, yada, schmatta! Fight that nonsense!

If you start believing what everybody is saying about you, and if you start wearing the labels that everybody puts on you, you'll start to think about it, and think about it, and think about it, until your feelings of defeat turn into discouragement, which turns into depression, which turns into despair. Once there, you cannot do a lick of good for the kingdom of God. You'll start believing the nonsense that the devil wants you to believe.

You must stop getting your identity from anyone but God! Some of you have defeated thoughts, like, "I'm just from a dysfunctional family." Welcome to the club! Adam and Eve jacked up everybody in the world, so we're all from a dysfunctional family. Just take some responsibility and quit blaming your folks or their folks! Stop believing you're a *victim* of your circumstances or your past. The Bible says you're a *victor* if you're saved by Jesus Christ.

It's time to take charge of what you believe about yourself. Will you believe the lie of the enemy, or will you believe the truth of God's Word? Henry Ford once said, "Whether you believe you can do a thing or not, you are right."[1] That statement shows how powerful your thought life is. And so are your words. If you keep saying your marriage or your job will never get any better, you're right—because death and life are in the power of the tongue (Prov. 18:21).

WATCH YOUR MOUTH

> O generation of vipers, how can ye, being evil, speak good things? for out of the abundance of the heart the mouth speaketh. A good man out of the good treasure of the heart bringeth forth good things: and an evil man out of the evil treasure bringeth forth evil things. But I say unto you, that every idle word that men shall speak, they shall give account thereof in the day of judgment.
>
> —JESUS (MATTHEW 12:34–36)

From this passage, you know that the words you speak reveal the condition of your heart and determine whether you are good or evil on the day you stand before the Lord to be judged. Notice that Jesus ensured you didn't think He would only judge you by your public confessions or social media posts. When He points out that you will be judged for "every idle word," He's speaking directly to the careless, negative, exaggerated things we say (whether in public or in private) when we're speaking outside the mind of Christ and, thereby, outside the will of God.

If the treasure in your heart is not established by Jesus alone, it is an "evil treasure," says the Lord. You must purge those negative, defeatist thoughts and stick to the truth of the Word of God. Even after getting this instruction written on your heart, you might still slip up from time to time, so you also need to get skilled at *quickly* repenting and cleaning up the damage those idle words may have caused, starting with the damage done to your mind. Take it captive and cast it down. I'm writing from experience, so please trust that the process is critically important and more rewarding than you can imagine.

If it's the truth based on God's Word, and if it's the Holy Spirit compelling you to speak, it needs to be spoken and even shouted from rooftops. Never forget that Jesus, John the Baptist, Paul, all the apostles, and many of Jesus' followers throughout history have been executed for speaking out boldly against evil and hypocrisy. I say it often: Jesus wasn't crucified for what He *did*; He was crucified for what He *said*. I've learned to be as bold as the Holy Spirit leads me to be and to tame my tongue when I cross lines that He has drawn, especially concerning my identity in Him. (See Matthew 10:27–28 and James chapter 3.)

FOREVER VICTORIOUS

Some of you are constantly self-berated by defeatist thoughts. Amid my harshest storms, I often thought, "Lord, You have never made a mistake, but You called the wrong cat into this deal." It can become very easy to believe the enemy's lies and attacks through the stuff people say about you. When this happens, it's only human nature to think thoughts like, "I am defeated," "I am a failure," or, "I did this wrong, and I didn't do that right, so they're right about me." If you keep thinking that way, you will never be able to escape the downward spiral. It's a trap set by the enemy. If that's you, rebuke that!

Weeping may endure for a night, but joy comes in the morning, says the Lord (Ps. 30:5). When you finally put on the whole armor of God, it will get better! And no matter how long it takes to get better, if you sincerely want the protection of the helmet of salvation, you've got to demolish those thoughts of defeat. God didn't tell you to suit up, boot up, and contend for the faith so that you can be defeated. He tells us to armor up because we are permanently victorious once we are born again. As my granny used to say, "Whether I go or whether I stay, I'm a winner either way" …in Jesus. Amen!

> There is therefore now no condemnation to them which are in Christ Jesus, who walk not after the flesh, but after the Spirit.
>
> —ROMANS 8:1

CHAPTER SIXTEEN

Helmet of Salvation: Part 2

THE HELMET OF salvation is designed to keep your mind fixed on things above because genuine salvation is the born-again experience that will transform your mind and eventually transform everything about you—some faster than others. In Mark chapter 5, we are introduced to a man who lived in the darkest imaginable state of defeat until he met Jesus.

> And when he was come out of the ship, immediately there met him out of the tombs a man with an unclean spirit, who had his dwelling among the tombs; and no man could bind him, no, not with chains: Because that he had been often bound with fetters and chains, and the chains had been plucked asunder by him, and the fetters broken in pieces: neither could any man tame him. And always, night and day, he was in the mountains, and in the tombs, crying, and cutting himself with stones. But when he saw Jesus afar off, he ran and worshipped him.
>
> —MARK 5:2–6

The Bible says that when Jesus was done casting the unclean spirit out of this man, the people found him sitting there, cleaned up and clothed. This guy was buck-naked before Jesus got off the boat, and suddenly he's fully clothed. Maybe Jesus and the boys carried around an Adidas bag of clothes for naked folks that got born again—as do some of our outreach ministers—or maybe He tacked on a little extra miracle. We'll probably never know this side of heaven, but the Bible said he was in his right mind, sitting in clothes (Mark 5:15).

The crowd freaked out once they realized what Jesus had done. They said, "Oh, hey there, Mr. Messiah, that'll be enough of that. You get in that rickety raft and go on." So Jesus got in that rickety raft and left. Do you know why? Because Jesus never stays where Jesus isn't welcome. America had better figure that out. Jesus got in the boat and went to the other side, but the city folks were freaked out. They were like, "Man, this guy was a loony bin, this guy cut himself with stones, this guy foamed at the mouth, this guy's hair stuck off his head like he'd put his finger into a 110-volt wall outlet, blood all over him, and he lived in the graveyard!"

This guy was evil, and he couldn't even think for himself. He was crying and mutilating himself twenty-four hours a day. Then he met Jesus and *BAM*! He was in his right mind. Why? Because genuine salvation transforms you.

THE ENEMY'S CHIEF WEAPON

Returning to our key verse on the helmet, Ephesians 6:17, we see the central word is *salvation,* meaning redemption and deliverance. This type of deliverance is not the same type as needing deliverance from the oppression or possession of evil spirits. Most of us deal with much subtler mental attacks than those of the demon-possessed man in Mark's Gospel, but all of us have been delivered out of one thing and into something else. We've come out of bondage, we've come out of Egypt, we've come out of the world, and we've been delivered into the land that flows with milk and honey. We've been delivered from darkness into light. We've been delivered from the kingdom of darkness into the kingdom of God's dear Son (Col. 1:13). We've been delivered from spiritual death to eternal life. Instead of facing eternal separation from God, we are granted everlasting life in His presence.

Once delivered, though you were formerly of the devil, you're born again through the grace of the gospel (John 8:44). There's a great change. You've put on the helmet, you have salvation, you're going to heaven, and you have been redeemed, but the devil does all he can to make you think otherwise. If he succeeds, you're going nowhere in your Christian walk. It's one thing to operate with a dirty mind and another thing to operate with a defeated mind. We need to clean those up, but the enemy's chief weapon is a seemingly benign five-letter word: *doubt.*

Why do we need a helmet to protect our salvation if it cannot be taken? Because the devil knows that if he can make you doubt your salvation, you will accomplish very little, if anything, for the kingdom of God. And if he can't have you, he'll ensure you can't help those around you and use you to cause others to stumble. Doubting your salvation enables both.

Many believers doubt their salvation because they base their salvation on things that give them no assurance. It's one of the greatest problems in Christianity. They simply don't base their salvation on the Word of God. They don't base their salvation on the authority of Scripture. They don't base their salvation on "Call unto me, and I will answer thee" (Jer. 33:3) or "Whosoever shall call upon the name of the Lord shall be saved" (Rom. 10:13). They base it on the nonsense they heard from someone they know. "Mama said," "Papa said," or, "The preacher said." I'm glad you liked what the preacher said when you accepted Christ, but that won't hold water in God's canteen when you get to the day of judgment. You're redeemed by what Jesus said, not by what Greg Locke or any other preacher said.

It's a Decision and Nothing More

If you know you've given your life to Christ, don't ever second-guess if you did it right or prayed the right prayer. Salvation isn't a religious act with a magic oath to say or a series of physical actions to complete. It's a decision made with an honest mind and a contrite heart. Do you honestly think you could kneel with repentance and humility and ask Jesus to take over your life, yet Jesus would reject you because you didn't do it right?

There is no pixie dust to sprinkle, and there are no hocus-pocus magic words to say. A prayer didn't die for you; a person named Jesus did. You could pray it fifty million different ways; it's not the prayer that saves you; it's Jesus who saves you. Stop doubting what God did for you. It doesn't matter if you were four or forty-four when you made your decision, yet people go through life constantly thinking, "Well, I don't know. I just don't know."

Personally, I *know*. I have zero doubts. If your decision to give your life to Him is real, you too will know, absent any doubts. You can't be born again without knowing it's real! You'll be a new creature in Christ, old things will pass away, and all things will become new (2 Cor. 5:17). You won't be perfect, but you *will* be different, and you'll know it. Knowing that you are changing how you think and act is evidence that you are this new person.

Before you were born again, you were an absolute colossal wreck of a failing mess, even if you didn't realize it at the time. You would have just kept getting worse and worse and worse, but now look at you. Stop doubting what God did for you. Victor Raymond Edman, a preacher from yesteryear, famously said, "Never doubt in the darkness what God has made clear in the light."[1]

The devil knows every time we start to doubt our salvation. He's the one who triggered it. Never forget that *doubt* is his chief weapon and tactic. He pulls that one out of the old toolbox and drills us and drills us and drills us because he knows that if you struggle with the reality of your salvation, the rest of your thoughts don't even matter. If you bebop through life with a think-so, hope-so, maybe-so salvation, you will not be used mightily by God because He only uses people with real faith.

THE THIEF ON THE CROSS

God changes our lives by faith. He fills us by faith. My Bible says, "whatsoever is not of faith is sin" (Rom. 14:23). Yet we've raised a generation of people who base their salvation on which church they go to or whose live stream they watch, not on what the Bible says. Remember the two thieves who were crucified along with Jesus? The King James Bible called them "malefactors."

I like those old King James words. They're loaded. Of these two bad dudes, one rejected Jesus, and one received Jesus. The first one said, "Hey there, Bucko, if you are who you say you are, why don't you jump down off that cross and help all of us?"

The other one argued back at him, "Who do you think you are? This guy has done nothing wrong, but we have hooked and crooked the government. We deserve to die!"

These guys are literally suffocating to death, yet they're having an argument—with Jesus in the middle. Then the repentant one turned to Jesus and said, "Lord, remember me when thou comest into thy kingdom" (Luke 23:42). That was it.

Do you remember what Jesus said? He didn't say, "Well, wait a minute, you've got to come off that cross and join a church." He didn't say, "Now, wait a minute, I've got to call for one of My disciples to get My credit card machine. It'll cost you $39.95."

He didn't say, "Wait a minute! You've got to talk to some dude who calls himself a father through a knothole in a phone booth!" Nor did He say, "Sorry, son, you've got to get off that cross and get baptized first!" Don't ever believe it when people say that baptism saves you. It's a lie. The thief on the cross didn't get baptized, but he entered God's kingdom—you can be sure of that.

Jesus also didn't say, "Well, you just don't look the part. I don't like the way you've got your hair cut. I don't like that tattoo. Your nails are dirty. What did you do last night?" Jesus never asks the stupid questions that church people ask, like, "Who were you with last week?" Who cares?

The thief was on a cross! I can guarantee he was with somebody he shouldn't have been with, doing something he shouldn't have done. Jesus just said, "Okay." There was no pretense. Jesus said, "Okay, *today* you will be with Me in paradise!" (See Luke 23:43.) And the guy dies. Isn't that amazing? That very day he transcended space and time and met Jesus in paradise. Not because of what he did or said but because Jesus already knew what was in his heart before he spoke a word. Don't ever forget that.

NO LONGER A THIEF

God knows everything about you and everything that crosses your heart and mind! You can't surprise Him, and you can't keep a single thought from Him. Notice that Jesus didn't give that guy a lot of gospel preaching to work with up to that moment. All he had to go on was Jesus' actions throughout His torture and crucifixion and the words Jesus spoke from the cross, and that was more than enough.

Some theorize the thief might have known of His miracles and maybe heard Him speak a time or two, but considering Jesus' dire straits and apparent powerlessness on the cross, any past interaction couldn't have meant much. This dude didn't even get to see proof that Jesus would rise again! But he *believed* He would. He spent the most epic day in world history witnessing Jesus fearlessly taking up His cross in obedience to the Father. That was all it took for this unnamed thief to believe the gospel, and he has been celebrated throughout history for it.

I look forward to meeting that guy. He isn't a thief anymore; I can promise you that.

Let me ask you—concerning your salvation—in what do you place your trust? If it's not the gospel of Jesus or His outrageous love and power proved on the cross, it's no wonder you doubt. I'm not trusting the word of my grand-daddy. I'm trusting the Word of God Himself. He said to me, "Today, today, today!" And I was like, "Okay." That was it, and I rest in that. Do you know why people can't make me doubt my salvation? It's because people didn't give it to me. I'm not going to live my life in dread, defeat, misery, and doubt, thinking God didn't do what He promised.

IT STARTED IN THE GARDEN

You've got to put on the helmet of salvation because if you doubt your salvation, the rest of the armor won't matter to you. If you're not born again, you'll go through life thinking, "Who cares about a belt? Who cares about shoes? Who cares about the sword? Who cares about the shield? Who cares about the breastplate? Who cares about praying?" You won't.

That's why many so-called born-again Christians have not worn the whole armor of God a single day in their lives. If they're not even sure they're born again, why would they try putting on something supernatural that makes no sense to them? To the unsaved, it all sounds like religious superstition. It all sounds too good to be true. From the enemy's perspective, the primary tactic of spiritual warfare is getting people to believe that God is a liar or that God is a lie. He's been doing that since Genesis chapter 3.

In the Garden of Eden, Eve was all cozied-up with that serpent when he said, "Yea, hath God said...?" And then proceeded to twist God's Word to convince Eve that the Lord was lying about death. Since then, people have tried to change the Bible for every twisted reason imaginable. The serpent said, "Oh, that's not what God said, and if it is, that's not what God meant."

Eve got all confused and discombobulated, and we can't blame her too much because her deadbeat husband, Adam, was ultimately to blame. Where was that joker, anyway? Not where God wanted him, that's for sure. You must understand that the devil has been slick and sly about getting people to doubt what God said for a long time.

THE BAPTISM OF CHRIST

At the end of Matthew chapter 3, we see John the Baptist in the murky, muddy waters of the Jordan River with people lined up as far as the eye can see, and he's dunking them left and right. It was great. Nonetheless, suddenly John looked over the hill and said, "Behold the Lamb of God, which taketh away the sin of the world" (John 1:29). This humble figure came forward and walked into the water, and John realized it was his first cousin, Jesus.

John the Baptist was six months older than Him, and he was the prophesied forerunner for Jesus—the table setter for the Messiah, as it were. John was "the voice of one crying in the wilderness, Prepare ye the way of the Lord, make his paths straight" (Mark 1:3).

Suddenly Jesus was in the water. He walked over to John and said, "Hey, John, I need you to baptize Me."

And John said, "No way! I need to get baptized by You!"

And Jesus said, "Oh, no you don't. The Bible says you're going to baptize Me, so that's the way we're going to do it."

So John grabbed Him and dunked Him in the water. As Jesus came up, the voice of God the Father said, "This is my beloved Son, with whom I am well pleased." The Holy Spirit came in the form of a dove and lit on His shoulder, and He rose out of the water as one—God the Father, God the Son, and God the Holy Spirit. (See Matthew 3:13–17.)

THE TEMPTATION OF "IF"

Immediately after John baptized Jesus, the Bible says, "Then was Jesus led up by the Spirit into the wilderness to be tempted by the devil" (Matt. 4:1, ESV). We know the three primary temptations the devil threw at Him:

1. Turn the stones into bread because You're hungry.

2. Jump from the top of the temple and see if God's angelic hosts will save You like the Scripture says.

3. Here are all the kingdoms of the world. Bow down to me, and I'll give them all to You.

Of course, Jesus knew exactly how to respond, and He used nothing more than the Word of God.

Here's what's fascinating about this time of testing for Jesus. The biggest temptation He faced in this attack is something most of us gloss over every time we read it. Every time the devil tried to tempt Jesus, he opened with, "If thou be the Son of God...." Let's slow down and consider that for a minute. "If...thou be the Son of God." Wow. Let's be piercingly honest. Even atheists will have to admit that's the biggest *if* in the history of mankind. Even today, there is no other if that impacts the world with greater force. Nations have been born and nations have died because of that if.

Don't let the gravity of this device escape you. The devil was trying to cast doubt into the character and identity of Jesus and to cast doubt concerning *to whom* Jesus belonged. If, if, if. But even in a weakened state, Jesus could easily defeat the temptation because, to Him, there was no if. There was absolutely no doubt. He knew exactly who He was and exactly who He will always be. Even in His walk as a man, He knew precisely to whom He belonged. He knew why He had come to this earth: to seek and save what was lost (Luke 19:10).

Why do you think the Lord allowed this incredibly powerful joust to occur? Why do you think Jesus allowed the devil into His space with an illusion of power? Because He wanted to teach us a lesson of warning so crucial that it warranted this unimaginable scenario. The devil knows that if he can trick you into doubting to whom you belong, you'll miss all the Lord has planned for your life, and he might just steal your soul.

NOT ABOUT FEELINGS

Some of you toss and turn in your bed, tormenting over the if. You're like a boat tossed back and forth on the ocean waves. "Am I, or am I not? I didn't have such a good day, week, or month, so maybe I'm not?" Sometimes I hear people say, "I just don't feel saved today." I have to wonder what being saved is supposed to feel like to these folks. So what if you've been stumbling hard and falling short? That doesn't mean you're a lost cause! Just because you've stumbled, that doesn't mean you're not born again.

I wake up some days feeling bad, but I'm still saved. I'm still born again. It feels good to be born again, but you're not born again because of your feelings. You're born again because Jesus did something for you that you couldn't do for yourself, and it sets you on a trajectory of transformation. He who knew no sin became sin for us so we might be made "the righteousness of God in him" (2 Cor. 5:21).

HERE AND NOW

As I conclude this chapter on the helmet of salvation, I want to challenge you to recommit yourself to Jesus and commit to *never* doubting your salvation from this day forward. He loves you more than you can ever grasp and longs for an intimate relationship with you. But as I hope you're starting to realize, intimacy is impossible if you don't wear the armor, for it represents the manifestation of the born-again life in Christ.

Once you are born again, you are His treasured child, His holy temple, His royal priest, and His spotless bride. He truly sees you that way, so don't you ever doubt it again. Get before Him right now, no matter how you *feel* about your salvation. If you're in a place where you can do this, please take a moment to get alone with Him and kneel at His feet, and maybe have a long overdue cry with Him. It will be the best food for your soul and grow your faith.

He won't dwell in us or work through us for His glory if we don't believe He's real, so take every opportunity to recognize He is more real than the air we breathe. Never forget that He's waiting for us to come to Him far more often than any of us realize and far more often than any of us do. Start taking Him and His Word more seriously every single day. He is not to be trifled with or put away on a bookshelf to reference only in times of despair. He is God, the real deal, and there is no other beside Him. Make sure you know that in your heart. Confess your salvation once and for all, and put on the helmet anew every day.

THE REAL LIFE BEGINS

No matter what you've done in the past, Jesus will never reject you. If you struggle to start a dialogue with Him, just talk to Him as a little child would talk to their daddy, their "Abba" (Gal. 4:6). That's the kind of relationship He wants with all of us. Just pour your heart out and love on Him, remembering how deeply He loves you—especially at moments of brokenness and transparency.

When this brief temporal life is over, the real life begins, just as it did for the thief on the cross and every other born-again believer before you. Until then, you'll have God Himself living in you in the person of the Holy Spirit, giving you access to the power of His armor, maybe for the first time in your life. Through it all, learn to relax and let it be. Be still and know that He is God (Ps. 46:10).

You don't have to be perfect while He starts transforming you. You just have to surrender to Him. You'll never be perfect until you're perfected with the Father in heaven, but you can and will instantly start the process of turning away from your sinful nature. Putting on the whole armor of God will ensure that. Just be patient with yourself (Ps. 37:7–9). He lives, and He loves you! Lift your head and rejoice!

> And when these things begin to come to pass, then look up, and lift up your heads; for your redemption draweth nigh.
> —JESUS (LUKE 21:28)

CHAPTER SEVENTEEN

Sword of the Spirit

And take the helmet of salvation, and the sword
of the Spirit, which is the word of God.
—EPHESIANS 6:17

W HEN I WAS growing up, we learned the "B-I-B-L-E, yes, that's the book for me. I stand alone on the Word of God, the B-I-B-L-E." Do you know that song? Sometimes we can dismiss that as a Sunday school sing-along, but its lyrics should represent the highest anthem for every Bible-believer reading this book. If any of us are going to say we believe the Holy Bible, we'd better *behave* the Bible that we say we believe.

As I've implied throughout this book, you cannot claim to believe the Word of God unless you also believe you must obey the whole Bible, not just your favorite parts. You must act on the Lord's instructions in His Word. Many people have the attitude, "Well, you know, I love Jesus, but I just don't take all the Bible at face value." If that's you, then there's something desperately wrong with your understanding of the Word of God. As noted earlier in our discussion of righteousness, in the armor of God, the sword of the Spirit is the raw material—the God-forged steel—that gives each piece its intrinsic strength. The armor has no strength or structure without the indestructible metal that is the Word of God.

THE WHOLE COUNSEL OF GOD

Even if they don't admit it to themselves, most people take a buffet approach to the Bible. "I'll have a little of this and a little of that. Give me some extra of this, but I'm going to subtract some of that. I don't want any of this, and I won't even look at any of that."

It's an approach that leads to destruction, no matter what you believe. We must believe the whole counsel of God, or we won't truly believe any of it (Acts 20:27–28). We can't just consume (or serve up) the yummy parts and ignore the parts that make us want to vomit because there are teachings in the Bible that deliberately kick us in the gut and show us who we really are. When we look in the mirror of the Word of God, we have a choice. We either change the problems we see in ourselves or distort the mirror to reflect what we want to see. Our culture has chosen the latter.

This generation refuses to change what they see in the mirror because they don't want to admit it is wrong, wicked, and abominable to God. They have fooled themselves into believing that ignorance of the truth is an excuse He'll accept when He returns. This culture has decided to discount and pervert the mirror, but I can promise you this—the Bible will still stand when you and I and our little brains are cold-dead and six feet in the ground.

When the universe is on fire, the Bible will rise—still fully alive—above and beyond all space and time, and only those born again in Christ will rise with it. The Word of God will usher in that final fire, and the destructive fires of the devil and his minions cannot consume it or stand against it.

The Bible tells no lies and has no contradictions. If you think you've found a contradiction in the Bible, it's because you consume too much fake news—too much anti-Christ propaganda—and not nearly enough of the Bible. The Bible is a self-defining, self-explaining manual. If you find something you cannot explain, the Holy Spirit will show you another Scripture to reveal its meaning. He'll use Scripture upon Scripture to explain Himself in revelatory ways. I am fully convinced that the Bible is perfect to those with eyes that see and ears that hear, but to all others, it will never add up (Matt. 13:13, Ezek. 12:2). The Bible was unquestionably created by our living God to prepare us for His kingdom to come! Only those who are born again into the kingdom life can grasp how true this is.

THE SYMBOLISM OF THE SWORD

In the first-century days of Jesus and the first apostles, the Roman army conquered much of the world. Of all their weaponry, their finely crafted, perfectly straight, double-edged swords were most symbolic of their dominant strength. A fully armored Roman soldier was an impressive sight, but absent his gleaming steel sword, he was deemed an easy target in battle. By no coincidence, first-century advancements in carbon-steel technology had produced the most powerful swords the ancient world had ever seen, as the Romans introduced the *Spatha*, the prototype for the swords used in battle to this day.

This three-foot-long, double-edged, hardened-steel masterpiece was lighter, longer, and stronger than any sword that came against it. A well-trained, fully-armored soldier wielding this sword struck awe into enemy combatants as well as those they protected—on offense or defense. It would shatter all other swords in battle and pierce through enemy armor with relative ease.

Until the modern era of warfare, when gunpowder and firearms gradually replaced swords as the primary weapons in battle, the sword has always represented warfare, honor, strength, and dominion. Paul surely had these firmly in mind as he penned the armor discourse. Every culture holds the sword in high esteem, but its history in Israel is especially rich.

When researching for this book, I learned a very interesting tidbit about sword-making technology in ancient Israel, and I think you might appreciate it. Though many history books will tell you that carbon steel was first used in swords during the second and first centuries BC in India and China, the oldest known carbon-steel sword is the Vered Jericho Sword, which dates way back to the seventh century BC. It is currently on display in Jerusalem's Israel Museum. Vered Jericho was a small fortress in the Jericho region during King Josiah's reign.

This profound artifact's archaeological discovery was made in 1982, but don't hold your breath while waiting for liberal historians and the media to ever edify ancient Israel. Most are too hell-bent on trying to erase ancient Israel from the historical record—which is one of the myriad reasons they're trying to ban the Bible from public discourse.

With this rock-solid evidence that the ancient Israelites were the first to create carbon-steel weapons, in all likelihood, this advanced metallurgy was one of the many lost technologies that King Solomon leveraged to generate his unprecedented power and wealth during the tenth century BC. While the discovery of the Vered Jericho sword is an inspiring glimpse into God's active handiwork through all of world history, I believe it also serves as a reminder

177

of all that can be lost if we ever choose to betray the Word of God in our daily lives—no matter our past godliness.

SOLOMON AND THE WORD OF GOD

Having mentioned Solomon, I would be remiss if I failed to use his tragic story as a teaching moment concerning the two-edged nature of the sword of the Spirit. Sadly, to please his many foreign wives late in his reign, Solomon built numerous temples and high places to worship their false gods. "And Solomon did evil in the sight of the LORD, and went not fully after the LORD, as did David his father" (1 Kings 11:6–8). These acts, caused by Solomon's perverse relationships, were an abomination to God, and the sword judged him harshly despite his unprecedented success as a man of God.

I don't believe it's a coincidence that the Vered Jericho fortress where the great sword was found is believed to have originated as one of those unholy temples to a false god. Regardless, due primarily to his establishment of all these evil high places, Solomon's story didn't end well. His technological breakthroughs and great wealth were scattered far and wide, and his wickedness led to the collapse of the Kingdom of Israel at its pinnacle. Does that sound familiar?

Despite having built the temple of God in Jerusalem and having penned Proverbs, Ecclesiastes, the Song of Solomon, and many of the Psalms, Solomon came under great deception, lost sight of right and wrong, wavered in his faith, and lost his grip on the Word of God with devastating results. If the wisest, richest, most powerful man in the history of the world can be so easily corrupted by the wiles of the devil, anyone can. Be careful what you prop up in high places, and don't ever lose your sense of awe and wonder concerning the sword of the Spirit, nor your fear of God. He cuts both ways, and He is jealous concerning His bride (Exod. 34:14).

> Therefore thou shalt keep the commandments of the LORD thy God, to walk in his ways, and to fear him.
>
> —DEUTERONOMY 8:6

TIME-OUT: WHAT DOES THE BIBLE SAY ABOUT SWORDS?

If you glanced at the table of contents, you might have wondered why the sword of the Spirit warranted three chapters while the other pieces of God's armor each received two. I have two great reasons. First, this is a book about the Word of God, so it stands to reason. Second, with the tyrants on the left working so hard to strip away our right to protect ourselves and our families with effective self-defense weapons, the Holy Spirit is compelling me to take an extended time-out to let His sword settle the debate.

This is an urgent matter during these buck-wild, tyrannical, uber-violent times, so I want to give it proper attention. Over the next four or five pages, I will dive deep into biblical self-defense and justification for the Second Amendment, starting with Jesus' often misinterpreted message of the sword. I believe you'll find it liberating.

At the very moment He was being arrested in the Garden of Gethsemane on the night before He was crucified, Jesus famously said, "All they that take [draw, wield, take up] the sword shall perish with the sword" (Matt. 26:52).

It's crucial to understand the context of Jesus' statement. Just hours before uttering those historic words, Jesus instructed the disciples that His earlier directions concerning the gear they carry while on a mission were no longer sufficient. He told them they must now start traveling with purses and money that He had earlier banned, and then told them explicitly to buy swords even if they had to sell their most valuable garments to do so (Luke 22:35–36).

In this discussion, He reminded them that all biblical prophecy must be fulfilled, and He foreshadowed the dramatic never-ending persecution that would begin that night. That's likely why Peter felt emboldened to draw his sword to attack one of the arrest party in the garden just hours later, cutting off Malchus' ear (John 18:10). At that moment, Jesus didn't rebuke Peter for having a sword, but for taking up the sword that night outside the will of God. Jesus then repeated the need for the Scriptures to be fulfilled through His arrest and crucifixion (Matt. 26:54), and He asked Peter, "Shall I not drink the cup the Father has given me?" (John 18:11, NIV). Furthermore, Jesus had already negotiated for the disciples' release, so He had eliminated their need to defend themselves with swords (John 18:8–9).

Peter gets a bad rap as a hothead and an emotional wreck, but I think many of us would have lost control in that situation once we realized what was about to happen. Still, we can learn a lot about what *not* to do from Peter's actions that night.

With all that in mind, it's crucial to realize that Jesus never retracted His instruction that they arm themselves—not that night nor any time afterward through the Word of God. Immediately after Peter hacked off the dude's ear, Jesus first told him to put his sword back into its place, and then He uttered

His famous axiom in Matthew 26:52. He didn't tell him to throw it in a ditch, sell it on Craigslist, leave it back in the car, or hand it over to the tyrants who were arresting Him but to put it back from where he drew it—in its sheath on his belt. Never forget, this is the Word of God. You can be sure Peter and the boys left the garden armed that night, just as Jesus instructed.

Some liberalized commentators irrationally and erroneously claim that the swords in the garden that night were just props to make them appear more like criminals, as if they helped fulfill the prophecy that Jesus would be "reckoned among the transgressors" (Luke 22:37). But don't you believe that nonsense. That would contradict Jesus' actual words that night, the full counsel of the Bible, the Holy Spirit's leading through history, and all common sense.

The temple guards were already committed to arresting Jesus no matter what they did in the garden, and they put Him on trial that night as a transgressor no matter what gear His disciples carried. If the swords played a role in His arrest, it would have been noted during His trial or one of His interrogations that night, but nada. Not once was it mentioned. Likewise, Jesus would never have told them to change their entire gear inventory if His instruction to start carrying swords was a silly, unnecessary, one-night gimmick.

Once Jesus ascended into heaven after His resurrection, the disciples continued preaching the gospel despite being treated like outlaws, and each eventually met arrest and execution. It's encouraging to know that the biblical record and other historical writings present no evidence that they ever had to use their swords to make violence or to make war by carnal means. From that, we can conclude that the swords served primarily as a defensive *deterrent*. The fact that Jesus told them that two swords were enough for their small group further proves this purpose (Luke 22:38). They obeyed Jesus and the Holy Spirit in all things, including when and if to draw their swords.

MODERN-DAY HEROES OF THE FAITH

Knowing all the above in proper context, we can see that anyone who misappropriates Matthew 26:52 to promote pacifism or ban our ability to purchase effective self-defense weapons ignores Jesus' lessons from that night in the garden. The only honest way to interpret His message of the sword is to see that Jesus was ensuring His disciples would confidently arm themselves for deterrence and self-defense in accordance with the Holy Spirit.

It was His last night with them before His death on the cross, and He was preparing them for the especially dangerous days at hand—and thank God He did. If we don't deter violence through the appearance of strength and protect those in vulnerable situations, who will? Certainly not the violent fascists or tyrannical government agency trying to disarm us. We don't have to go too far back in history to imagine what could happen. Remembering the fate of Holocaust Jews after their government disarmed them gives us a horrifying glimpse.

The tangible weapons we carry today are intended for deterrence, survival, and defense of the defenseless as we continue to follow the Holy Spirit across the increasingly dangerous prophetic timeline. Socialists in our government are trying to erase our biblical right to effectively arm ourselves as a deterrence, just as the Nazis did to their citizens in the years leading up to WWII. We must send them the message that deterrence and defensive capability are non-negotiable.

If the miracle-working apostles were instructed to purchase swords to fulfill their mission, the same is true of us. Someday our Father will send many legions of angels to fight on our behalf here on earth (Matt. 26:53), but until then, we need to hold the line with our deterrent capabilities, just as He instructed. I believe the founding fathers who wrote the U.S. Constitution had this biblical truth firmly in mind when they wrote the Second Amendment, so the church is more than justified to fight for this right as directed by the Bible *and* the law of the land. I will cooperate with every single governmental policy until it goes against the Word of God and the counsel of the Holy Spirit. That's where we all have to draw the line.

This lawless government aims to cast the Bible out of the public forum and ban it, and I'm sure you can see that by now. They're coming after our self-defense weapons now, but never forget that their ultimate target is the Bible and the Judeo-Christian moral code. We've been on a tragic slippery slope in America, and the enemy has already taken far more ground than we should have allowed. This is why the church must fight to protect the Constitution—as written. Hold the line!

> Defend the poor and fatherless: do justice to the afflicted and needy.
> Deliver the poor and needy: rid them out of the hand of the wicked.
> —PSALM 82:3–4

THE TWO TYPES OF PACIFISTS

Looking back to the first-century disciples where the use of steel swords is concerned, we can trust that they indeed traveled with the posture and attitude of peacemakers and eventual martyrs (Matt. 5:9–10). Knowing this, I would be shocked to have seen these disciples ever draw their swords. When deterrence didn't work for them, it's clear that they trusted the Holy Spirit to have His way once they were arrested. These were the men and women who introduced the Word of God to the world, much of which they had penned, so fighting for the proliferation of the Word was far more important for the survival of the church than fighting for their own lives. As we learned from the life of Paul, who penned much of the New Testament while imprisoned, there was nothing to gain if they had perished by the sword while fighting to avoid his imprisonment.

The same cannot be said of this nation's Christian warriors who died to secure religious freedom and end slavery, or the Christian soldiers of WWII who gave their lives to liberate Europe and the Jews from the Nazis, or the people of Asia and the Pacific from the brutal Empire of Japan, or the Christian peacekeepers who die in the line of duty every day, or the untold numbers of Christians throughout history who heroically sacrificed their lives to save others.

History has proven that taking up the sword and dying by the sword *was their calling.* Can anyone in their right mind say these heroes sinned against God by arming themselves to defeat evil? Only a demon or a wicked fool would suggest or believe that. When Jesus said that "all who take up the sword, perish by the sword," was He in any way saying that such a fate was sinful? Absolutely not. That's why I call it an axiom. It is entirely true whether the sword wielder is good or evil, but it can't be considered sinful when it is directed by the Holy Spirit. If Jesus intended to condemn the carrying of swords, He would have said so on the night of His arrest or elsewhere in the New Testament. He certainly wouldn't have told Peter to purchase swords to begin with, nor would He have told Peter to re-holster his sword at the very moment He stated this axiom.

The New Covenant of Christ brought a lot of Old Testament practices to a close, but defending the innocent was not one of them. Anyone who believes God expects us to sit back passively while millions are being massacred by evil tyrants, while dozens are being murdered by a domestic terrorist, or while their children are being attacked by a drug-crazed home invader has lost their mind. They're the deluded puppets that make these horrors possible.

EXPOSING THE DELUSION OF BIBLE PACIFISM

While the first disciples were never called to sacrifice their lives in mortal combat like the heroes noted above, they boldly and sacrificially waged war against evil in the spiritual realm, wielding the sword of the Spirit with great force, no matter who was offended, no matter how many laws they broke, and no matter how many times they were arrested; even when they knew their execution was imminent.

Recall when Paul and Silas were beaten and imprisoned. They lived to obey the commands of God over the man-made laws of godless governments. And like the other first-century apostles, Paul gave his life to ensure two thousand years of saints could eventually read the Bible. This is what I mean when I say there is no such thing as biblical pacifists.

We all must take up *that* sword no matter who we offend and no matter who turns on us—and that can be painful. As we discussed earlier in the book, Jesus said that His peace is not worldly peace (John 14:27), and in direct reference to this aspect of the sword of the Spirit, He also said:

> Think not that I am come to send peace on earth: I came not to send peace, but a sword. For I am come to set a man at variance against his father, and the daughter against her mother, and the daughter in law against her mother in law. And a man's foes shall be they of his own household. He that loveth father or mother more than me is not worthy of me: and he that loveth son or daughter more than me is not worthy of me. And he that taketh not his cross, and followeth after me, is not worthy of me. He that findeth his life shall lose it: and he that loseth his life for my sake shall find it.
>
> —JESUS (MATTHEW 10:34–39)

This seldom-preached verse can be gut-wrenching, but don't miss His point. This is one of the more powerful examples of Jesus' *comparative* teachings using family bonds and our very lives as extremes to emphasize the seriousness of His commands. He has no desire for division in our homes, nor that we ever get executed for our faith, but if that's the consequence of walking in the gospel and wearing God's armor in Spirit and truth, so be it. Like the first disciples, we can trust the Holy Spirit to protect us and our families while ensuring we fulfill God's prophetic plan for our lives—no matter the cost.

THE FINISHER OF THE FAITH AND HIS SWORD

In the Book of Revelation, we learn that Jesus will soon return as the conquering warrior King with this two-edged sword coming from His mouth. With it, He will bring a close to His finished work in startling fashion, all of which is revealed in this final book of the Bible (Rev. 1:16). This vision of

Jesus gives us the most accurate picture of the sword of the Spirit—the Word of God—from Jesus' perspective.

Later in Revelation, we learn that upon His return, He will use this sword to judge and cast down the nations that stand against Him (Rev. 19:15). In the Gospel record alone, Jesus warns us of His judgment and the horrors of hell no less than sixty times. One warning should be enough. We must come to terms with this fact: the same sword that equips the saints to enter His kingdom will cast the devil and his minions into the eternal hell, called the lake of fire (Rev. 20:10–15). Very soon, the Author of our faith will finish His work on this earth, and those who are born again will enter the kingdom of heaven while everyone else will be cast out into the fiery abyss of hell.

Never forget that this is the reason for our urgency in putting on the whole armor of God and drawing the sword to fight the good fight in these last days. Not only do our homes and churches depend on it, but every soul alive depends on it, and Jesus commissioned our generation for this final rescue mission to the nations (Matt. 28:16–20). Despite the silence in the church over the past quarter century, hell is a soon-to-be reality that we must avoid, no matter the cost on this side. We must stop letting the culture, the media, the government, and unbelievers in public forums attack our faith and intimidate us for living and speaking out boldly in obedience to the Bible. Their eternity depends on it—and so does ours.

THE REAL GLOBAL WARMING

> And whosoever was not found written in the book of life was cast into the lake of fire.
>
> —REVELATION 20:15

Jesus spoke of everything we're seeing today. There has never been a season so ripe with biblical prophecies coming to life. The end of this world will come as written in the Word, yet Bible-deniers constantly cry, "One day soon, global warming is going to destroy the world." Even from a secular perspective, that's science-denying nonsense, but we must remember that they believe this planet and our universe was born of chaos. The devil has them believing they have time to lord over us and future generations—unless global warming scorches the earth before they can. Do you want to know what global warming really is?

The day of the Lord will come as a thief in the night; in the which the heavens shall pass away with a great noise, and the elements shall melt with fervent heat, the earth also and the works that are therein shall be burned up.

—2 PETER 3:10

There will be massive climate change; they're ironically right about that. But Jesus will cause it, and only born-again believers will survive it.

Others say, "I worry one day there's gonna be a nuclear war, and a massive atom bomb will destroy everything." Not a chance. Jesus spoke the world into existence, and He alone can speak the world into oblivion.

The same Word of God that says, "In the beginning...let there be light," is the same Word of God we are holding in our hands today, and it alone has the power to destroy or save the world. That's why the government can't stand it. That's why the public school systems can't stand it. That's why rebellious people can't stand it. And that's why the devil is pulling out all the stops to rip it out of our hands—and the hands of our children. That's also why most churches would rather preach fake news and self-help than the Bible. The sword of the Spirit will not leave you to wallow in your sin. It will cut you free, or it will cut you to pieces. The choice is yours. The Word of God will make you increasingly uncomfortable until you get right with Him, or it will judge you harshly on that last day.

Choose wisely.

He that rejecteth me, and receiveth not my words, hath one that judgeth him: the word that I have spoken, the same shall judge him in the last day.

—JESUS (JOHN 12:48)

CHAPTER EIGHTEEN

Sword of the Spirit: Part 2

So shall my word be that goeth forth out of my mouth: it shall
not return unto me void, but it shall accomplish that which I
please, and it shall prosper in the thing whereto I sent it.
—ISAIAH 55:11

LET'S REVISIT THE devil tempting Jesus in the wilderness in Matthew chapter 4. The devil tempted the Lord three times, leading off with "if thou be the Son of God" while he tried to trip Jesus into doubting who He was to the Father through each temptation.

Do you remember how Jesus responded on all three occasions? He didn't say, "Well, I'm glad you brought that up, devil. Let Me sit down on My stool, open a Red Bull, and chitchat with you for a little while—psychologically and philosophically speaking—and just talk to you dogmatically about what I learned in seminary." No. He said, "It is written, it is written, it is written," and the devil got a snout full of the Word of God before running for safety. Then the angels came to minister to Jesus. From this, we learn that we are only strong when we are fighting the enemy with the sword of the Spirit—the

Word of God—leading the way. Do this as Jesus did, and you too can count on angels to come to your aid in times of need, whether you realize they are angels or not (Heb. 13:2).

WORTHY OF OUR LOVE AND HONOR

As discussed earlier, John chapter 1 tells us that Jesus *is* the Word. Don't ever gloss over that. *The Word* must be the most loaded name for Jesus in the Bible. It's easily the most weaponized. This amazing name points to the tangible, unchanging, omnipotent, omnipresent, and omniscient nature of Jesus, revealing Himself as the Author and Creator of all we know. This is a divinely powerful reality.

The Word represents Jesus expressing Himself through the history of everything we know. Calling Jesus *the Word* also reminds us that His creative power is so great that He can speak universes and dimensions into existence with a single thought. Though the men who penned and printed the Bible through history are indeed heroes of the faith, Jesus is the sole Author who spoke it all into existence, so the Word is God's manifest presence in our hands—thus the sword of the Spirit. This is why we can read the books penned by Solomon despite his latter fall. He was just a vessel—until he wasn't.

I praise God for every second of the amazing creative process that went into producing the most historically authenticated, most printed, most translated, most world-changing, most desired best seller in the history of books—more in these evil days than ever before. I could never teach long enough or write enough books to express the awe and wonder I feel toward the Word of God and all He continues to reveal in these last days. I love to see Scripture anywhere, in any form, at any time. I hear Jesus' voice whenever I read it because that's what it represents. It's His spoken Word delivered to us on a golden platter at a very high cost. The weight of that reality should remind you why we still put our hands on a Bible in a court of law and most swearing-in ceremonies for high offices in government (for now, anyway).

When you recognize and touch a Bible, you're recognizing God's omniscience and omnipresence in the room as a witness to your integrity and all you do. That's why those who hate Jesus are trying to strip it out of the public domain. The devil knows that the Bible is exactly what we claim it to be—Jesus' supernatural instruction manual. His sword! It's His bundle of previous love letters and the way, the truth, and the life that leads His children home to heaven with the Father. The Word of God reveals His heart concerning every matter under the sun and beyond it.

So Valuable It's Invaluable

The Bible simply cannot be assigned a value—it's well beyond valuable. As I mentioned, though we in America have mostly lost this heavenly perspective on the Word of God, people worldwide are begging for Bibles. Americans can have forty of them lying around the house and never sincerely read one of them. Most people only open their Bible when the preacher says, "Hey, let's open up our Bibles." And even then, most folks these days click the app on their iPhones and can't even remember the last time they flipped through actual inked pages.

I love all the power we gain through the high-tech redneck stuff in this culture. You might love the Bible on your phone, and that's cool. I know people who are highly effective and efficient at studying the Bible on their iPads or computers, and that's legit. I get it. I use my MacBook to quickly research and cross-reference Scripture while writing, so I'm grateful for all of it. But there's just something about holding a printed Bible in your hands that's immeasurably powerful.

When I see a believer holding a printed Bible, it moves me. Having the ability to touch the Word of God, to leaf through the pages and feel its weight and read "thus saith the Lord" printed in ink, is something most saints through history could only dream of—and many gave their lives so we could have it. In the same way, carrying a printed Bible reminds us of the presence of God wherever we go. You can't say your phone or tablet does that. Carry your Bible as often as possible, wherever you go—not just when going to church, but especially when you do. We need to honor our Bibles and send the message to our kids and the world that we treasure the Word of God.

The Sword We Carry

Reflect on our discussion of the symbolism of actual swords during the first century. Roman soldiers would evoke strength, honor, dominion, and even fear when citizens saw their steel swords gleaming in the sunlight. A far more powerful response can be triggered when someone sees you carrying your Bible. A steel sword in a soldier's hands is provocative, but the sword of the Spirit in your hands can provoke revelation in the hearts of the lost.

The sword of the Spirit is the Word of God, and it is the strongest, most disruptive weapon in the history of the world. Over sixteen hundred years, forty-plus writers (most of whom never saw each other a natural day in their lives) were all in agreement. From continent to continent and from era to era, all these writers agreed on one thing: Scripture is the living Word of God breathed into them by the Holy Spirit, and no worldly power or doctrine of demons can stand against it.

My church is called Global Vision Bible Church for a reason. We preach the Bible. We love the Bible. We honor the Bible. We have nothing other than truth to stand upon, so we literally stand on the Word of God. When constructing a new pulpit, we typically place a Bible in a glass case and build it into the floor directly behind the lectern to remind every speaker of this fact.

WOULD YOU MISS IT?

The way most people treat the Bible reminds me of this story about a father who sent his son to college. Before his son headed out, the father said, "Son, when you get to your college, make sure that you live a pure life, make sure that you live right, make sure you live godly, make sure you go to church, and make sure you read the Bible." The father gave a litany of rules, regulations, and boxes to check, and the son just nodded in agreement.

Over the following year, the son visited a couple of times and returned home for a short stay at Christmas, and when summer rolled around, he finally came home for an extended stay. So, his father sat him down for a serious discussion and asked, "Have you been reading the Bible?" Then he went through his lecture all over again.

Once he was done, his son said, "You know, Dad, I have been reading the Bible. As a matter of fact, I have some massive questions about Matthew, Mark, Luke, and John. Do you think you can help me?"

Dad said, "Sure," as he walked into the kitchen and reached atop the refrigerator to pull down his own Bible. He brought it into the den, sat next to his son, and flipped it open to Matthew but couldn't find it. He looked for Mark, Luke, and John but couldn't find them either. Sincerely bewildered, he leafed through Acts, jumped to Romans, and even went back to Malachi, wondering if he was having his first senior moment. Then he jumped back to Genesis, flipped back to the maps, and even skimmed through the index and the concordance, but still couldn't find the four Gospels. He looked where he knew it should be one more time before throwing his hands up in exasperation. He looked at his son and said, "My goodness, Son, I can't find Matthew, Mark, Luke, and John."

His son replied, "Dad, after our talk last year, I tore them out of your Bible for safekeeping, and you mean to tell me in the span of a full year you've never once missed Matthew, Mark, Luke, and John?"

AMERICANS AND THE BIBLE

That story illustrates a sobering point. Most people in Western nations would never miss a single page of their Bible, even if they were all torn out. Yet there are people around the world that risk their lives to hold and study just a few loose pages. They don't have whole copies of the Word of God, but the pages they do have are passed around so everyone they know can memorize it, love it, revere it, and worship God through what little they have.

That is what it looks like to wield the sword of the Spirit. They love every single bit of the Word of God and plead for more. Meanwhile, we have bookstores with thousands of copies gathering dust on their shelves or in their warehouses, and some of you have twenty-five seldom-used copies spread around your house like movie props, yet we wonder why we don't see biblical obedience or revival. Most American Christians simply don't read the Bible. Let's just admit it.

Most born-again believers quickly want to take hold of the defensive pieces of armor (and the virtues they represent), but they still struggle to draw the sword. Whether that's because they're afraid of what it will say to them or simply a matter of laziness and twisted priorities, when the enemy charges into battle against someone who does not take up the sword, wield the sword, or obey the sword in this regard, they will be ripe for the slaughter. Consider Solomon. He knew the Old Testament texts virtually word for word and penned a good bit of it, but as soon as he stopped wielding it in battle, the devil destroyed him and the entire Kingdom of Israel with him.

This sword is the only weapon Jesus will use to defeat His enemies upon His return, and there will indeed be violence on that day. How much more should we use it to prepare for His return, just as He instructs? If ever there was a case where we cannot afford to be on the wrong side of history, this is it. The Word of God is the only weapon that can effectively fight on defense *and* offense. In a scrum, where the battle breaks down to hand-to-hand combat, the greatest defense will be our ability to use the sword on offense. Nothing compares to the offensive power of that sharp two-edged sword.

MARINATING IN THE WORD

Blessed is the man that walketh not in the counsel of the ungodly, nor standeth in the way of sinners, nor sitteth in the seat of the scornful. But his delight is in the law of the LORD; and in his law doth he meditate day and night.

—PSALM 1:1–2

In the context of this passage, the word *meditate* means to marinate or to soak. If somebody is about to grill some meat and do it right, they marinate it first. They let the juices soak deep into the meat before they put it on the grill, and even then, they'll typically brush on more of the marinade while it's cooking. God says that someone who marinates in the Word day and night "shall be like a tree planted by the rivers of water," and "whatsoever he doeth shall prosper" (Ps. 1:3). Notice that it's not a tree in the desert, it's not a tree on an asphalt parking lot, and it's not even a tree in the backyard, but a tree planted by "the rivers of water" with its deepest roots soaking in the richest soil possible—an inexhaustible resource of nutrients and life-giving water feeding it continually.

If you're not a spiritual person or are always troubled by what others say or do, it's because you are not meditating on the Word of God. "Great peace have they which love thy law: and nothing shall offend them" (Ps. 119:165). If you walk around with a chip on your shoulder or feel offended all the time—like most of this generation in this culture—this explains why. If you're easily offended, it's because you are not really in the Bible. You might be skimming through it, but you're not meditating on it. You can be sure of that.

The Bible tells us that great peace comes from this great Book, and you will not be easily offended when you properly use the sword of the Spirit. The Word of God tells us to wear the armor and use the double-edged sword of the Spirit. You can fight back against the enemy's attacks with nothing more than your obedience to the Word of God.

THE BIBLE "ELEVEN"

Of all that the Lord says about His Word, there are eleven analogies—metaphors the Bible uses to describe itself—that I find especially practical where the whole armor of God is concerned. The enemy cannot stand against the sword of the Spirit when it is wielded by a fully armored believer with a healthy prayer life, so let's look at how the Word can prepare you and strengthen the armor for battle. The first and highest analogy is the two-edged sword. The

Word is the most powerful defensive *and* offensive weapon in His arsenal, and as we learned earlier, it will be the very weapon He will use to smite His enemies upon His return. It cuts going in, and it cuts coming out. It cuts to the left, and it cuts to the right. It cuts to defend, and it cuts to offend. The sword of the Spirit cuts both ways, no matter the context.

THE BIBLE IS A SWORD

> For the word of God is quick, and powerful, and sharper than any twoedged sword, piercing even to the dividing asunder of soul and spirit, and of the joints and marrow, and is a discerner of the thoughts and intents of the heart.
>
> —HEBREWS 4:12

Let me tell you what you *don't* do with a sword. You don't ever have to defend a sword. Let me explain what I mean. Have you ever noticed how many people waste the entirety of their life trying to defend the Word of God, as if the Bible needs defense? If I were in a sword fight with someone trying to kill me, I wouldn't waste any time telling the attacker, "This big old sword right here is a sharp sword, this is a shiny sword, this is a real sword that can cut through anything." No, I would just try to chop his head off with it.

I wouldn't explain how it works or try to convince anyone that it's really a sword. But some people timidly go around saying things like, "Let me tell you about the Bible because I need to prove who Jesus was. I've got to prove His resurrection. I've got to prove it's all true." No, just pull out the sword and watch it cut. Whether on defense or offense, let the Bible prove itself. You don't have to spend all your time on Twitter arguing with people and worrying about what they think about the Bible. Let the Word of God speak for itself.

If you're walking in obedience to the Word, all you need to do is pull it out, and the sword of the Spirit will chop up the enemy. It is a sword that was designed for spiritual warfare, and it must be used in battle. But the problem is that most Christians act like, "Oh my goodness, I don't want to whip out the Bible and start quoting it. I might offend somebody." You absolutely *will* offend somebody. God is counting on it. Do you know why you're saved? Because the Bible eventually offended you.

Do you know why you're born again? Because God said you were lost, dead, doomed, and damned in your sin, but the blood of Jesus Christ—another man's blood—saved you. That's offensive at first, but without that offense, you cannot be born again.

Read Jesus' discussion with the Pharisee Nicodemus recorded in John chapter 3 for evidence. In fact, read pretty much any confrontation Jesus had with religious folks and other lost folks, and you'll see what I mean. The Bible is a weapon to be used in conflict, and you'd better realize by now that we're deep in conflict in this nation and around the world. We are in the most serious spiritual conflict in the history of mankind, so keep the sword of the Spirit well in hand.

THE BIBLE IS MILK

As newborn babes, desire the sincere milk of the word, that ye may grow thereby: If so be ye have tasted that the Lord is gracious.

—1 PETER 2:2–3

When I first got saved in 1992, I couldn't get enough of the Bible. I was like a little bird in a nest, "Feed me! Feed me! Chirp, chirp, chirp!" I just had to have it nearly every waking hour. I was so hungry for this milk that I wanted to bring a sleeping bag to the house of God.

You would have had to put a stick of dynamite in the back of my britches to get me out of church in those early days. I just wanted to be there to hear the Word. I wasn't going because of discontent in my life but because the Word was suddenly all I wanted. I'd kneel at the altar because everything was going right. So I just kept going to church every day possible. I loved hearing the Word, and I loved preaching the Word. Church was suddenly the coolest place on earth. If it got me reading the Bible, I was all in.

I'm not some sort of super-brainy person or one of those crazy nerds, but when I was living at the Good Shepherd Children's Home, as soon as I got home from school—while everybody else was out playing sports and running around—I'd lock myself in my bedroom, and I'd put on some sermon tapes. (In case you're too young to know what cassette tapes are, they're those cute little plastic cases with little reels of tape inside.)

I'd listen to those fiery preachers until I passed out in the wee hours of the morning. Those old preachers would throw down, wide open, heaven-bound with the hammer down! I'd spend all my free time memorizing Scripture. I'd get 3x5 index cards and write the verse on one side and the reference on the other. I'd pace back and forth wherever I was, reading and reciting the Word at every opportunity. Even after I had traveled the world as an evangelist—at the age of thirty, when I started Global Vision—I'd still walk around memorizing scripture. Even though I had long before moved on to the meat of the Word, I just couldn't get enough.

I know I'm an extreme case, but I'm not alone. Some of you can relate. When you first get born again, there's something about the milk of the Word that nourishes your body like nothing else. A baby needs milk. It needs those simple nutrients. It needs those easily digested vitamins. It needs to add strength to their soft bones. But the time comes when we must quit living off milk and get some meat.

THE BIBLE IS MEAT

> For every one that useth milk is unskilful in the word of righteousness: for he is a babe. But strong meat belongeth to them that are of full age, even those who by reason of use have their senses exercised to discern both good and evil.
>
> —HEBREWS 5:13–14

In this passage, the Bible is compared to meat for those who are mature and able to "discern both good and evil." If you're a grown-up and you walk into my church sucking on a baby bottle, I will ask you to come back when you've kicked that disgusting habit. In fact, if an adult ever came walking into Global Vision sucking on a bottle while I was preaching, we'd call 911 because that dude would have to be crazy.

Milk is amazing when you're a newborn, but after a while, you've got to graduate to solid, staple food. I'll be honest with you. A church like ours can sometimes get so meaty that our preaching can make the milky crowd sick to their stomachs. When people are used to being bottle-fed with cherry-picked verses, paraphrased sermons, and self-help messages packed with rainbows, Skittles, unicorns, and cotton candy, their bellies are so full of junk food that if you put a T-bone steak in them, they'd go from zero to projectile in no time. They just can't handle it. If a kid has been filling themselves with chocolate milk, Red Bull, potato chips, and other greasy stuff, you can't give them red meat without making them sick.

Sometimes when I'm deep into my meatiest preaching, I expect someone going to one of those milk-bottle, watered-down churches to start gagging right there in the service. The point is, you eventually have to graduate from milk, and you've got to get the meat of the Word of God. This has always been true.

Let's recall what Jesus said about the meat in the Olivet Discourse. The Lord put special urgency on teaching and studying the meat of His Word in these last of the last days, which He called the due season in the context (Matt. 24:45).

Regardless of your age, I strongly encourage you to get busy consuming whatever "portion of meat" you can digest (Luke 12:42). I pray that you crave the sizzling steak of God's Word and just go after it. Marinate on it, think about it, chew on it, and savor it. It will do what it's supposed to do regardless of the size of your portion. It's good meat for the soul, and we all need to start craving it.

THE BIBLE IS FIRE

> Wherefore thus saith the LORD God of hosts, Because ye speak this word, behold, I will make my words in thy mouth fire, and this people wood, and it shall devour them.
>
> —JEREMIAH 5:14

After the Lord spoke these words to Jeremiah, He later asked him, "Is not my word like as a fire?" (Jer. 23:29). Yes, the Word of God is indeed like a fire. That's why some people don't want to touch it. The Bible will burn you. It will sizzle you. It will incinerate and devour everything that is not of God and will set your heart on fire for Him. It will consume you. In Luke chapter 24, the resurrected Jesus hid His identity while walking and talking to two of His disciples on their way to Emmaus.

After they realized who He was during this post-resurrection dinner, one of them said, "Did not our heart burn within us, while he talked with us by the way, and while he opened to us the scriptures?" (Luke 24:32). I call that "holy heartburn," and the whole church needs it. I don't want Pepcid, Tums, or anything else to quench that fire. I just want to let it burn.

As the Word of God gets inside you, it begins to burn out all your sin. It will burn out disobedience, doubt, misery, depression, nastiness, and ungodly behavior. Don't you want to burn all that darkness and dross out of your life? That's what the Word of God does—it's a fire that burns, and I'm sure you can see how it strengthens the steel of your armor. Have you ever noticed how often the Bible distinguishes His fire as a *consuming* fire? It's a fearful thing to fall into the hands of the living God. He is an all-consuming fire, and He burns for your salvation.

I watched a documentary about Mount Sinai and learned that if you went there today, you'd see the top of the mountain is still scorched. Below a certain height, the entire mountain looks normal, but the top is blacker than coal dust. The glory of God burned it before Moses for all generations to see. When God comes through with His holy fire, He's an all-consuming fire. We sing about the name of Jesus, and devils shake and quake in their boots. Demons flee just by hearing His name. It's the only name by which you can be saved.

During the days of the Old Testament, when the scribes and priests would write God's name—whether Jehovah, Yahweh, or Elohim—they would do the most remarkable thing. Once they got to a place in the text where they wrote God's name, as soon as they wrote it, they would go home to shower and shave and change their robes all over again. Then they would go back and finish the text! Can you imagine what that was like when they got to a passage where God was mentioned fifteen times? That's the degree of reverence they held for the name of God.

Here's a revelatory observation for you. The Bible says that God has exalted His Word above His own name (Ps. 138:2). From this, we know there is only one thing in the universe that God said is more powerful than His name—including the only name by which you can get born again—and it is this book we call the Bible. If God exalts His Word above His name, a name that we know we are to revere, don't you think we ought to love, cherish, and honor this book we call the Bible? If His name is a terror to demons, don't you think His fire, the sword of the Spirit, is also a terror to them? Yes, and it should burn within us to an all-consuming degree. Amen?

THE BIBLE IS A HAMMER

> Is not my word like as a fire? saith the LORD; and like a hammer that breaketh the rock in pieces?
>
> —JEREMIAH 23:29

The Lord also told Jeremiah that the Bible is like a hammer. If you have a cold, stony, concrete heart, the Word of God will beat the hardness out of you (if you'll let it). A preacher doesn't have to beat it out of you. A book or a video doesn't have to beat it out of you. Your spouse doesn't have to beat it out of you. The Word of God will break off the stoniness and beat out all the rough edges.

I'll be the first to admit I've got some rough edges that need the hammer, and if you're honest, you'll admit it too. When our hard places become set in stone, sincerely taking hold of the Word of God will work like a jackhammer. When you get busy reading the Bible, God will break all the craziness out of your relationships, home, workplace, and every part of your life that displeases Him.

A lot of people just want the Bible in delicate, little doses. They never want God to hit them in their head with His Word. They stay away from anyone they consider to be a Bible thumper. People call me a Bible thumper on social media, and I say, "Yep, I'm a Bible-thumping fool." I'll thump you with the Bible, and I'll thump myself with the Bible. After all, it's like a hammer, and we all need more of its transforming power.

Only the Word of God can break up the bitterness and unforgiveness you've held on to for decades. Only the Word of God, like a great hammer, can break the ungodliness out of us. Men, if you were to dig up a diamond today and give it to your wife, saying, "Look, honey, I got you a diamond!" she would laugh at you. At this stage, it's little more than a muddy rock. It's a nasty, ugly, disproportioned rock with nothing sparkly about it. But if you got busy chiseling on it like a master jeweler, putting a little fire on it and hammering away—bing, bing, bing—you'd finally have something worthy of her hand, and she'd finally see that the ugly rock was a diamond in the rough all along.

A diamond is just a dirty, unformed rock until you put a hammer to it, and we all start out like those dirty rocks. We are hardened, we are crusty, we are seemingly worthless, and we need some breaking. Then Jesus tells us to come to Him so He can make diamonds out of us, and the breaking hurts. Oh man, does it hurt. But when you take it as one who truly trusts in Him and His Word, you'll embrace it (Job 13:15). Even David said, "Make me to hear joy and gladness; that the bones which thou hast broken may rejoice" (Ps. 51:8). Sometimes God will take that hammer of the Word and beat all the foolishness out of our life. If you let Him do His work in you, once the hammering is finished, you'll thank Him with all your heart.

THE BIBLE IS AN ANCHOR

Wherein God, willing more abundantly to shew unto the heirs of promise the immutability of his counsel, confirmed it by an oath: That by two immutable things, in which it was impossible for God to lie, we might have a strong consolation, who have fled for refuge to lay hold upon the hope set before us: Which hope we have as an anchor of the soul, both sure and stedfast, and which entereth into that within the veil.

—HEBREWS 6:17–19

The Bible also likens the hope in God's Word to an anchor for our souls. In the context of this verse in Hebrews, He's talking about the immutable, unchanging counsel and eternal promises of God. Numerous times throughout the Bible, we are reminded that it is impossible for God to lie. Now, the Lord says that the Word of God is an anchor for your soul. I'm not much of a fisherman or boater, but I have enough sense to know what an anchor does.

If you throw an anchor in the water, it holds your boat in place. It will keep your boat from drifting. Do you know why the American church has drifted from the Word of God? Because all our possessions become an anchor—not the Bible. We've drifted away with the culture. We've drifted from the truth. We've drifted from sound doctrine. We've drifted from real science and history. We've drifted from what the Bible teaches about morality, justice, mercy, and honor because we are no longer tied to the right anchor.

When you finally have the right anchor and make the Word of God your foundation, when you let the Bible be all that you stand on, stand by, stand for, and stand with, it will hold you firmly in place when the tide and the waves and the storms try to push you farther into the cultural abyss. The anchor of your soul will hold. The Bible says the Word of God is an immutable promise from God. It will never change.

Contrary to the popular opinion of the lukewarm church, God hasn't changed His commands—we have. God hasn't moved—we've moved. God hasn't lied—we've lied. God hasn't drifted—we have. The Bible is an anchor that we can cast out into the waters and wait for the day of His return. The Word of God is the only thing that can hold your home in place. It's the only thing that can hold the church in place. And you'd better realize this by now— it's the only thing that can hold this nation in place.

The United States has drifted far from God because we've allowed godless forces to lift the anchor and let other things replace it. There was a time that the Bible was the anchor and the foundation of the United States of America. Our founders were very clear about that, and even the non-Christians among them realized this anchor was our only hope to survive in this great experiment we call the USA.

We were once the bedrock of morality around the world because we (and our Constitution) were founded upon the Judeo-Christian moral code that is the Word of God. But over the past two hundred years, we've allowed the enemy to creep in and pull up that anchor while dropping a few of his own.

David asked, "If the foundations be destroyed, what can the righteous do?" (Ps. 11:3). I'll tell you what we'll do. We'll just repent, put on the whole armor of God, and start wielding the sword of the Spirit. We'll just start being righteous and fight the good fight of faith with the Word of God as our most potent weapon.

President Andrew Jackson is well known around the Nashville area. Our Mt. Juliet church is just a couple miles from his historic homestead called the Hermitage. Jackson was a controversial man, and I don't agree with much of what he did in the early 1800s, but it was a different world with far different challenges than we face today. Undoubtedly, he did much to fight the godlessness and elitist evil that still plagues our governments today, so I identify with Jackson in that regard.

You can visit the Hermitage and pick up a lot of factoids about the man, but there's one thing the secular humanists who are scrambling to rewrite history won't tell you about Andrew Jackson. It is said that a man's last words are his most important.

When Andrew Jackson was on his deathbed, getting ready to cross over to the other side, right beside him on the nightstand was his old Bible that he had faithfully read all those years. Let me tell you what your kids won't learn in public school—they are the last words of President Andrew Jackson as he was taking his journey into God's presence. He rolled over in an uncomfortable position, pointed at the Bible on the nightstand, and said, "That book, sir, is the rock on which the republic rests." God knows he was right.

> But he that heareth, and doeth not, is like a man that without a foundation built an house upon the earth; against which the stream did beat vehemently, and immediately it fell; and the ruin of that house was great.
>
> —JESUS (LUKE 6:49)

CHAPTER NINETEEN

Sword of the Spirit: Part 3

The woman saith unto him, Sir, thou hast nothing to draw with, and the well is deep: from whence then hast thou that living water? Art thou greater than our father Jacob, which gave us the well, and drank thereof himself, and his children, and his cattle? Jesus answered and said unto her, Whosoever drinketh of this water shall thirst again: But whosoever drinketh of the water that I shall give him shall never thirst; but the water that I shall give him shall be in him a well of water springing up into everlasting life.
—JOHN 4:11–14

L ET'S CONTINUE OUR look at the Bible's eleven analogies, starting with water. Natural water can do two primary things for humans. It can quench our thirst and wash us when we're dirty. In Ephesians 5:26, the Bible says that we need to be washed in the water of the Word. In John chapter 4, after Jesus told the woman at the well about His living water, she told Him she was thirsty for it. And Jesus basically replied, "Yep, I know it, and you're going to keep being thirsty unless you drink what I can give you.

I'll give you water that fills you with righteousness, authority, and power and puts some pizzazz in your life you've never imagined. You'll never thirst again!" This woman had gone from man to man, to man, to man, to man, to man (yes, six of them), and then to her surprise, this Jewish man was waiting for her at the well—and her soul was thirsty. Through a single interaction, she found that there was something about the message Jesus gave her. With the hope of the gospel, He quenched that thirst.

The Bible's good news is like water to a thirsty soul (Prov. 25:25), and water that washes over us and cleans out all the filth, wickedness, perversity, ungodliness, and impure thoughts from our lives. It washes us clean. I call it taking a Bible bath or taking a Scripture shower. When you get in the Word of God, the Word of God will get in you.

In the Bible, a man named Job made a very interesting analogy. He said, "I have esteemed the words of his mouth more than my necessary food" (Job 23:12). Food, of course, is necessary. You'll die without it. But Job said, in effect, "No Bible, no breakfast." He said, "Before I even feed my body, I'm going to get into the Word of God and feed my soul." Make sure you don't spiritually starve yourself to death.

At the children's home where I spent the better part of my youth, they had a little phrase they'd use on you after you had been there for a while. They'd say, "Babies get fed. Everybody else feeds themselves." That's a good rule for the church right there. If you only consume what a pastor spoon-feeds you every Sunday and Wednesday, you will become spiritually malnourished and starve to death. You've got to feed yourself every day in between.

Likewise, if you're not washed in the water of the Word, no wonder you have so much chaos and confusion in your heart. Your mind is so impure that you can't focus during a television program or phone call, let alone a sermon. If you're not being washed in the Word, your heart and mind are soaking and corroding in this world's filth; as we've already learned, the filth will take you over.

THE BIBLE IS A MIRROR

But be ye doers of the word, and not hearers only, deceiving your own selves. For if any be a hearer of the word, and not a doer, he is like unto a man beholding his natural face in a glass: For he beholdeth himself, and goeth his way, and straightway forgetteth what manner of man he was.

—JAMES 1:22–24

In the King James Version, the word *glass* refers to a mirror. What's interesting about a mirror is that it shows who you are without any misrepresentations—unless you go to the fair or the circus and find those funhouse mirrors. I'm not talking about those; I'm talking about the mirror in your house or car or the type some of you ladies might carry in your purse. If you look into one of these mirrors, it will show you the unvarnished truth. That's what the Bible does, and that's why people get nervous around it.

Have you ever noticed that you can take virtually anything to work with you? But don't you dare take a Bible if you want to avoid persecution. You can even take a cross with you to work. People might think you're a vampire slayer, right? They'd be cool with that. They wouldn't even mind if you brought a Bible-verse coffee mug or wall-hanging with an uplifting message, especially if the verse reference was tiny or not there at all. But take an actual printed Bible to work and see what happens.

If you try taking a Bible to some restaurants, they might ask you to leave. You can get tossed out if you flash a Bible in public places like government buildings. Let your kids take a Bible to public school and see what happens. They might go crazy, saying things like, "What on earth! We can't believe your kid is bringing Bibles to this safe place! How dare you expose the other kids to that book! Don't you know that the ACLU will sue you?!"

Kids should take their Bibles to school every single day of the week. They have the right, the privilege, and the freedom as a United States citizen to carry their Bibles anywhere they please. Don't you forget that! They're doing enough to remove the Bible from public settings; don't you dare help them.

TIME-OUT: THE PUBLIC EXPERIMENT

Let me ask you to take part in an experiment. Go somewhere public with your Bible this week. Blame it on me if things go sideways fast, and maybe we'll make a video about it. Take your Bible where there are a lot of folks around, and just lay it right in the middle of the table. Then stand back and video the reaction; you don't even have to draw attention to it. You'll see folks walking by with the most disturbed expressions as if thinking, "What on earth is this doing here?" And they'll look around all nervous like it was some sort of illegal contraband.

People freak out when they see a Bible in public because that's how the devil wants them to react, and we only have ourselves to blame. Sometimes, I'll carry the Bible into a public place just to send a message. I hope you'll join me in taking back some public territory for the Word of God.

There's a well-known bar in town called the Rusty Nail. I've been in it just once, and it wasn't to drink, praise God. It was about 1:30 in the morning, and the place was packed tighter than a tick. We had a guy in our church who was in his fifth marriage. He kept running through women because he wouldn't quit drinking. His new wife called me pleading for help one night, just squalling, and that was it. I had begged that man and warned him that I would embarrass him on the spot the next time he went in there, so it was go time.

I put on a little tie, grabbed the biggest leather-bound Bible I own, and walked right through the front door of the Rusty Nail. When our eyes met, you would have thought that dude stepped in something. He knew something was up when, at 1:30 a.m., the preacher came walking in with a giant family Bible under his arm.

I wasn't nearly as bold back then as I am now. I should have shouted to the crowd, "Hey, is it open mic night? Let me chitchat with all you good folks for a little bit. Praise God!" Nonetheless, I made sure that my Bible was easily seen by all, and you should have seen their reactions. It was both hilarious and disturbing. People are afraid of the Bible, and some even hate it because it's a mirror.

Did you know that some Christian writers and pastors avoid mentioning the blood of Jesus because it makes people feel bad? They don't want anyone to feel like a sinner, even though they are. They don't want to risk hurting people's feelings because they might lose a nickel or a nose, so they don't use heavy biblical words like *abomination*. I can hear them in their circles saying, "Oh, my goodness, *abomination*? No. I don't think so. Let's just call it an alternative lifestyle. That sounds better. And we don't want to use judgmental words like *adultery*. It creeps me out when I feel that chill go through the congregation when someone slips and says the 'A-word.' We've got to be more careful! Let's just call it an extramarital affair."

People don't want to call it what it is, so they try to rename everything. It's revisionist reality. That's the real pandemic. We have to strip it down to the bare foundation and get back to the naked truth. We need to get back to saying what God says about an issue so we can deal with it the way the Bible says to deal with it. We need to use biblical terms and call sin what God calls it because only the mirror of His Word can show us the unvarnished truth about it all.

THE BIBLE IS A SEED

> He also that received seed among the thorns is he that heareth the word; and the care of this world, and the deceitfulness of riches, choke the word, and he becometh unfruitful. But he that received seed into the good ground is he that heareth the word, and understandeth it; which also beareth fruit, and bringeth forth, some an hundredfold, some sixty, some thirty.
>
> —JESUS (MATTHEW 13:22–23)

One of the most loaded parables Jesus ever uttered, the parable of the sower recorded in Matthew chapter 13, tells of a man who went out and sowed good seed, which represents the Word of God. Once we receive this seed, we, in turn, are compelled by the Spirit and the Bible to sow good seed wherever we go. Psalm 126:6 says, "He that goeth forth and weepeth, bearing precious seed, shall doubtless come again with rejoicing, bringing his sheaves with him."

If we want to be successful in our spiritual life, if we want to be kingdom-minded, then we're going to have to sow the seed of the Word of God in our churches, in our homes, at our workplaces, in Dollar General, in our communities, in our nation, on social media, and everywhere else we go. We have to sow the seed of the Word of God. We're not responsible for what happens to the seed because some plant and sow, and some water and nourish, but God gives the increase (1 Cor. 3:7). God produces the results and saves the souls; we just sow the seed. That's our primary role in the rescue mission, and we don't even have to travel overseas to do it. We can do it right where we are, wherever we are, no matter the time of the day or day of the week. We're supposed to be seed scatterers for the kingdom of God.

Isaiah 55:11 says that God's Word will not return to Him void and will accomplish what He set out to do. You will never share the Word of God and find it coming back void or invalid. You may not immediately see its effect because the seed is planted in the soil of the heart. If the soil doesn't reject the seed, the seed will inevitably grow. People have been saved twenty and thirty years after their mama or their preacher sowed the seed into them. I know of people who went forty years ignoring God, and suddenly, they remembered a sermon they heard as a kid and knew God was calling them. These occurrences aren't coincidences. They're divine providence, the call of Christ.

THE BIBLE IS A LAMP

Thy word is a lamp unto my feet, and a light unto my path.
—PSALM 119:105

They didn't have iPhones with built-in flashlights back when the Bible was written. They didn't have Edison bulbs or streetlights either. It was dark as a dungeon along those winding roads and narrow paths. They didn't have concrete or asphalt, and in the Middle East, they didn't even have much gravel. These roads were bumpy and very difficult to navigate in the dark. Historians tell us that, during the time of King David, night travelers and warriors would wear shoes fixed with small lamps or candles. That was some high-tech stuff back in the day. They'd have these little candles on their shoes to free their hands for a journey, and they were just bright enough for the next step.

Our problem is that we want to know where God wants us to be in six weeks or six years, while most don't even know where God wants us in the next six seconds. The Bible is a lamp unto your feet and a light unto your path. As we journey through these dark days, there are going to be holes, there are going to be rocks, and there are going to be stumbling blocks that might break an ankle or sprain a knee if we don't know where our next step will fall.

The Bible is a lamp that shows the way for every step we take, especially the next one. The steps of a good man are ordered by the Lord (Ps. 37:23), and the *stops* of a good man are ordered by the Lord as well. He shows me the way. He lights and illuminates my pathway. The days are getting exceedingly dark, and I believe one of the major problems in the church is that our eyes are getting comfortable with it. Our eyes are adjusting to the darkness. Instead of allowing the Word of God to light the way, we're tolerating darkness and losing our way. If we want to navigate out of this darkness, we must light our lamps, the Word of God, and take each delicate step in its light.

THE BIBLE IS A TREASURE

The fear of the LORD is clean, enduring for ever: the judgments of the LORD are true and righteous altogether. More to be desired are they than gold, yea, than much fine gold: sweeter also than honey and the honeycomb.
—PSALM 19:9–10

The Bible tells us that the Word of God is more valuable than gold, more valuable than silver, and more valuable (and *sweeter*) than the honeycomb. Do you consider the Bible a treasure? It's not a Marvel comic book, it's not a phone book, and it's not a novel. It's the living Word of God. The content of the Bible is so valuable that it's invaluable. It is without question the most valuable book in the history of the world—not for what it costs in the bookstore, but for what it cost to get it. Sometimes we forget how much blood has been shed to get the Bible into our hands all these centuries after Jesus finished it, and it neither started nor ended with the most precious blood of Jesus. Many have shed their blood and given their lives to ensure we could read the Bible.

For most of its existence, the Bible wasn't available in English or any other common language. The Bibles that common people throughout history would have seen chained to the altar at a cathedral or heard recited by a priest were written mostly in Latin, the ancient language that died along with the Roman Empire during the fifth and sixth centuries.

For the next thousand years, by the dictate of the Roman Catholic Church, the Bible was produced primarily as a version we call the *Latin Vulgate*. By doing so, the Vatican ensured that only those in the elite Catholic hierarchy (who still learned Latin) could decipher what the Word of God said. Only popes, cardinals, bishops, priests, monks, and whoever else they appointed could possess a Bible or read the Word of God. Even worse, they would only read it publicly during a sermon, and the people would listen to the reading in a language they didn't even know.

Can you imagine going to a church that hid the Word like that? After their Latin reading of the Word, they finished their sermons in the common language while sticking to a mostly scripted commentary (produced and distributed by the Vatican) that seldom explored the Latin text through the lens of Christ. At the same time, they made it illegal to translate the Bible into any common language, which made home churches or even personal study impossible (and, in effect, illegal). They simply didn't want people reading the Bible for themselves. They liked the total control they gained by owning that treasure and keeping it from the masses.

TIME-OUT: A TREASURE LONG BURIED

As we pause to look at the rich and painful history of the Bible as a treasure, I want to acknowledge that some Catholics are devout followers of Jesus, and they're working hard as secret agents, as it were, to change things from the inside out. If you are still loyal to religious organizations like the Vatican, I believe you are finally being made free by the truth. Otherwise, you wouldn't have reached this point in this book. I love Catholics just like I love Mormons and Muslims. It's the misuse and abuse of the holy Scripture, and thereby the children of God, that I hate.

Many of our people at Global Vision were raised in these religions, including several of my staff, and I thank God for their deliverance through the one true gospel. If you still identify as a Catholic, please don't take my commentary as an assault against you and your ancestry. I'm just a messenger and a watchman on the wall, and I love you enough to give you the unvarnished biblical/historical truth, so please don't bail now! The Bible is a treasure, and it's important that you know the beautifully painful acts God did to finally put this treasure in our hands.

THE RISE OF THE VATICAN MONARCHY

Following the collapse of the Roman Empire, powers at the Vatican had the people enslaved to a heretical form of Catholicism, and they knew all too well that the Bible would expose them if they ever learned the actual Word of God. The Dark Ages had begun, and they began their thousand-year campaign to keep commoners in the dark and ensure they could never put on the armor of God and draw the sword of the Spirit to remove them from power. We can't wield what we do not know, so—just as the media and corrupt government officials do today—they hid the truth and controlled the masses with lies. Because of this wickedness, for most of Western history, the people heard little more than the false and perverted doctrines (lies) of the elitists in the Vatican. That's still a very real problem in Catholicism today.

We must never mix the doctrine of men with the Word of God, but the popes have built an empire doing just that. I'm not writing a book about the dark history and continued heresies in the various "religions" that misappropriate the gospel and the Bible, so I'll save that subject for another writer or another day. The bloodthirsty inquisitions, the ongoing practice of demonic rituals, the plague of institutionalized pedophilia, and their continued global-elitist corruption are finally exposing these institutions for what they are. However, what I do want to discuss are the acts of the saints who put on the whole armor of God and risked all to fight for our right to hear, read, and know the treasure that is the actual Word of God—the sword of the Spirit—for themselves.

CASE STUDY: FINDING THE TREASURE

During the Protestant Reformation of the sixteenth century, protestors like Martin Luther and his contemporaries around Europe went to war against the Vatican, and their defiant (and ironic) battle cry was *Sola Scriptura!*—which is Latin for Scripture Alone. Since those days, many thousands have been hunted down and executed as they fought for the Word of God because the enemy is hell-bent on keeping the sword of the Spirit out of our hands.

The Bible says we've got to get our theology from the Bible and only the Bible, Sola Scriptura. We must get our truth from the Bible, the whole Bible, and nothing but the Bible—not from what Greg Locke tells you, not from what Global Vision tells you, and certainly not from a perverse pope and his small club of elitist men who dress like women.

While Martin Luther was setting Germany on fire by translating the Word of God into their common language, a priest named William Tyndale came onto the scene to ensure England took part in this revival of God's Word. If you're not a history buff, his name might be more familiar to you as the namesake of Tyndale Publishing House. The Oxford- and Cambridge-educated priest had mastery over eight languages and was widely considered one of the greatest minds of his day.

Despite all this worldly favor, Tyndale stood with Luther to defy the Roman Catholic Church that trained them. He basically said, "I don't give two flips of a wooden nickel what you clowns at the Vatican think about your heretical doctrine or your indulgences. I don't care about confessing to men in a phone booth to receive forgiveness or about the Catholic Church being the only way to salvation. I'm gonna print the Bible in the English language even if it kills me."

So Tyndale got busy with his English translation and eventually acquired the newly invented Gutenberg press to ensure even the poor could finally hold the Word of God. This guy was a certified genius, and he began to get as much of the Bible into the hands of common people as fast as he could. He, of course, started with the Gospels and the New Testament. As you might expect, revival broke loose. Can you imagine what it was like for people to finally be able to hold a Bible in their own hands, in their own homes, and to read it in their own language for the first time? Please try to imagine the feeling and remember that feeling the next time you see one of your dusty, unused Bibles lying under your bed.

At this point, the Roman Catholic Church told Tyndale that he would be labeled a heretic for disobeying the Vatican. No surprise there. They said, "If

209

you keep it up, we're going to burn you at the stake in front of your wife, your kids, and anyone else who wants to watch." Many of us can relate to that evil intimidation tactic in these dark days.

I get that threat from anonymous cowards every week, but I still can't relate to how it must feel when you know it will probably happen. Tyndale knew. I've mentioned this several times throughout this book, and I'll keep repeating it in all my writings to ensure we never forget: Over the past two thousand years, more saints than we can count have died horrific deaths so that we could hold the Bible. You'd better appreciate that.

I believe everyone should read *Foxe's Book of Martyrs*. Knowing how many devout men and women of God have been tortured to death for defending the true Word of God will make you want to go bear hunting with a switch. I know it does that for me. It's unimaginable what people did so that you and I can have the Bible, but they should inspire us to value this treasure even more.

TYNDALE'S LEGACY

In the face of real death threats, the man of God, William Tyndale, basically said, "Whatever! I'm just going to keep printing it!" He had escaped to mainland Europe but knew his days were numbered. So he kept translating and printed and smuggled as many copies of his translation back to England as he could (thousands by most accounts) before they finally hunted him down and arrested him.

Agents of the church were able to convince King Henry VIII that Tyndale was public enemy number one to England, so they locked him away in the worst of prisons before conducting his public execution. His wife, kids, and the whole town showed up, and agents of the church were there in force, all turning down their thumbs on Tyndale as they set him on fire in the public square. History tells us that his flesh was already burning when a wind rose and put the fire out. That ticked off his inquisitors all the more, so they had the executioners wrap a chain around his neck to finish him off.

Through it all, his wife and kids continued singing hymns from the sidelines because Tyndale had told them, "Don't weep for me. I'm doing God's work!" So the executioners took hold of the chain wrapped around his neck to choke the life out of him, all for putting the Bible in the commoner's language. However, Tyndale wasn't dead yet, so the story doesn't end there.

As they were wrapping that chain around his neck—with all the bishops and their hierarchies there to relish the fact that this man, this instigating troublemaker, this rogue Bible printer, this government-defying insurrectionist, was about to die a horrible death—William Tyndale opened his mouth with great zeal and said, "Lord! Open the King of England's eyes." Then they quickly choked him to death.

Seventy-five years later, in 1611, King James I finally put the full Bible in the commoner's language. He agreed that the Roman Catholic Church had no right to keep it veiled in the Vatican and chained up in their altars. Thanks to the revival started by Tyndale, King James decided to assemble a massive team of scholars to finish his work, and they used the Tyndale Bible as a primary source. The King James Bible we read today is the product of that beautifully painful chain of events inspired and empowered by the Holy Spirit. When a man or woman of God puts on the whole armor of God and wields the sword of the Spirit for the sake of the least, they can change the world.

LOVING THE BIBLE

Now the Holy Spirit is calling *us* to the front lines of the battle to preserve His sacred treasure. Dark forces controlled by the devil continue to twist it, hide it, chain it, and even eradicate it wherever they can, so this is our due season. Do you sense the urgency yet? Are you willing to contend for the faith before we find ourselves in a modern-day government-imposed inquisition? It's coming, and from my perspective, it has already begun, so we'd better armor up.

When I hold the Bible in my hand, I believe I hold the complete, inerrant, perfect Word of Almighty God—from Genesis 1:1 to Revelation 22:21—from the beginning to the end. All 791,328 words, all 31,101 verses, and all 1,189 chapters. It is written! It is written! It is written! This is the living Word of Almighty God!

I worked with a young man in Nigeria, West Africa, by the name of O'Drew. He was my interpreter while I was preaching there; at the time, he was just twenty-six. I'll never forget O'Drew. Every time we stood to preach, just before we started, he would always kiss his Bible for all to see. I'll never get over what that sincere display of love for the Bible did to me. It was convicting. That young man treasured the Word of God, and there is no doubt about that. I pray we also treasure it like O'Drew—and like Tyndale. It doesn't matter who you are, where you live, how much you make, or how many friends you have on social media. Just love the Bible out loud wherever you go and see what God does.

May we all love, value, and esteem it highly—at home and in public—for Christ's sake and our own. That's how we wield the sword of the Spirit in battle. Speak it, bring it, read it, hold it, digest it, spread it, plant it, apply it, obey it, and love it. Drink it up and pour it out. Use the double-edged sword defensively and offensively as the Holy Spirit leads you, no matter what people, the church, or the government say about you or how they threaten you. Stand firm in battle with Scripture alone—sola scriptura—the sword of the Spirit, the Word of God.

> It is written, Man shall not live by bread alone, but by every word that proceedeth out of the mouth of God.
>
> —JESUS (MATTHEW 4:4)

CHAPTER TWENTY

Prayer

Watch and pray, that ye enter not into temptation: the
spirit indeed is willing, but the flesh is weak.
—JESUS (MATTHEW 26:41)

GOD GAVE ALL of us free will to weave through this tangled reality as we approach the end of the Bible's prophetic timeline, and each of us must choose whether we serve Him or serve ourselves, whether we'll armor up or fall away. As we've unpacked the power and the process of putting on each supernatural piece of armor—each weapon of our warfare—I trust you've committed to following through on each. Make sure you don't let yourself feel overwhelmed. Ultimately, it all boils down to being Christlike, but don't be mistaken. The Lord wasn't just waxing poetic when He gave us His armor with such powerful words.

The fact that all His instructions aim to lead you home to Him should be all the motivation you need. He's our loving Father, and He wants to bless our socks off. We need to maintain an ongoing conversation with God through every transformative step. We need to pray continually.

If reading this book has opened your eyes and caused you to finally put on the armor of God, you may already feel its transformative power. That's kingdom power from the King. As you put it all on, the Holy Spirit expands in you, your faith grows, and you begin to walk in His power twenty-four/seven. I hope you want that because the enemy is still on the prowl. Just because we're coming to the end of this book doesn't mean we're approaching the end of the spiritual war. We're just getting started. Now let's discuss how to fully activate the armor and keep it that way.

> Praying always with all prayer and supplication in the Spirit, and watching thereunto with all perseverance and supplication for all saints.
> —EPHESIANS 6:18

As I begin this chapter on the armor activator that is prayer, notice that the final verse from the armor discourse concludes with the words *all saints*. The Lord wants to ensure we realize that the act of putting on the armor of God is designed not just for ourselves as individuals but also for the corporate gathering of the body. The more we realize we are in this spiritual war together, the more we need to pray together in the Spirit. That's why the unity of the body of Christ is so very crucial. That's why it's so very powerful.

Knowing that I'm not alone in this fight keeps me inspired. I'm in this with you, and you're in this with me. We, the saints, are all in this together, just as the Lord repeatedly tells us. Though one person alone can do a lot when armored up, a bunch of us working together can turn the world upside down with the gospel of Jesus Christ.

One glaring problem at the core of all other problems in the church is the simple fact that we can't figure out how to get along and work together for the sake of the gospel. It has never truly happened. We may not have the same traditions, tastes, or personalities as individuals and individual churches, but there's no need to disagree on any of that. As long as we all believe the same foundational truths of the Bible and fully agree on who Jesus is, we should be able to unite and get along. We may have different philosophical approaches to things, but if Jesus is our common denominator, we should be eager to armor up, put aside our differences, and join forces in the war against evil. To that end, let's commit to embracing our fellowship as saints and recognize why He calls us to pray for each other and all believers around the world.

Once the armor is properly put on, it can only effectively serve its purpose by getting properly activated and appropriated for specific applications. In our study of Ephesians 6:10, we learned that the indwelling of the Holy Spirit is the power source for the armor, but the Holy Spirit doesn't just take us over like we're some sort of remote-controlled drone without a brain. Remember, we're talking about God. He is indeed in control, but we must do our part where spiritual warfare is concerned. We must activate the power source with the act of prayer. This isn't religion to practice like robots. It's the divine design of God to walk out as heirs, and it's incredibly beautiful.

THE IRON MAN ANALOGY

Pardon me for often using analogies from Marvel movies, but most of you have seen a few of them or are aware of their characters from the comic books, so I believe they serve well in speeding up your learning curve. Consider the Iron Man suit. It's a great-looking suit. It's a powerful-looking suit. But in the context of the storyline, it's nothing but a clunky metal costume until he puts that arc-reactor power source right in the middle of the breastplate.

If you've seen the Iron Man movies, you can probably imagine the "power up" sound effect of the arc-reactor when it starts firing up in his suit. In the films, we learn that the suit is powerless until Iron Man plugs it in and gets it all lit up. With this analogy in mind, prayer is the act of powering up the whole armor of God for battle. Prayer does this by accessing the power of the Holy Spirit within us. Prayer lights up the armor and activates the power to do the miraculous. That might seem like a silly analogy, but it works, and my whole family gets a kick out of the Iron Man movies, so please roll with me.

PRAYING ALWAYS

In the context of our key verse, God says you can have all this beautiful, shiny, strengthened steel all over your body, but it won't be activated until you start "praying always." Praying "without ceasing" will light you up (1 Thess. 5:17)! "Praying always with all prayer and supplication" will fire up your spirit, and the Holy Spirit responds in kind. If we are powerless, it's because we are prayerless. God said we must pray always. Not sometimes. Not now and again. Not even most of the time, and certainly not just when asked to pray by others, but always.

I know why the church in America is powerless and doesn't have enough Holy Spirit infusion to blow the fuzz off a small peanut. It isn't because we lack programs or the tools to reach people. We have plenty of programs and ministries and different types of Bibles and best-selling books to buy. We have plenty of high-tech stuff like big screens and live streams to give them all the multimedia pizzazz anyone could ever want. In this generation, we have more access to the truth of the gospel through social media and technology than at any other time in the history of the world. Yet the church in America, spiritually speaking, is dead as a nail without a hammer.

We are weak, we are anemic, and we are powerless. We talk about turning the world upside down, but we can't even turn Waffle House upside down. The reason? The church no longer prays. Not really, and not always. God said we need to be an always-praying church, not an always-playing church. We are called to pray for each other no matter where we are, whether alone in our prayer closet, out there in the streets with those in need, or corporately as we congregate in church and other gatherings.

In Luke 18:1, Jesus said, "Men ought always to pray, and not to faint." I used to wonder why God mentions praying and fainting in the same verse, but not anymore. If you've ever prayed alone where no one can hear or see you, the devil will try to make you sleepy. If you have insomnia, let me tell you how to fix that. Just start praying and reading your Bible. The devil will make sure you get sleepy. How's that for a sobering truth? Before you know it, you'll be nodding off. If you can't sleep on a given night and decide to watch Netflix in response, you'll stay awake until four o'clock. But if you just start reading your Bible, your head will bob like a chicken pecking corn before you can finish two chapters. The devil knows a praying Christian is a powerful Christian, so he'll fire all the arrows needed to keep you from praying always. Whenever you brush off prayer, you know the devil has found his mark.

PRAYING IN HUMILITY

In the context of prayer, Jesus said, "Everyone that exalteth himself shall be abased; and he that humbleth himself shall be exalted" (Luke 18:14). First, we're reminded that prideful, self-glorifying (or crowd-pleasing) prayers are powerless, and will ultimately cast us down. Then we learn that prayers from a humble (meek) spirit will elevate and fill us with power.

There's nothing like a sincerely humble connection with God. In the Sermon on the Mount, when Jesus told us the meek would inherit the earth (Matt. 5:5), He was pointing to the blessings we receive in this life when we establish that humble connection to Him in all we do, especially during our prayer time. Once your prayers are grounded in selfless humility, whether alone in your quiet time or standing before dozens or thousands in a corporate setting, it will light a fire in you that activates the rest of the armor.

When you're always praying in the right spirit, the sword of the Spirit becomes more amazing. When you're always praying with a humble spirit, you're always growing your faith. When you're always praying, you have full confidence in your salvation. When you're always praying, you'll start sharing the gospel with bold excitement as you walk through your day. When you're always praying, you'll stand in greater righteousness and truth as you transform and tune your mind to the mind of Christ (Rom. 12:2, Phil. 2:2–5). When you're always praying as led by the Spirit (and never for the approval of men), the armor of God is always active, and the Word of God is full of power in your heart and your hands. Our Father knows exactly what we need. We're the ones who need clarity, and that is only found in Him.

HOW NOT TO PRAY

> But thou, when thou prayest, enter into thy closet, and when thou hast shut thy door, pray to thy Father which is in secret; and thy Father which seeth in secret shall reward thee openly. But when ye pray, use not vain repetitions, as the heathen do: for they think that they shall be heard for their much speaking. Be not ye therefore like unto them: for your Father knoweth what things ye have need of, before ye ask him.
>
> —JESUS (MATTHEW 6:6–8)

I could write a full chapter about the sin of using vain repetitions—memorized rote prayers and other long, lifeless, flowery words spoken with a religious spirit—but I won't. When Jesus Himself says *not* to do something, you'd think every follower would realize it is a mic-drop command, yet many pray that way following their denominational doctrine, and that's a mind-blowing error.

Some of my staff raised in the Catholic faith tell stories of confessing their sins to a priest in a phone booth and being instructed that to receive forgiveness, they had to kneel and pray "ten Our Fathers and twelve Hail Marys" or even larger numbers depending on the severity of their sins. In addition to the gross error of that counterfeit path to forgiveness, if ever there was an example of a "vain repetition," that is surely it.

We should memorize Scripture for use in many settings, and prayer time is indeed one of them, but converting Scripture into vain rote babbling is not acceptable to the Lord. And before you Evangelicals pooch your lips out, we're not much better in that regard. We need to stop speaking all these short, lifeless, memorized pseudo-prayers over meals and at bedtime. Those are also "vain repetitions," right?

WHAT ABOUT THE LORD'S PRAYER?

I know that nearly all Christians traditionally use an adaptation of the Lord's Prayer (Matt. 6:9–13) in all sorts of settings, and I'll admit that there is something beautiful about it when spoken with sincerity and a real connection to the meaning of each word. But it's still a vain repetition when it's not. Its public use is a carryover from our Catholic roots, as that's the rote "Our Father" prayer used in their confessional rituals noted above. In the Sermon on the Mount, Jesus delivered that prayer to instruct the crowd on how to pray, not what to pray. It is correctly considered to be a brief model prayer, a framework for the intimacy, intent, and humility we should express while we pray. That said, it may be the most memorized scripture passage in the Bible, so I'll never dismiss its power and impact when used as a sincere prayer, but I have to discourage its use as a rote repetition in all but the most secular public settings.

When I hear many voices rise in unison to recite the Lord's Prayer in the right spirit, it can be especially inspiring and moving, so I get it. I well up with tears nearly every time I say it. But Jesus told us not to pray anything to impress those listening, so it's a dangerous practice in that sense. He doesn't even count it as prayer unless it's spoken (or groaned within; see Romans 8:26) for an audience of one—God Himself.

Jesus reminds us that He already knows what we need and what we should ask for, so prayer is your opportunity to make sure *you* know what those needs are and honestly, intimately, and transparently lay them before the Lord. Prayer must be born of your heart, spirit, and fully focused mind, not your memorization skills.

HOW TO PRAY

When you start praying with this degree of seriousness, you'll find yourself thinking about a thousand different things, and it will be difficult to focus on God. Don't let that discourage you. God knows your heart and every thought in your mind. He'll honor your effort if you're committed to growing your personal relationship with Him through your prayer time. Like Mr. Miyagi from the *Karate Kid* movie used to say, "Your focus needs more focus," right?

While it can feel like a struggle early on, if your heart is in the right place, you'll start to recognize the body posture and locations where you can overcome the distractions and take every thought captive to focus on the Lord.

This is the deepest meaning of the "prayer closet" Jesus speaks of in the passage from the Sermon on the Mount (Matt. 6:6–8). Yes, an actual physical prayer closet is beautiful when used in the right spirit, but your prayer closet can exist anywhere at any time if you're willing. In the context of Jesus' sermon, the actual closet is found through the door to our inner temple— our heart, mind, soul, and spirit—the essence of who we are, as discussed in our study of the breastplate of righteousness. The closet is the metaphor Jesus uses for "the secret place" that we see so beautifully portrayed in Psalm 91. We can and must go there whenever we pray, even in corporate settings, which, I admit, can be a challenge even for a seasoned preacher like me. It can take some practice, but if you're coming from a place of faithful humility, you'll eventually master how to close the door to your inner closet—your secret place—even when praying before thousands.

WHY MOST FOLKS DON'T "PRAY ALWAYS"

I realize that not everyone can kneel beside a bed for two hours and call out to God the entire time. Some of you have that spiritual gift and thank God for it. But some of us have ADHD issues. Some of us deal with so much activity and uncertainty in our daily lives that we have to do something physical to calm our bodies (our temples) and clear our minds before we can close the door and truly pray. We know by now that those distractions are among the devil's favorite darts, so we must counter them through righteous means.

I go on a run or a brisk walk or take a hard ride on my bicycle before I get alone with God in my closet for prolonged personal prayer. I've learned many such approaches that help me get "more focus in my focus" for every type of prayer, personal or corporate, so if you're like me in the ADHD department, I encourage you to find approaches that work for you. You might think, "I can't believe a pastor like Greg Locke has trouble focusing during prayer." Well, I did, so don't roll your eyes at me. I know most of you get distracted just like me, and I know that's why you're not always praying.

The reality is that most folks—like most churches—struggle to pray without ceasing, and that's why we're powerless. And what is true of the body is true of its members. You might start with great intentions, but before you know it, you'll find that you went several days or weeks without getting alone with God in prayer even once. That's why our marriages are in a mess. That's why our kids are losing faith. That's why addiction and depression are at an all-time high. Through the devil's deceptions and distractions, folks tend to accept a life of misery even when they know the answers and the power to overcome are found by always praying in God's presence—without ceasing. We all know it, but few do it.

OUT OF TIME?

Some people don't pray because their lives are too busy. To that, I say, "Join the club." I have kids and pets. I have ministry responsibilities and a busy job. We all have busyness to deal with, and there's a simple solution: get honest with yourself and make the time. You know better, and so does God. Flip the script, and instead of telling yourself you can't afford to make time for prayer without ceasing, tell yourself you can't afford *not* to.

I bet you'd hate for me to look through your phone and look up your screen-time stats. That little app that tells us our screen time is the most convicting tool I've ever found in a phone. When you look at how much time you spend on your phone every day, it should embarrass you. It should humble you. And it should drive you to repent for all the prayer time you've lost to the enemy.

Some of you spend three and a half hours on Facebook every day. Some of you spend more. Don't you realize the Lord knows what you're filling up with while neglecting your time with Him? Don't you know He knows you could get out of Facebook and get your face in His book or seek His face in prayer?

I'll never forget when I checked my app and shouted, "What? I just spent two and a half hours on Twitter?" When that happened, I immediately knew the Holy Spirit was telling me to stop choosing Twitter over the prayer closet. I could have rationalized that it's part of my job as a preacher and social media commentator, but that would be weak. If I can't do my job without stealing from my time alone with God, I need to cut back or cut it out entirely.

What are you allowing to eat up all your time with the Lord? A hobby? Netflix? Sports programming? The mainstream media and news? Something dark and shameful that you'd never want to admit? Or is it just your job? Once we put on the belt of truth to get honest with ourselves about this critical issue, we should quickly realize we have plenty of time throughout the day to shut out the world, the other voices, and our flesh to get alone in prayer with God. Just as the individual pieces of the armor can't work without the activating power of prayer, praying always isn't possible unless you've put on every piece of the armor. So get honest, hunger for His righteousness, walk in the gospel, celebrate your salvation, grow your faith, and let the Word of God have its way with you. Do these, and you'll start praying by default—and the demons will fear you.

CORPORATE PRAYER

Some denominational people think it's strange when we gather and break into groups for corporate prayer in the middle of a church service—especially when it's live streamed. When we pray, we don't care who's watching or listening. We don't care who's here visiting, and we don't care who jumped online expecting something else.

Our people agree that we are powerless unless we're always praying. It's our most beautiful and tender time with the Lord in a corporate setting all week. People will gather in groups or sit alone to pray for others—including our online members who send in prayer requests—while others just pour down and get down low around the altar to enter their prayer closet in transparent humility.

Whatever the posture, we all start calling out to God and praying in unison, wide open, like no one else was there but God and the souls we're praying for. Sometimes visitors or folks online are like, "Doesn't that make people uncomfortable?" Oh, yes. That's why we do it! We've learned all too well how to get so very comfortable at church, haven't we? We have our heat and air, our padded chairs, and our lights and music all tuned to make us feel cozy and insulated.

I used to wonder what would happen if we ripped away all the comforts and just got some folding chairs. Would people come back the next week? Then the chaos of 2020 revealed we had a core membership that would show up to worship the Lord and study the Word even if they had to stand in a driving rainstorm—which literally happened—on Easter Sunday, no less. Yes, a lot of comfort-seekers and lukewarm believers suddenly felt out of place, but for every family that left us, ten more drove in from around the country to take their place.

Born-again children of God will go to great lengths to fight a good fight, and I'm still amazed how the Lord has blessed Global Vision with people from all over North America—and all over the world—to take part in a church that is always praying, come what may, regardless of the comforts or lack thereof. Read *This Means War* for the amazing full story of how revival broke out at our church when 99.9 percent of the churches in America were shut down. A church alive is worth the drive!

CASE STUDY: THIRD-WORLD HUNGER

Do you know why the living church in third-world nations is lit on fire right now? It's because they don't care about their comfort or the condition of their buildings. They only care about growing their faith and experiencing the presence of God. Once they gather, they pray, and they pray, and they pray. The first time I went to Ghana in 2001, I was preaching in a little Ghanaian village on New Year's Eve, shortly after the events of 9/11. Though I was still in my twenties, I was already a preaching machine, and I was excited. I was lit up in the Spirit, but being in a non-English-speaking culture, I needed an interrupter (I mean an interpreter).

I would speak in small chunks, and then the interpreter would immediately repeat what I said in their language. That back-and-forth process continued to the very end of the message. What's crazy is that when I would say two or three short little sentences, he would often rattle on and on for what seemed like a paragraph or two. I'd be standing there, silently thinking, "What on earth? I didn't say all that. There is no way I said all that!" And then I could quote a whole passage only to hear him utter five syllables! As odd as that was, it wasn't even close to being the most unusual part of that first-time experience. That honor goes to what happened when I finished my sermon— at midnight.

Because it was a New Year's Eve service designed to have me preach out the old year and preach in the new, the service didn't start until 10 p.m. I intentionally preached until about 12:10 a.m. I figured midnight plus ten minutes would take care of the symbolism of the gathering. It was a tiny little building, and they had two hundred people packed into a small room to hear me preach. It was so tight that even the standing space was completely used up. When I was finished, I was completely worn out. Preaching with an interpreter is exhausting in and of itself, but I had already preached several times that day, and this was the grand finale for me. So I closed my Bible and prepared to exit the platform, but a particular deacon had other plans. During the services at this church, it was his job to come down the aisle and poke you in the back of your head with a long stick if you nodded off.

I remember thinking about the many churches back in the States that need one of those sticks, right? Nonetheless, once the deacon with the little stick realized I was ready to leave, he perked up and said, "Mr. Greg? Mr. Greg! Encore, encore, encore!"

CRAZY PEOPLE

I was still a carnal twenty-something back then, and I thought, "It's 12:10, deacon. I ain't gonna encore anybody! What are you talking about with all this encore nonsense?" But there I was at 12:15 in the morning, and everybody began chiming in with, "Encore! Encore!" I'll never forget the feeling when I realized I would have to preach again and that it would be at least 1:30 in the morning before I'd be heading back to my hotel. What's worse was remembering that I still had a two-hour drive across Ghana before I'd get to the place I was staying, and I had to be up by 7 a.m. to start preaching in five different churches that day. All I could think was, "You people are crazy. Don't y'all ever sleep?" Yep, they were crazy—crazy about Jesus.

So I preached till 1:30 in the morning, and when I finally got in the car to start our trip back to my lodging, the man in the car waiting for me said, "Pastor Greg, we're going to have a prayer meeting!"

And I said, "Brother, I don't know where you've been hiding, but we just left the prayer meeting."

But then he said, "No, in the car. We're going to have a prayer meeting in the car."

And I'm thinking, "We're going to have a sleep meeting, Jack. I've been preaching all day, and it's 1:30 in the morning. You are out of your mind!" Some things you think, but you just don't say, right?

For the entire two-hour trip, those men prayed, cried, and called out to God! I don't know if I've ever felt as small as I did that New Year's Eve. There I was, wishing I was asleep while these faith-filled men were just whooping it up, calling down fire, and having an amazing time in the Lord.

IT'S ALL ON US

It's no wonder that the entire New Year's Day experience changed me. You could have walked into that church and just said "boo," and half the crowd would have gotten born again. There was real power, enthusiasm, encouragement, and hunger for prayer in that room. I could have walked on the stage, quoted one verse, and three people would have run the aisle.

Does that give you a glimpse into why the American church is so powerless? Those people love to pray always; in contrast, we're prayerless. At Global Vision, we will always be a church of bold preaching, but we have learned that becoming an unapologetic, unashamed church of prayer is even more important. We're going to pray for people! We're going to love people.

We're going to stand in the gap for people. We are going to pray without ceasing. It's the way God wants it. And it's all on us to make it happen.

Even before the lockdowns, 85 percent of Christians were sitting at home every Sunday. Do you know why? Because people are sick of the show. People have grown sick of the religious behavior in church. I've learned that the body of Christ is sick of all the comfort and pretense and just wants the raw truth and real prayer. Most of you just want your pastors to open up and say what needs to be said. You also want to open up the windows of heaven and pray and worship until God shows up, absent a script or a time clock.

Some people think, "Well, my goodness, Pastor Greg, if my preacher gets too fired up, he might go on too long." If you attend live services at Global Vision and think this way, that's cool. We're meeting in a tent right now, so there are a lot of back doors for you to slip through until you finally catch fire like the rest of us.

If that's you, I sincerely hope you come back next week, but don't think I'm ever going back to doing church on your time clock. I'm not looking for nickels and noses. I'm looking for the power of the Holy Spirit. If five people show up, then five people show up. If five thousand people show up, then praise God, five thousand people show up. God gives the increase, so I pray you can get your local pastor to wake up to that reality.

WHEREVER YOU GO

Be sure to realize when God says we should be "Praying always with all prayer," that is not a suggestion. It's a command. He is telling us to pray about everything that warrants our attention. If the thing keeping you from prayer is on your mind that much, you should be praying about it—talking to the Lord about it—not dwelling on it, rehearsing it, re-creating it, rewinding it, and replaying it. I pray about all sorts of stuff you wouldn't assume.

I still ride my bike for fun, but until a few years ago, I was a competitive ultra-endurance mountain biker. Riding a bike across the continent on rough terrain becomes a rolling altar, praise God. So even now I'll be on my bicycle zooming through parks, and I'll pray the Lord will direct me when I get to a fork on the Greenway because if I take the wrong turn, I might accidentally run into someone crazy who hated my last video. Nonetheless, I've learned to love keeping in touch with God in every way possible, no matter where I am or where I go.

If I'm already thinking about something, especially when I'm deliberating over it, it's beautiful and powerful to recognize His presence and ask Him to guide me through the thought processes. That form of prayer helps make sense of His command to pray without ceasing. I'm learning the Holy Spirit is ready to flow through us with wisdom and power as soon as we're ready, even if that's every waking minute of the day.

Sadly, a dying world has lost contact with God. The church must turn from prayerlessness and return to His presence where we belong—always praying without ceasing. I try to be conscious and cognizant of the Holy Spirit at all times—not because I'm uber-spiritual but because I have a massively great God who wants to lead me and guide me through all things, and I can't resist something that I never want to resist.

Walking in constant prayer isn't always possible, but when it is, don't forget to try. As you stay attuned with God, He'll guide you away from temptation, deliver you from evil, stand as your shield, stop the devil's darts, and bring you into opportunities He has ordained for you. It's something He loves to do for everyone who fully armors up.

> He that dwelleth in the secret place of the most High shall abide under the shadow of the Almighty. I will say of the LORD, He is my refuge and my fortress: my God; in him will I trust. Surely he shall deliver thee from the snare of the fowler, and from the noisome pestilence. He shall cover thee with his feathers, and under his wings shalt thou trust: his truth shall be thy shield and buckler. Thou shalt not be afraid for the terror by night; nor for the arrow that flieth by day.
>
> —PSALM 91:1–5

CHAPTER TWENTY-ONE

Prayer: Part 2

Ask, and it shall be given you; seek, and ye shall find; knock, and it shall be opened unto you: For every one that asketh receiveth; and he that seeketh findeth; and to him that knocketh it shall be opened.
—JESUS (MATTHEW 7:7–8)

SOMETIMES FOLKS USE words like *intercession, prayer,* and *supplication* as if they're interchangeable. But they're different aspects of a biblical prayer life. In our opening verse above, Jesus gives us an overarching understanding of prayer. Earlier in history, God told Jeremiah, "Call unto me, and I will answer thee, and show thee great and mighty things, which thou knowest not" (Jer. 33:3). When we pray in this way, we're asking God to meet our personal hopes. In contrast, intercession is the act of praying on behalf of others. So we intercede for others, and we simply ask for ourselves.

The Bible tells us that Jesus was resurrected and ascended to heaven, where He sat down at the right hand of God's majesty to make intercession for us (Rom. 8:34). I find that to be one of the most awesome, amazing, and humbling verses in all the Bible. If you ever feel like no one is praying for you, be reminded that the Lord Jesus is always praying for you. Now that He is in the heavenly dimension—outside space and time—He is always actively involved in our lives. I know that can be difficult to wrap our heads around, but it's true. Jesus is Lord, and He's praying for everyone who calls Him Lord through belief in the gospel. Don't ever minimize that most beautiful reality. If He's praying for you, how serious do you think He is about His instruction that you ask for all you need in His name?

> And whatsoever ye shall ask in my name, that will I do, that the Father may be glorified in the Son.
>
> —JESUS (JOHN 14:13)

SUPPLICATION

Supplication is a word of humility. It's a word of positioning and posturing. It points to getting down before the Lord with a lowly and meek attitude. I currently pray best when I ride my bicycle, when I go on long walks, or when I'm pacing at my personal burning bush that is my tree. Some people pray best in the car, right? On that note, let me add that some people need to pray a lot more when they drive! In all seriousness, here's what I want you to realize. Sometimes, the active moving posture of those prayers won't suffice because we are instead called to deep levels of supplication in stillness.

We pray over our meals, families, and others. We pray when doing something with a purpose. Those most common types of prayers are all very important, but supplication takes prayer to a far more passionate level. You might wonder if you always have to be on your knees when praying. No, you don't, but when you do, it should help you go deeper with the Lord, as kneeling before the Lord—bowing and lowering yourself—is intrinsic to supplication. There are times when we are greatly burdened due to stress or emotional distress or during times of fasting, perhaps. These are instances where prayers of supplication are in order.

You may also know the term *travailing*, which is the most intense form of supplication. In John 16:20–22, Jesus gives us an example by referencing a woman who weeps and laments while suffering severe labor pains. These are the times we are profoundly passionate about something we must endure or when we have an acute need to know the will of God and discern the mind of the Spirit. These are the times that we absolutely should kneel and bow our heads before God our Father (if we are physically able), and sometimes we'll even lay out on our faces, prostrate before the Lord, as did David in his darkest hours (2 Sam. 12:16). Laying out prostrate is simply bowing and kneeling in the most submissive posture possible—face down, flat on the ground. Only these physically humbling postures speak to the proper order of the matter and of who is really in control of the conversation. All of this is humble supplication—getting meek and lowly in the presence of God.

HUMILITY

If my people, who are called by my name, will humble themselves and pray and seek my face and turn from their wicked ways, then I will hear from heaven, and I will forgive their sin and will heal their land.
—2 CHRONICLES 7:14, NIV

Humility is so central to prayer that I'm going to double back on it. It can't be overstated. "God resists the proud, but gives grace to the humble" (1 Pet. 5:5, NKJV) As we consider 2 Chronicles 7:14, we know God was initially speaking to the nation of Israel when He said, "If my people," and some people say, "Well, I'm not an Israelite, so that doesn't apply to me." But God specifically said, "If my people, which are called by my name." You may not have one ounce of Jewish blood in your veins, but if you are called by His name, this verse addresses you and me and everyone else who is born again in the Spirit. This profound verse has become a popular mission statement for the saints in these dark days, but sadly, most pastors are ignoring its implications—even as they recite it.

In this deeply prophetic verse, God says, "If my people, which are called by my name, shall humble themselves." That's the first thing He states in this conditional promise, and that's a huge "if." Then, after requiring humility, He requires three more crucial behaviors: praying, seeking His face, and turning from our wicked ways (repentance). Each of these is vitally important, but you won't be able to do any of them if you don't first humble yourself before God.

From the text, we learn that humility comes before prayer, before seeking His face, and before repentance. We will do none of those with any positive impact if we live in the strength of our flesh and pride. In this state, we cannot put on the armor of God, and the enemy will have his way with us.

IT'S ALL FOR HIM

Some of us are not being used mightily by God or blessed by Him because we can't handle what He wants to give us. Most of us don't have the capacity for real humility in these dark days, and God knows it. He knows that if He blesses us in our fleshly state, we'll become even more arrogant, and God will share His glory with no one. Either He gets the glory, or no one does. That's why I always want to divert praise and glory back to God and would rather take the difficult roads that draw persecution than settle into a comfy-cozy mega-church trajectory where I'd get lots of nauseating pats on my back. To God be the glory, great things He has done!

I didn't open any doors. I didn't do anything to earn a blue checkmark on social media. I don't have any magic sauce or talents deserving of praise. I can do one thing: stand and preach and deliver the truth of the Word of God, and God takes care of everything else. No matter what the haters say on social media, the Lord knows this is true of me. He's the only reason you're reading this book, and I believe you know that. Whatever led you here, the fact that you've made it to the last chapter is proof. My testimony and my biblical revelations can indeed preach, but it's little more than soil for the seed that is the Word of God.

Our humility brings us in direct connection with God, praying always, with supplication. Are our prayers always filled with crying and begging with urgency (travailing)? No. But God said there are times when we must be willing—in strict adherence to humility—to fall before Him and say, "Lord, I'm nothing. I'm a zero with a circle rubbed out. I have nothing to offer. 'Nothing in my hand I bring, but simply to thy cross I cling.'" If we get to a place where we think we can figure it out, or think we can do it, or think we can control it, God will let us try, and we will fall and flail and bounce all over the floor in misery, rottenness, and ruin.

When you think you can do what only God can do, He will allow you to try; He'll turn it into a learning experience for you and those watching you because "There is a way which seemeth right unto a man, but the end thereof are the ways of death" (Prov. 14:12). So don't ever make the mistake of believing God is in your corner just because you pray. Without humility and total submission and surrender to Him and His Word, you're a disaster in the making.

HUMILITY IN RELATIONSHIPS

Have you ever noticed that humility always disarms a battle, even in our relational connections to others? "A soft answer turneth away wrath: but grievous words stir up anger" (Prov. 15:1). Think about the last spat you had with a loved one. A soft answer turns away wrath. I've had men tell me in counseling, "Pastor, my wife just came out firing at me full force." Grievous words stir up anger, sir. All you've got to say is one stupid, hard thing, and you are stirring up the pot of strife in your marriage.

I've taken the time to learn what makes my wife tick, but I also know what ticks her off. If I'm in a distracted, cavalier, Greg Locke mood, it won't be long before I tick her off, and it takes humility to admit I'm wrong and make things right. No doubt, that's hard to do, especially in the heat of the moment. It's hard in any relationship, but especially in a marriage.

Humility isn't something we naturally embrace, and it's seldom our first response in conflict. We want to fire back at someone in conflict no matter how much we love and care about them. And those of you who just close off in conflict, don't confuse that with humility. Passive-aggressive silence is an especially prideful and destructive form of manipulation, and there's nothing humble about it. So, whether you fire back with incendiary words or with icy silence, it's all fleshly pride, and the armor of God is powerless in either case.

HUMILITY IN PUBLIC SETTINGS

We also lack humility in our relationships at work. We're guilty of it in our relationship with our bosses, immediate subordinates, and coworkers that rub us wrong, and all it does is choke the joy and sense of purpose in the workplace. That's why so many of you hate going to work when it should be a primary mission field in your personal ministry. The Lord reminds us that anyone with friends must be friendly (Prov. 18:24). So if you're one of those "I just keep to myself" people, it's time for a correction. If not, don't whine when no one shakes your hand or hugs you at church.

Humility will put you in a position to be a blessing to God and, thereby, to be blessed by God as you've never imagined. Let me slip in a quick word about the sin of paranoia. If you go into a situation already thinking everyone is against you, you're exactly right. They will respond to the negative vibe you are putting out. And when you exhibit a lack of humility, whether through arrogance or passive aggressiveness, they will inevitably come at you with toxic pride of their own. It's one of the more common vicious cycles in this culture. On the flip side, if we're truly humble with one another, it connects us in a way that blesses God. This, in turn, leads Him to bless us well beyond our expectations—if we maintain our posture of humility while praying always to Him.

PRAYING IN THE SPIRIT

Returning to our study of Ephesians 6:18, Paul says, "Praying always with all prayer and supplication, in the Spirit, and watching." Notice that all prayer and supplication must be done in the Spirit. Sometimes you'll feel so beaten down, burdened, discouraged, defeated, depressed, and broken that you need a breakthrough from God. At times like this, you often don't even know what to pray, so the Bible says, "The Spirit itself maketh intercession for us with groanings which cannot be uttered" (Rom. 8:26). Sometimes we get to a place where we simply don't know what to say in prayer. This is when the Holy Spirit of God intercedes and makes supplication for us.

If you're from a cessationist background like me, don't let the phrase "in the Spirit" freak you out. The acts and gifts of the Spirit operating through us have never ceased. So—like me—you need to put away that false doctrine regardless of what Granddad told you. The Bible is clear about this, praise God. You connect to God in your spirit by His Spirit and only by His Spirit, so we must be in tune with the Holy Spirit in our prayer time. This is critically important, so please don't gloss over this. Just remember that the armor is powerless without the indwelling of the Holy Spirit, and so is prayer. The Spirit of God is the power in us and the armor.

PERSEVERING FOR OTHERS

In the final phrase of our key verse, which is the final phrase in the teaching on the whole armor of God, notice that He closes by commanding us to always be "watching thereunto with all perseverance and supplication for all saints." He is telling us to never give up and to never quit, to remain dedicated, committed, and consistent. Sometimes I'm powerless because I haven't been praying about my powerless situation, so I have learned to persevere—praying always in the Spirit.

In the closing instruction of the armor discourse, I'm also told to pray for what you're dealing with. I'm called to intercede for you through your brokenness, disconnectedness, hurt, all the difficult things you are dealing with, and all the fires, waters, and floods you are walking through. He also says to do this with great perseverance, without wanting to quit. Sometimes we persevere in prayer for people for a very long time, only to see them get worse. As a pastor, I've been there often, so I get it.

There have been people that I've intensely prayed would get saved, and all they did was become bigger jerks. Isn't that crazy? There have been situations where I've prayed for a guy to get right with God, and instead, he turned further away from God. There have been times I've prayed for a lady to have a better attitude, and then the bottom falls out, and she develops an even worse attitude. This is why our perseverance is vitally important to our prayer life. We simply can't change people. Only God can change people.

If you walk through life trying to be the Holy Spirit for everybody else, you'll fail miserably, and you'll, in effect, disconnect yourself from God. You are not the Holy Spirit. You are not God. Never tell others how they're supposed to live just because you're praying for them. If you think you have any power in the situation, you are dead wrong, and you're walking in disobedience. The Holy Spirit may give you a word of knowledge for that person (1 Cor. 12:8), but it won't be a thought you conjured up. Be very careful what you lay at the feet of God, especially when you feel led to utter something you believe He is saying to you by the Spirit. Just stay armored, pray for them, and let the Holy Spirit do the work.

SOMEONE ELSE PRAYED YOU HERE

Don't forget that the enemy is tirelessly trying to deceive you and destroy you and sometimes it's difficult to discern his minions within a crowd, so be careful who you allow to lay hands on you in prayer. God's full armor will protect you, but don't let just anyone walk behind your shield. As you grow, you'll gain the discernment necessary to keep all threats at the proper distance, so don't freak out, just armor up and remain circumspect.

On the other hand, I'm sure you have born-again folks laboring, fasting, and praying for you with perseverance right now. In fact, I know something beautifully true about you, whether you are seeking God or already born again: Every move you make to get closer to God is the product of someone else's prayer time. Isn't that an awesome reality? You're reading this book because someone else has persevered in prayer for you. If you're born again, it's because someone prayed for you to get born again. It might have been your mama or your grandmama, or it might have been someone you don't even know. My grandmother, who is in heaven now, prayed for me without ceasing.

When I was an absolute jerk of a juvenile delinquent who was arrested six times, on probation five times, smoking dope, and running off to a children's home for four years just to stay out of jail, my grandmother would pierce through all the darkness and say to me, "Just wait, you're gonna be my little preacher."

And I'd say, "What on earth? What do you mean I'm gonna be a little preacher? How is that even possible?" But she prayed and prayed and prayed with perseverance.

The extreme rebellion of my youth finally hit a wall when good old Judge Heywood Berry said to me, "Son, listen, twenty-five years ago, I put your father away in the Tennessee State Penitentiary. If you ever stand before me again, I'm gonna lock you up, boy. I'm sick of this. I'm tired of this. You have cost the state of Tennessee Department of Juvenile Corrections tens of thousands of dollars, and we're done with it!"

Then he turned to my mama and said, "Woman, you've got six weeks to find a place for this boy, or we'll do it for you." I walked out of that court-room thinking, "That's the dumbest thing I've ever heard. They ain't putting me anywhere."

I was a typical rebel without a cause, so I despised authority. Do you know what my mama did next? She called my grandmama for prayer. So, every day at lunchtime, my grandmama would pray over the phone that God would open a door leading me to Him. I don't know the most accepted theological terminology for what I'm about to write, so don't judge me. There's something extra powerful about elderly saints who pray. They seem to get a special pass to the front of the line with God.

When a gray-haired saint starts praying for you, you'd better make sure you're ready for what comes next. You'd better make sure you're ready to get right with God. Where would I be if my grandmother had not prayed for me all those years or spoken that simple word of seemingly impossible destiny into my life with such consistency? Only God knows. I praise Him for using my grandmama with love, power, and grace. That woman had some power in her prayers, so you can be sure her armor gleamed like the morning sun in the eyes of the Lord.

PRAYING FOR ALL THE SAINTS

I hope you now understand why we must earnestly stand in the gap as prayer warriors for others. If you are not praying for other people, you need to get right with God on this matter. I believe God honors our own personal, private, self-directed prayers if, and only if, we take the time to pray for the needs of others "with all perseverance and supplication for all saints." I don't know exactly how that works, but I do know God in heaven wants to pour out mercy, give out rewards, and even bless people who seem unblessable and love people that seem unlovable. He hears the cries of all His kids at the same time, and He discerns every single word.

Why would we avoid praying for others when we earnestly and sincerely hope others are praying for us? Why would we overlook intercessory prayer when we know it activates our armor? You'll never, ever, ever hear me say I don't need others praying for me. Oh, no. Instead, you'll hear me say, "I need more prayer. My family needs more prayer. My church needs more prayer. My pastors need more prayer. My entire life needs more prayer." I don't just want to stand in the gap for others; I want them to stand in the gap for me! Asking others to pray for you is a righteous thing to do, just like asking others if you can pray for them. They're two sides of the same coin.

If you expect the armor to be activated and full of power, you must realize your prayer life needs to flow both ways. The growth of your faith and the power to fight the good fight should be motivation enough, but I can promise you without exception, someone on this planet is desperately banking on your prayers. So I'll ask you to answer this question: Who are you praying for today? Over time, your answer should become long and fruitful.

Let's put on the whole armor of God and light it up! Praying always with all prayer and supplication, in the Spirit. If we're going to utilize the armor God gave us, we'll have to pray to activate that armor and walk into our calling from this day forward—armored up and fully armed with the weapons of our warfare, as mighty soldiers of Jesus Christ!

> If ye abide in me, and my words abide in you, ye shall ask what ye will, and it shall be done unto you.
>
> —JESUS (JOHN 15:7)

CONCLUSION

WHEN I TAUGHT my sermon series on the whole armor of God at Global Vision in 2019, I knew it would do some surgery on a few hearts and open some wounds that desperately needed it. I also knew it would stir up some homes that needed to be stirred. Sure enough, chaos broke loose in our church. I counseled more people than ever before and witnessed more people sobbing, more problems being exposed, and more drama than I could have imagined. If you've been applying the Lord's instructions detailed in this book, chapter by chapter, maybe you know exactly what I'm talking about. At the same time, some folks immediately armored up and caught fire. Through it all, we became a stronger family, and I was reminded of an inescapable spiritual truth: When you start exposing the devil, that joker doesn't take it lying down. He rears his ugly head in anger and starts pulling out all the stops to keep you from putting on God's armor. He knows that if you do, you are no longer easy prey but have become a legitimate threat to his destructive plans.

After teaching that series, a pastor friend asked me why I would teach on spiritual warfare when I knew it might disrupt a calm season in our church. The fact that a pastor could ask fear-based questions like that revealed a lot to me about the state of the church in America, and I'm convicted. It's time we stop avoiding the meat of God's hard teachings. That's how we got into this mess. In *This Means War*, I prefaced Part I of the book with a sobering parable from Jesus' Olivet Discourse (Matthew chapters 24 and 25). In that prophetic message, Jesus commends those who obediently teach the meat of His end-time instructions and condemns those who don't. I just want to obey Him.

I'm never surprised when the Word of God is fulfilled—I'm amazed and inspired, but never surprised. I take heart in the fact that God knows I'm doing all I can to shake up and wake up the lukewarm while also taking the fight to the enemy, as we've discussed through this book. I'm contending for the faith, no matter the consequences. As I stand on the Word, fully armored up, it's good to know that my church family and I are standing on the right side of God's prophecies concerning the last of the last days, and for that, we're standing on the right side of history. If you're not already in our camp, I hope you'll join us.

I hope you've gained from reading this study and are committed to suiting up and booting up with intentionality and Spirit-infused power every day for the rest of your life. The spiritual war is still ramping up, so please don't lose your sense of urgency. As you know, I made sure this book is packed with Scripture that speaks to the entirety of the born-again life. I hope you'll reflect on it often, but even more, I hope you'll use it to aid your deeper study of the Word so you can better serve the meat of the Word to everyone you know—and many you don't know.

We're in a fight for the faith in our nation, and we're on a rescue mission for the lost everywhere. We have been born into the war that began in the Garden of Eden, and we just may be entering the final battle before Jesus returns as the warrior King—wielding His swift double-edged sword. He could return anytime, even today, so make sure you're ready. Though I pray He gives us more time for the sake of the lost in every corner of the globe, I still say, "Come quickly, Lord Jesus!"

You may have what some call a life verse or a life passage, and I'd like to close with mine. In Luke chapter 4, we read of the day Jesus revealed who He was to His hometown of Nazareth. He was in the town synagogue, and everyone present knew Him and His family and the scandalous array of rumors surrounding His birth. They also knew the stories of His sudden, inexplicable notoriety. A priest handed Him the scroll of Isaiah, and He read what we refer to today as Isaiah 61. Within minutes, the priests and the crowd were so enraged by His words that they tried to throw Him from a nearby cliff to kill Him. They failed. A moment in the life of God, a prophetic gift to us. Please meditate on His promises in Isaiah, saying "Yes, and Amen!"

> The Spirit of the Lord GOD is upon me; because the LORD hath anointed me to preach good tidings unto the meek; he hath sent me to bind up the brokenhearted, to proclaim liberty to the captives, and the opening of the prison to them that are bound; To proclaim the acceptable year of the LORD, and the day of vengeance of our God; to comfort all that

mourn; To appoint unto them that mourn in Zion, to give unto them beauty for ashes, the oil of joy for mourning, the garment of praise for the spirit of heaviness; that they might be called trees of righteousness, the planting of the LORD, that he might be glorified.

—ISAIAH 61:1–3

To be continued...

Notes

CHAPTER 5

1. Erwin Lutzer, *God's Devil* (Chicago: Moody Publishers, 2015), back cover.

CHAPTER 9

1. Tony Reinke, "The Nail in the Coffin of Our Hearts," Desiring God, October 1, 2017, https://www.desiringgod.org/articles/the-nail-in-the-coffin-of-our-hearts.

CHAPTER 15

1. "Henry Ford Quotes," BrainyQuote, accessed May 22, 2023, https://www.brainyquote.com/quotes/henry_ford_145978.

CHAPTER 16

1. Dr. Wallace Alcorn, "Every Saying Has a Beginning, and Some Never End," Wheaton College, posted November 11, 2016, https://www.wheaton.edu/about-wheaton/why-wheaton/mywheaton-alumni-blog/archive/2016/november/every-saying-has-a-beginning-and-some-never-end/.